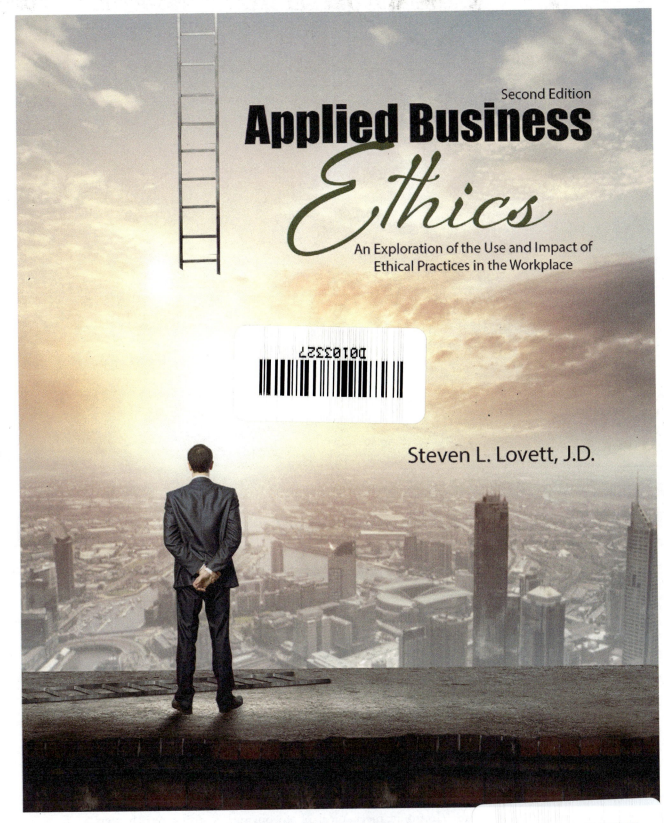

Second Edition

Applied Business
Ethics

An Exploration of the Use and Impact of
Ethical Practices in the Workplace

Steven L. Lovett, J.D.

Kendall Hunt
publishing company

TABLE OF CONTENTS

CHAPTER 12   Using the Toolkit   193

PREFACE

Roughly two years ago, I was having a conversation about ethical business practices with a colleague of mine. I had (and still have) a tremendous amount of respect for this gentleman, and because he, like myself, had years of experience representing, advocating for, and counseling a wide variety of business clients, I knew he was constantly confronted by the same two philosophical questions with which I was wrestling:

1. *How* does a *businessperson* know what is ethical?
2. *Why* should a *businessperson* strive to make ethical decisions?

The answers *feel* obvious. They *feel* like they should be easy to answer. But, absurdly, they aren't.

The answer to the first question is challenging because it relies on something that is largely unempirical. Acting "ethically" is commonly understood to mean a person or entity is acting "morally," according to a certain set of values—usually Aristotelian values and principles, such as integrity, honesty, and fairness. *How* a person can know what is "ethical" is something that is apprehended intuitively more than being understood systematically. Paradoxically, a businessperson needs to be able to determine what is ethical objectively, not subjectively. Virtuous characteristics—principles of Aristotelean ethics—usually does very little regarding most of the dilemmas faced by a businessperson. In fact, there are situations in which the commonly used definition of "ethicalness" could lead to enormous risk for a businessperson, such as insisting on the virtuous characteristic of transparency or honesty when dealing with a trade secret, an inherently (and necessarily) secretive asset.

Because of this, the concept of "ethicalness" needs to be taught and explained through the lens of a dispassionate, near-objective framework—a framework with the look and feel and *applicability* of systematic and empirical principles. In effect, a businessperson needs to be able to determine something that feels more qualitative than quantitative but do it in such a way that it can be applied to a quantitatively driven purpose—to make a profit over time by delivering value. This brings us close to answering the first question postulated above.

The point of being in business is not to be ethical; it is to *remain in business*. What, then, is the *role* of ethics in business? The role of ethics should not be—but has been for a long time—framed by a circular argument.

Businesses should act ethically because acting ethically is the ethical thing to do, and the ethical thing to do is what is considered to be "ethical."

We, as a society, want our businesses, our marketplaces, to be conducted in certain ways. Some of our concerns are important enough we translate them into laws. Others, almost as important, we translate into regulations (rules that interpret laws) or best practices (informal rules commonly accepted as the preferred methodology within an industry). Beyond these parameters, however, our expectations become a lot more fuzzy, more difficult to define, and more difficult for businesses to ascertain and to apply. When our expectations are not met, we ostracize, criticize, and castigate the offending business or business person. We will say the offender's actions are "wrong," "unethical," and "immoral." We will make our consumer, employment, and investment decisions based on our fuzzy, ill-defined, and inexact expectations. For these reasons, businesses are, or should be, very concerned with conducting themselves in such a way as to be perceived as "right," "ethical," and "moral." Businesses want to "*act ethically because acting ethically is the ethical thing to do*," and we reward businesses for being "ethical" by purchasing from them, working for them, and investing in them. This is the role of ethics in business: to advance the business purpose. And this brings us closer to answering the second question postulated above—*why* a business should act ethically.

Because these two questions are so cunningly difficult to answer, they are equally difficult to teach, or at least difficult to teach if the teacher is committed to providing a student with a real-world decision-making framework to use throughout the vast array of issues and dilemmas that come with any career. Unwittingly or not, this is where most ethics instructors, and the books they use, fail.

The key to understanding the proper context for both questions is to zero-in on the word, "business-person." Indeed, these two questions might have vastly different answers if the context of "business" was eliminated from their inquiries. Because "business" gives us the proper context for answering our two questions about ethics, we can (disturbingly perhaps) surmise two things that may help construct a near-objective framework for determining ethical conduct in a business situation:

1. "Ethicalness" can't be derived from the law. The law only provides the fundamental, mandated boundaries agreed on by our society. The law only offers the most basic framework—a formative scaffolding standing apart from the millions of buildings built by business people, designed to properly build, sometimes repair, and sometimes demolish, but never to serve as the building itself. The law is the outer marker—the ring of compliance—inside of which *all* businesses must conduct themselves without subjective interpretation.

2. "Ethicalness" can't be derived from a moral code. Morality, much like law, provides a fundamental, but very personal (even when shared by millions of other humans), framework for answering how and why a person believes in things that require faith. Apologetics might justify or substantiate morals, but morals are ultimately the result of pure trust. Morals offer definitions for what is "right" and "wrong," but they do so because of personal reliance on a particular set of beliefs. This, in fact, is an area in which a circular argument is perfectly permissible and, because of faith, perfectly applicable: Something is "right" because I believe it is "right" because of what I believe. This framework, of course, is ill-suited for the nearly infinite number of business scenarios, decisions, and dilemmas that are disconnected from the stalwarts of morality, such as life and death, truth and deception, and finiteness and infiniteness.

In my discussions with my friend, we talked through the uncomfortableness of these two suppositions, and, if they were correct, where they left the concept of "ethicalness"—a concept that should be fairly static and that should lead to better outcomes. What we happily concluded is that *ethics in business*—divested of legal and moral meanings—would have to rely on philosophical frameworks designed to help a business person make a decision and resolve a dilemma constructively and sustainably (meaning "can be repeated over time") so that the decision or resolution would lead to prosperity in the long term. Ethics, in this sense, becomes subordinate to, and aligned with, the primary purpose of business. Ethics becomes the tool a businessperson can reliably utilize in order to achieve a business' purpose and to continue achieving that purpose over time. The law and morality still have their place—the mandated boundaries they would impose—but ethics are the toolkit for the vast multitude of decisions and situations faced by businesses every day in which the law, or a set of moral beliefs, provide little if any guidance.

"Ethicalness" can be determined by super-imposing a philosophical frameworks on whatever business situation or dilemma is being faced. By acting "ethically," businesses are able to rely on the positive impact, and positive impression, their decisions make on us—their consumers, employees, and investors—over time.

The effort to explain this function of ethics in the marketplace, and to provide a functional toolkit a businessperson can use, is what drove the writing and publication of this book. The purpose of this book is to provide an "ethical toolkit" that remains true to, allows for, the internal objectives of each unique business, but which also leads to beneficial outcomes for other stakeholders and society at-large. Instead of falling back on a recitation of illegal practices (e.g., "don't embezzle") or social reforms (e.g., "workplace safety should be a priority") or environmental concerns (e.g., "wind energy equals ethical energy"), this book attempts to refocus the conversation about ethics in the workplace around each businesses' primary goal: to make a profit by delivering value over the long term. Instead of long laundry lists of "do's" and "don't's," students will be taught to carry a "multi-tool" that can be practically and successfully applied to a myriad of different business situations.

That is the hope. But it will take an open mind, an energetic spirit, an engaged attitude, and a desire to really make the marketplace a better place—not a confused battlefield of political, social, and personal convictions. I wish you the very best.

Steven L. Lovett, J.D.
Spring, 2017

ABOUT THE AUTHOR

Steven Lovett, J.D., is an Assistant Professor of Business Law and Ethics at Emporia State University's School of Business (AACSB Accredited), and Director of Career Services for Business Administration at Emporia State University. He teaches Business Law and International Business Law courses, along with Business Ethics, Social Responsibility, and Sustainability, at the undergraduate and graduate level. Mr. Lovett is also Of Counsel to the Carrillo Law Firm, PC, where he is senior counsel. Mr. Lovett has served as counsel for a multi-billion dollar credit union, regional banking clients, and private companies on a wide variety of corporate governance issues, compliance and regulatory issues, best practices, outside counsel management, and business-to-business transactional matters. He received his B.A. degree from Texas A&M University and his J.D. degree from St. Mary's University School of Law. Mr. Lovett is the author of Corporate Counsel Guides: Practice Basics (1st ed., ABA Publishing, 2013) and several trade and journal articles, book chapters, and scholarly papers. He is a member, or former member, of the American, Federal, Texas State and New Mexico State bar associations and has served on the ABA Corporate Governance, Commercial & Business Litigation, and Financial Institution Litigation Committees.

UNIT ONE

THE MEANING OF ETHICS IN BUSINESS

In the next three chapters, we will explore what it means to be "ethical" in a business context.

Chapter 1 will take a look at the paradoxes ethical conduct can create when it is applied in real-world contexts. This will challenge how we perceive issues such as fairness, justices, freedom, responsibility, the law, and social expectations. In this chapter, we'll also formulate a way by which we can define "ethics" apart from "morals" and how that definition fits with the purpose of every business: *to stay in business*.

Chapter 2 will review how individuals make personal decisions in contrast to how business organizations make decisions. We will learn about critical thinking and how that skill can offset the pitfalls of rationalizations and logical fallacies—pitfalls that may not mean much on a personal level but that can be catastrophic at an organizational level. After exploring various ethical paradigms, we'll learn about how those paradigms can provide frameworks for decision-making in business situations.

Chapter 3 will take what has been learned in the preceding chapters and begin to look at those things that influence decision-making within an organization.

This first unit is intended to redefine "ethicalness" in a practical way for organizational decision-making. What ethics means to an organization is different than what it means to an individual.

CHAPTER 1

ETHICS AND BUSINESS: BEYOND THEORY

The fact is, most business dilemmas do not pose any clear, morality-driven choice. Instead, business organizations routinely co-opt a mixture of ethical paradigms in order to process a vast array of operational decisions, conflicts, problems, and stakeholder concerns and interests. Just like financial accounting procedures for a business are likely to be very different from how an individual handles his or her personal finances even though both may share similar notions of profit, loss, expenses, income, and taxes, ethical decision-making for a business is likely to be very different from how an individual may approach personal, ethical dilemmas.

© kentoh/Shutterstock.com

This does not mean morals do not, or should not, play an essential role in an individual's life. A person's morals are going to be fundamentally instructive when faced with "right" or "wrong" dilemmas. For example, stealing company resources is "wrong." If a

© Rawpixel.com/Shutterstock.com

person doesn't already have the kind of moral plumb-line inside him or her to know that stealing is unacceptable behavior, a course on business ethics isn't going to do much good. However, because most business dilemmas do not have a clear "right" or "wrong" construction, basic moral tenets often have a tendency to be overly simplistic or too limited to be of much use.

This is why ethics, for business purposes, should be understood and used as a critical thinking tool for corporate decision-making processes, separate and apart from moral value systems. To really be useful, we need to take a look at the practical implications and applications of ethical decision-making far beyond the theoretical (philosophical) understanding of ethics.

LEARNING OUTCOMES | OUTLINE

1.1 Fairness and Justice in Business

1.2 Freedom versus Responsibility

1.3 Societal Expectations and the Law

1.4 The Compass of Prosperity

1.5 Morals and Ethics—Articulating an Important Distinction

© 3D_creation/Shutterstock.com

- Describe the importance of, and the difference between, fairness and justice.

- Describe the role of freedom and responsibility in business.

- Describe the influence of the law and societal expectations on business decision-making.

- Understand the meaning and application of "prosperity" to business-related issues and dilemmas.

- Analyze the distinction between "morals" and "ethics" and understand the significance, and distinct application, of each concept.

OPENING THOUGHT EXPERIMENT

Marsha, your best friend, called you up and asked to meet you for lunch.

"What's up?" you asked.

"I've got great news I want to share with you!" she said excitedly.

Later that same day, sitting at a corner table in a fancy restaurant, Marsha finally says, "Well, I did it! The small, virtual tourism company I started last year just hit its first, major financial benchmark, and I'm meeting with my broker tomorrow to talk about a private placement offering for some really deep-pocket investors." Her eyes sparkle, and her mouth breaks into a huge grin. "He thinks we can expect $3 million in the first round of offerings. I'm going to go from five employees to twenty overnight with a huge marketing and technology budget."

"That's fantastic!" You raise your glass and say, "Congratulations! Here's to you and your future success."

Marsha takes a drink, but then her eyes drop. "Thanks, but I'm struggling with something I can't seem to reconcile." She looks up. "I thought you could help. You seem to have a clear sense of right and wrong, and I know you took a great class in college about business ethics."

"Okay," you reply. "What's going on?"

"Well," she begins, "it's really not a complicated issue. The investors who've already expressed a genuine interest in the stock offering will expect solid returns on their investments, which I'm positive my company can generate with the right kind of growth. However, I just finished going over our options with my marketing director and with my accountant, and there's no doubt we're going to get the biggest bang for our buck if we purchase a new software platform and move our physical offices to Ireland. They've got the right kind of technological infrastructure there, a very affordable workforce, and one of the lowest corporate tax rates."

"That doesn't sound like a problem to me! Your company is going to get the money it needs, *and* you get a free ticket to live abroad. What's the issue?"

Marsha winces. "Yeah, it's an incredible opportunity, but. . ." she pauses and looks out the window. "This means I'm going to have to fire four of the employees who've been with me since the beginning. There simply isn't any financially reasonable, or logistically reasonable, way to keep them onboard after we buy new software and move overseas. They've all got families, and I know they were hoping to be a part of the company's future growth. They sacrificed a lot to work with me."

You sigh and lean back in your chair to think about Marsha's dilemma. Different ethical approaches cross your mind that would support the consequences of the company's growth: the company will be acting fiscally responsible to its investors; the company will be able to hire more people and benefit more families; the company will be able to provide better services to a greater number of consumers; and Marsha will be able to fulfill her hard-won dream of owning and running a prosperous and sustainable business. You also think of ethical approaches that would be critical of a decision to grow the company in the way described by Marsha: the company would be causing harm to employees (and their families) with whom it had a long-standing relationship, and the company would be causing harm to a local or domestic economic environment by moving off-shore.

You look at Marsha. "Is there anything illegal about these changes you're considering?"

"Not at all," she says. "I'm just struggling with this situation because of how it *feels*. I'm just not sure if it's the 'right' thing to do."

You nod in understanding. "Okay," you respond, "here's what I think you should do. . ."

ENGAGEMENT—What Do You Think?

What advice would you give Marsha? Would your advice be "ethical"? Why? Would it be the "right" thing to do? Why?

_____

_____

_____

_____

_____

_____

_____

© Rawpixel.com/Shutterstock.com

Section 1.1 Fairness and Justice in Business

For most people there is a general, widely-held opinion that ethical outcomes—the results of actions—can be categorized as "good" or "bad." This point of view likely comes from a fundamental need to determine within a social or organizational context those actions that will be tolerated and those actions that will not be tolerated. The categories of "good" and "bad" are derived from people's values, that is, the significance they attach to the consequences of an action. However, the value people attach to the consequences of an action is many times not as clear cut as simply applying a "good" or "bad" label. The moral value attached to an action's consequences isn't always a shared value. For instance, we can presume that robbing a bank is likely to be perceived as "bad" and "unethical" because it deprives other people (the bank's account holders) and the bank of their

© MJgraphics/Shutterstock.com

right to possess money they lawfully own. However, if the account holders and the bank are seen in an unfavorable light, then the robbery of that particular bank might be "good" and "ethical" because it can be validated as a matter of "fairness" or "justice"—think of the legendary example of Robin Hood or the local support for Jesse James during his spree of robberies, or even the social theory of "wealth redistribution."

> **CHALLENGE QUESTIONS:**
>
> Do you think every business dilemma has a "fair" solution? Do you think every business dilemma has a "just" solution? What do you think happens when a "just" solution causes an "unfair" outcome?

These kinds of statements and conclusions seem self-evident and might be easy to teach, discuss, and learn in a classroom where real-world consequences feel faraway. However, the philosophical concept of "ethics" as a synonym for words such as fairness, justice, reasonableness, impartiality, equality, and objectivity becomes inadequate and unwieldy when applied to most dilemmas faced in the business

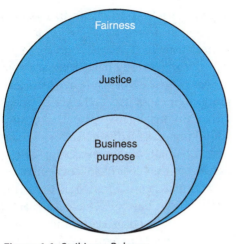

Figure 1.1 Striking a Balance
Source: Courtesy of Steven Lovett

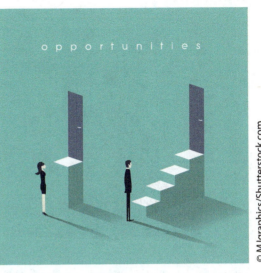

world. (See Figure 1.1.) "**Fairness**" represents a general concept of equality, which a majority of people in a society would consider to be reasonable: applying judgment or decision-making in an unbiased, or non-discriminatory, way. "**Justice**" represents a more surgical concept of fairness, which allows for one inequality (i.e., a higher tax on the wealthy) in an effort to correct another perceived, or real, inequality (i.e., the disadvantages of being impoverished). These concepts are useful (even if hotly debated) and, as concepts, are fairly universal. However, a person's ambition to be "fair" and to be "just" can also present seemingly irreconcilable dilemmas in a business setting. In a business setting, what might be "fair" or "just" might also be fatal to the business' ongoing interests (such as Marsha, in the Opening Thought Experiment, opting to keep her current employees and to remain in the United States), or they might lead to illegal conduct (such as hiring illegal immigrants out of an altruistic desire to help someone who might be less fortunate), or they might result in lost opportunity, reputational harm, or heightened litigation risk.

FAIRNESS

In an organizational setting, this means equality, freedom from bias, or dissimilarity.

JUSTICE

In an organizational setting, this means creating inequality or disparity in order to achieve equivalence, opportunity, or validity.

ENGAGEMENT—What Do You Think?

In your own words, describe the concept of "Fairness." Describe the concept of "Justice." Why do you think it is important to understand the distinction between these two concepts?

_____

_____

_____

_____

_____

_____

_____

Businesses, and persons who participate in business organizations, are most often driven by a passion to succeed. Success in business usually translates into financial success, and financial success has long been seen as a sign of a high quality of life and a positive measure of a business' and a person's reputation. Success can certainly be measured in ways other than financial gain—essentially, "success" is the concept of taking on a challenge and achieving a desirable result—but no matter how success is calculated, the critical question of the "cost of success" must be addressed. If fairness and justice are adopted as the justifications for actions that might have also have a negative impact on certain persons or social or economic groups, then when is that negative impact too high of a cost? What if acting "fairly" toward one group of stakeholders results in a negative impact on another group of stakeholders? What if applying "justice" to correct one inequality simultaneously leads to the creation of another inequality?

Ultimately, a successful business person must come to grips with how ethical conduct constructively intersects with business-related goals and ambitions. A business person must employ a more well-rounded view of "fairness" and "justice," and understand how those aspirations can be balanced with conflicting expectations and viewpoints.

Section 1.2 Freedom versus Responsibility

FREEDOM

In an organizational setting, the lawful ability to make business decisions, uninhibited by any regulation, obligation, or external responsibility.

RESPONSIBILITY

In an organizational setting, this means the lawful compulsion to make business decisions based on regulation, obligation, or external expectations and/or commitments.

Balancing the concepts of "fairness" and "justice" with conflicting expectations and viewpoints introduces the tension between exercising **freedom** in business and **responsibility**. As a starting point for purposes of our discussion, let's take a look at the outward discord between capitalism (often seen as the hallmark of "big business") and socialism (often seen as the hallmark of social responsibility and social equality).

For purposes of this discussion, we will attempt to avoid the ideological implications typically associated with capitalism and socialism. Universal definitions for either of these concepts do not exist, and an attempt to define them herein will likely push our minds toward one or more ideologically entrenched perspectives about these concepts. Instead, we want to use these concepts as archetypal frameworks for examining freedom and responsibility. To do this, we will limit our examination of capitalism and socialism to their recurring themes.

The conceptual framework of capitalism thematically includes:

- An emphasis on individual rights and ownership interests.
- A reduction of, or an absence of, political constraints.
- A reliance on "objective laws" that primarily are designed to protect individuals instead of organized groups (such as political parties or social classes).

The primary purpose of starting and running a business is to earn a profit. Because of this, a business' economic activity is driven by self-interest, that is, the actions taken by a business are intended to produce a profit for that business. The financial gains of businesses can translate into a vigorous development of culture, the arts, and an improved quality of life for a society at-large. A business' lawful ability to make decisions, uninhibited by regulation, obligation, or external responsibility aligns with an individual's lawful ability to pursue his or her own interests, therefore, capitalism is associated with "freedom." This does not, necessarily, equate capitalism with psychological egoism (in which all actions are selfishly motivated and purely altruistic actions do not exist). However, the majority of decisions within a capitalistic framework are driven by self-interest in the anticipation of profitable gain.

Conversely, the conceptual framework of socialism thematically includes:

- An emphasis on the community (organized groups) over individual rights or ownership interests.
- A lattice of governmental/political constraints to ensure communal economic policy and centralized control.
- A reliance on "subjective laws" that primarily are designed to protect the specific interests of specifically organized groups or communities.

CHALLENGE QUESTIONS:

What do you think is more important in business: freedom or responsibility? Why? How can both of these ideals co-exist constructively?

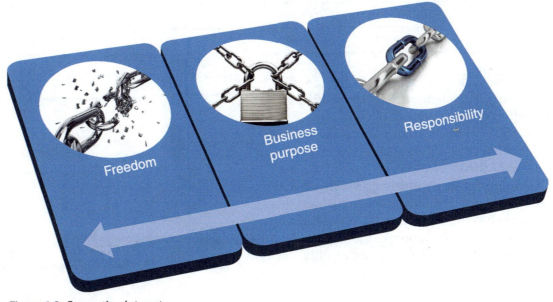

Figure 1.2 Competing Interests
Source: Courtesy of Steven Lovett, using images from Shutterstock.com

In some ways, a community-oriented urge also exists within businesses. No one business can survive on its own. Every business needs other businesses to also be viable and thriving; sometimes, businesses actually need competitors to be viable and thriving—this can help protect the communal interests of specific industries or it can help to leverage production capacity or resource availability. However, socialism takes the communal urge a step further and removes all, or most, control from individual businesses in order to ensure community-oriented interests are prioritized and protected. In this sense, socialism attempts to enforce a heightened standard of "responsibility" through centralized control, government ownership over individual ownership, and a flattened, instead of hierarchical, homogenous society.

Capitalism, generally speaking, favors the idea of free activity—freedom in the marketplace and within organizations to make decisions which result in profit and prosperity for the decision-makers. Socialism, also generally speaking, favors the idea of responsibility—restraint in the marketplace and within organizations which results in the betterment of everyone in society, even if a person or other entity is not directly connected to the decision-maker. In the real-world, ethical decisions in business are usually much more clearly identified somewhere between these two polarizing positions.[1]

ENGAGEMENT—What Do You Think?

Describe a situation—real or hypothetical—in which a business would actively be able to accomplish its primary business purpose by balancing characteristics of "freedom" with characteristics of "responsibility."

_____

_____

_____

_____

_____

_____

_____

Ethical decisions in business are constantly entangled with the potential effect on profit and the potential effect on other persons or entities, even those who may not be directly connected to the decision-maker. Effective and constructive ethical decision-making must, therefore, take both possible results into account. Just as there must be a balance between the concept of fairness and legitimate business goals, freedom must also be balanced with responsibility. A well-balanced ethical decision will ultimately advance the long-term viability—the sustainability—of a business.

Section 1.3 Societal Expectations and the Law

Every society possesses its own sense of what is, and what is not, acceptable conduct, and for every society some, or all, of that sense of permissible conduct changes over time. For instance, during World War II, cigarette smoking was so widely accepted that cigarettes were even included in American soldiers' C-rations. Fifty years later, smoking was banned in all federal buildings and all cigarette billboard advertisements were replaced with anti-smoking messages. In 1900, it was legal and commonplace for children to work as paid laborers, but by 1938 the Fair Labor Standards Act effectively outlawed the employment of children under 16 or 18 years of age. Up until the passage of the Civil Rights Act of 1964 and the Voting Rights Act of 1965, "Jim Crow" laws continued to be enforced in many southern states, permitting lawful racial segregation in public places and by private businesses. Social expectations, and a society's sense of appropriate and inappropriate behavior, usually predate changes in the law and in many instances may not even be reflected in the law. For instance, living a physically healthy lifestyle is perceived as a positive and preferable way to live, but while certain laws attempt to help people live healthier lives, the law does not mandate a physically healthy lifestyle. Social expectations are informal, but failing to meet those expectations may sometimes cause unwanted consequences for businesses, such as a consumer boycott, reputational damage, or even the loss of its workforce.

On the other hand, laws represent the most fundamental standards that all persons and businesses within a particular society must follow in order to avoid formal consequences and penalties. Essentially, laws provide a basic, or "lowest," boundary by which to determine the acceptableness of any given action. For business purposes, laws give rise to the need for "compliance," the requirement to obey whatever statutory or regulatory mandates that apply to specific business enterprises.

Increasingly over time, businesses have not only recognized the importance in making sure they comply with the law but also the importance in recognizing how their actions align with, or meet, social expectations. This is widely known as acting in a socially responsible way.

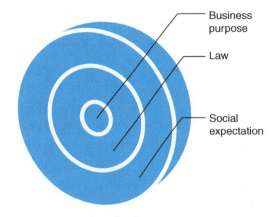

Figure 1.3 Finding the Center
Source: Courtesy of Steven Lovett

© Rawpixel.com/Shutterstock.com

CHALLENGE QUESTIONS:

Why do you think the idea of "social responsibility" has become so important to our society? Do you think following the law, or being socially responsible is more important? Why?

Being **socially responsible** is a standard that incorporates both the law and social expectations. Essentially, this means that a business acts in such a way that it benefits the community in which it operates—operating legally is beneficial and satisfying social expectations is beneficial. A study cited by James Epstein-Reeves (Covey, 2014) indicates that:

> **SOCIALLY RESPONSIBLE**
>
> In reference to a business, this means to be aware of the impact of business activities on external interests and to strive to make business decisions, which will positively affect those external interests.

- More than 88% of consumers think companies should try to achieve their business goals while improving the society and the environment.
- 83% of consumers think companies should support charities and nonprofits with financial donations.
- 83% of employees would seriously consider leaving their job if their employer used child labor in sweatshop factories.
- 65% would seriously consider leaving their job if their company harmed the environment.
- 32% would seriously consider leaving their job if their company gave no/little money to charity.[2]

Today, most business leaders feel internal pressure to produce profits and feel external pressure to meet social expectations. These pressures many times cause conflict and can change the focus of a business and its decision-making frameworks.

Of course, if social responsibility was the paramount and driving concern of a business, it might end in failure. For instance, if a paper manufacturer decided to put "social responsibility" ahead of long-term business sustainability, it might stop purchasing all of its raw material from logging companies

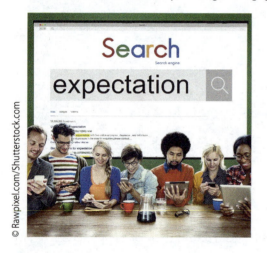

because of the possibility—even if remote—that deforestation, even well-managed deforestation, could harm the greater environment. If a landlord decided to put "social responsibility" ahead of long-term business sustainability, he or she might stop collecting rent because of the possibility that a low-income family might not be able to afford the rent and might be left homeless. While examples such as these might seem extreme, they demonstrate the logical outcome of using an ideal (i.e., social responsibility) as a decision-making framework.

Somewhere between "what is legal" and "what is socially responsible" is where most businesses will find constructive, compliant, resourceful, and sustainable solutions. Moreover, between these two boundaries is where *ethics* can take us.

Section 1.4 The Compass of Prosperity

The idea of "prosperity" has been aligned—or *mal*igned depending on who is speaking—with the concept of capitalism, free markets, and "big business." This is largely the result of the ethical paradigm called "shareholder theory" (championed by Milton Friedman, Nobel Laure-ate, friend and advisor to President Ronald Reagan, and an anchor scholar at the world-renowned Chicago School of Economics for decades) in which business decisions should be made in the pursuit of profit—that is, on behalf of the owners—within the limits of (1) the law and (2) the ethical custom. Since Friedman posited "shareholder theory" in the 1960s, there has been a wealth of debate in favor of, and against, this ethical approach. In the process, the concept of "prosperity" has become synonymous with a hands-off approach of pure capitalism espoused by Adam Smith.

Prosperity—stripped of its philosophical and economical ankle-weights—really means "making something better than it was before." A plant is prosperous if it is able to flourish in the right balance of sunlight, temperature, nutrients, and water. An idea is prosperous if it leads to useful and positive actions. A social movement is prosperous if it advances constructive and long-lasting change. An investment in education is prosperous if it leads to a healthier, fuller, and more enjoyable life. Similarly, the idea of prosperity, balanced with the appropriate ethical paradigm (decision-making framework) can act like a rudder for a boat. Prosperity means value. It means growth. It means resiliency and sustainability. When those kinds of results are helping to steer business decisions—decisions which are already being vet-

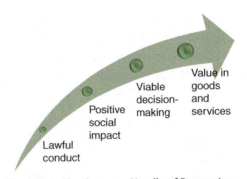

Value in
goods
and
services

Viable
decision-
making

Positive
social
impact

Lawful
conduct

Figure 1.4 The Compass Needle of Prosperity
Source: Courtesy of Steven Lovett

CHALLENGE QUESTIONS:

What is your impression of "prosperity"? What does it mean to you? Do you think business decisions should be informed by the concept of "prosperity"? Why or why not?

---

ted through an ethical paradigm—then it helps eliminate outcomes which ultimately cause harm over the long-term, and it provides a consistent baseline value. (See Figure 1.4.)

Section 1.5 Morals and Ethics—Articulating an Important Distinction

For most people, morality—a framework of moral values—is seen as objective and universal. This point of view pairs with a theory of morality called "moral objectivism" that includes the following presumptions:

1. Moral standards are not constructed by individuals or societies. Moral standards are universally inherent and transcend individual or social interpretations.

2. Moral standards are unchanging. They are not susceptible to historical epochs or geography.

3. Moral standards are collective. The same moral standards are shared by all people at all times, regardless of differences such as race, gender, social standing, economic standing, or culture.

While there is a contrasting theory called "moral relativism," most people believe there are certain, fundamental values that are objectively universal even if all values are not as strictly interpreted as they are in moral objectivism. Some of those fundamental values are identifiable in our laws. Values such as property ownership, the need to be truthful, the ability to participate in government, to have access to education, and the ability to live free from the fear of physical violence. However, the law only contains the "bare bones" of a shared moral framework, and that framework is mostly limited to a localized perspective about what should be legal versus illegal. Most issues that can be characterized as moral issues are not resolved by the law. Accordingly, the law cannot provide a morality-based direction for most issues or dilemmas.

This begs the question: *if the law does not, or cannot, provide a comprehensive and universal moral framework, then what <u>does</u> provide such a framework?*

In point of fact, nothing does. Very few people, much less thousands or millions of people, actually share a single, indistinguishable, and universal moral framework. Sometimes a group of people agree on a specific standard that serves such a purpose (as do, for example, religious groups or sects), but there isn't any macro-framework for resolving moral issues or dilemmas within complex societies or the world at-large. The absence of a single, universal framework for resolving moral issues and dilemmas has become a problematic reality for decision-makers in business organizations. It has become a problem mostly because society uses the term "ethics" synonymously with the term "morals." In common parlance, ethics is understood as being a set of moral principles—values based on a moral framework. But if there isn't a universally shared set of moral principles, how can there be a universally shared definition of what is ethical and what is not?

Philosophers have long understood a fine, but significant, distinction between the concepts of morality and ethics. While morality deals with values, ethics involves systematizing, defending, and arriving at conclusions based on a coherent set of criteria. For instance, a person's moral values may assert that lying is immoral (wrong), but the same person may willing lie in order to keep another person from harm. The willingness, and even the justification, for lying in this instance is the result of applying a systematic approach to resolving a dilemma in which telling the truth may result in harm. That systematic approach is the essence of ethics.

The concept of morality, and the argument over whether morality is universal or relative, is critical for understanding how and why people live their lives in the way they do. Morality provides a framework for understanding who we are, our place in the world around us, and where we are headed. Morality underpins our belief systems, our shared values, our passions, and the basis of our social fabric. However, for the purpose of understanding *ethics*—especially ethics in the workplace—we need to begin articulating a distinction. This doesn't mean we ignore our morals or downplay the significance of our morals. Articulating a distinction between *morality* and *ethics* means we will be able to use the right tool for the right situation.

Morals represent a belief system that—for purposes of decision-making—helps us to determine "right" from "wrong." **Ethics** represent a framework that should help us to find the "best" or "most constructive" solution to almost any problem. This distinction between morals and ethics is extraordinarily useful in business because most problems faced in the business world do not have a "right" or "wrong" answer (at least in a moral sense). For instance, if a growing manufacturing company was faced with

MORALS	ETHICS
A system of beliefs, individual or shared, which provide a basis for understanding the world around us and for understanding who we are, and which provide fundamental standards of behavior for decision-making.	A set of principles based on a specific paradigm (perspective), which provide a framework for decision-making, which may, or may not, conform with an underlying belief system.

deciding whether to buy a turn-key software program to handle its bookkeeping, or to hire three new employees to handle the same bookkeeping need, there is unlikely to be a morally "right" or "wrong" answer to this dilemma. In this situation, most moral belief systems would feel clunky—too vague or unconnected to be useful in this kind of practical, business situation. In fact, the company's decision-maker could decide to buy the software or to hire the new employees and still be acting "morally." Using morals to resolve this dilemma wouldn't be using the right tool for the right job. On the other hand, using a particular ethical paradigm (a decision-making framework) would probably offer a much clearer, pragmatic direction, and a clear rationale. Utilitarianism (which we'll cover in the next chapter) would tell the decision-maker to select the outcome that would benefit the greater good (i.e., if the software is more efficient and error-free, then this might be the best solution in order to continue growing the company). The Ethics of Care (which we'll also cover in the next chapter) would tell the decision-maker to hire the new employees because this decision would positively impact those new employees by providing a job for them. The point is to recognize that morality has a clear, and important, role in all our lives, but for the purpose of most business dilemmas, ethical paradigms offer a much better toolkit for solving problems.

© iQoncept/Shutterstock.com

> **CHALLENGE QUESTIONS:**
>
> In your own words, how would you distinguish between the concept of "morals" and the concept of "ethics"? If you don't think they are distinguishable, why not?
>
> What is a situation you can think of which would demonstrate "ethical" conduct that is also "immoral"?

Many times, morals and ethics are intertwined. What is morally "right" is also ethically "correct" or the best option, but this does not mean morals and ethics are the same thing. I may be a very upstanding, moral person, but I might also not care very much about making a profit as a business owner. To a Free Market Ethicist, I might be "unethical" even if I am moral, but to a Virtue Ethicist, I would be "ethical" because I am moral. Sounds difficult?

If making a distinction between morals and ethics feels strange and maybe even uncomfortable, think about it as if it was the same as the concept of finance. In our personal lives, each of us might handle money in the way we see fit. Maybe we spend too much on entertainment, or maybe we save every penny we earn. We are accountable for our personal finances, but only in very specific ways, such as filing taxes, or making sure that we have enough money to take care of the loved ones we support. However, in business, finances must be handled very differently. There are far more layers of accountability and responsibility for how a business' money is handled. Employees and vendors must be paid. Shareholders must be paid (or be able to see growth in their investment). Lenders must be repaid. Taxing and licensing agencies must be paid. Independent contractors must be paid. Landlords must be paid. Handling the finances

© Gajus/Shutterstock.com

of a company is much more complex than handling personal finances even if these two areas of money-management use a lot of the same terminology and the same principles. The concept of morals would be analogous to handling personal finances. The concept of ethics would be analogous to handling a company's finances.

If you are still struggling with making this distinction, be patient. We'll spend the next chapter better refining the idea of "ethics" as a "tool," separate and apart from morals.

SELECTED READINGS

- Solomon, Robert C. *It's Good Business: Ethics and Enterprise for the New Millennium* (Lanham, MD: Rowman/Littlefield, 1998).
- *Nicomachean Ethics.* (translated by W.D. Ross, Oxford University Press, 1915).
- Smith, Adam. *The Wealth of Nations.* Edited by Edwin Cannan. Later Printing edition. New York: Modern Library, 1994.
- Rawls, John. *A Theory of Justice* (Cambridge, Mass.: Harvard University Press, 1971).
- Hayek, Freidrich von. *The Road to Serfdom* (Highpoint Press, 1940).
- Barnes, The Central Question: Critical Engagement with Business, pg. 49

TAKE-AWAY QUESTIONS AND IDEAS

What is the distinction between fairness and justice?
How can the concepts of freedom and responsibility both be manifested in a business setting?
How are societal expectations distinct from the law? Why does this distinction matter?
What is meant by the "compass of prosperity?" What does this concept offer a decision-maker in a business setting?
How are ethics distinguishable from morals? Why is this important to understand?

- In business, fairness and justice must be central components to evaluating dilemmas and making decisions. However, these concepts are not always easily discerned or defined. Be wary of rushing toward what appears to be a "fair" or "just" solution. Challenge yourself to find possible harm or harmful outcomes, and let that process also inform your decision-making.

- Freedom is essential for businesses to remain viable, competitive, flexible, responsive to markets, and sustainable over the long-term. That freedom must be tempered by "responsibility"—understanding and planning for consequences of certain actions, while always keeping an eye toward societal expectations.

- Law can act as a baseline, and social responsibility can serve as a worthwhile vision, but these two concepts typically provide poles between which businesses must find long-term, sustainable solutions.
- Morality underpins who we are as human beings and who we are collectively as a society. Morals establish our belief systems and our shared values. Ethical paradigms work best as frameworks for daily decision-making, providing rationale and predictability to the vast majority of dilemmas, which do not have an obvious moral implication.

KEY TERMS

- Ethics
- Fairness
- Freedom
- Justice

- Morals
- Responsibility
- Socially Responsible

ENDNOTES

1. From *Introduction to Business Ethics* by James Fieser and Alexander Moseley. Copyright © 2013 by Kendall Hunt Publishing Company. Reprinted by permission.
2. From *Open for Business* by Brock Williams and Dane Galden. Copyright © 2015 by Kendall Hunt Publishing Company. Reprinted by permission.

ENGAGEMENT—WHAT DO YOU THINK?

Write down your own thoughts about what you've learned in this chapter. Consider the differences we've tried to explore between fairness and justice, freedom and responsibility, and morals and ethics. What are your perspectives about the concept of "prosperity" acting as the "compass" for business decisions?

CHAPTER 2

ETHICAL THEORIES: LEARNING THE LANGUAGES OF DECISION-MAKING PROCESSES

Until recently, ethical theories—paradigms—were given the greatest audience in philosophy classes. According to Webster's New World Dictionary (1979) it means:

1. Having to do with ethics; or of conforming to moral standards.

2. Conforming to professional standards of conduct.

3. Reflection on moral standards and decision making processes.

MORAL TEMPTATION

The inducement to violate a fundamental belief that would, according to that belief, be considered "wrong."

ETHICAL DECISIONS

For business purposes, regardless of the ethical paradigm being used, this means a decision based on a determination of what is constructive/productive and sustainable (repeatable over time), and which will lead to prosperity (improved circumstances).

© Amir Ridhwan/Shutterstock.com

Rushworth Kidder, in his book *How Good People Make Tough Choices: Resolving the Dilemmas of Ethical Living,*[1] suggests that decision-making is driven by our core values, morals, and integrity, and falls into two categories: **moral temptations** and **ethical decisions.**

"Moral temptation" is understood as a decision clearly based on the core values each person possesses and determining whether that decision leads to "right" or "wrong." The key here is the concept of "core values." Core values are traits or qualities that are not just worthwhile, but also represent an individual's highest priorities, deeply held beliefs, and fundamental driving forces. Most often, core values are immutable and cannot be (or should not be) flexible or alterable. Each person has a distinct set of core values. Because these are distinct to each individual (even if they are, in some ways, shared by others), and because these are absolute, core values—morals—do not provide a useful "common language," or a *lingua franca*, for business purposes. This doesn't mean core values are absent in business settings, or that they should be marginalized. This just means core

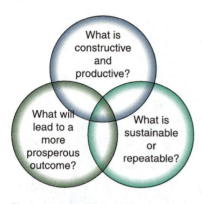

Figure 2.1 An Ethical Decision's Three-Part Structure
Source: Courtesy of Steven Lovett

values do not offer an efficient, constructive, and effective way of communicating, problem-solving, and decision-making within organizational settings involving numerous different persons and entities with a vast variety of beliefs, objectives, risks, and expectations. Thankfully (as we continue to gently pry apart "morals" from "ethics"), ethical paradigms provide exactly the right kind of "common languages" to use in business settings.

Rushworth Kidder would say "ethical decisions" are defined as dilemmas which are "right versus right." For instance, it might be "right" to protect an endangered species, and it may be "right" to protect the jobs of those persons employed by logging companies or mining companies or commercial fishing companies. Ethical decisions arise from genuine dilemmas precisely because every option (or most options) appears to be "right" based on a set of core values. And it is these types of decisions and dilemmas that most often plague a business organization. Because of this, ethical paradigms are ideal tools for resolving these types of dilemmas; they provide a framework for evaluating options and consequences, and they provide a reasoned basis—a rationale justification—for each decision. They can be utilized to create a common correlation between a vast number of stakeholders (affected persons or entities), even if those stakeholders all hold different core values. (See Figure 2.1.)

In the following chapters, we'll discuss how all of this occurs and why it occurs, but for the purposes of this chapter, let's concentrate on learning about the different ethical theories so we can better understand how each theory can be used as the "right tool" for the "right job."

LEARNING OUTCOMES | OUTLINE

2.1 How Individuals Make Decisions

2.2 How Businesses Make Decisions

2.3 Critical Thinking, Rationalizations, and Logical Fallacies

2.4 Ethical Frameworks and Philosophies

2.5 Using Ethical Languages in the Decision-Making Process

- Understand how individuals typically make decisions, using moral reasoning.

- Understand how businesses typically make decisions, using ethical paradigms.

- Describe the significance of critical thinking, the hazards of rationalizations, and the commonplace consequences of logical fallacies in business-related decision-making.

- Understand and analyze the various ethical paradigms that formulate the most common frameworks for business-related decision-making.

- Understand how ethical "languages" promote and facilitate the decision-making process in business-related activities and dilemmas.

© Sergei Kardashev/Shutterstock.com

OPENING THOUGHT EXPERIMENT

After your luncheon with your best friend, Marsha, you are walking home, feeling good about the advice you gave her about her growing company. You're lost in thought until someone suddenly calls out your name from across the street. You look over, and Sam, an old college roommate is waving at you and jogs over to greet you. You knew Sam had joined the State Department out of college, but you haven't seen him in years.

After catching each other up on how your lives have been going, Sam says, "You always were pretty smart. You mind if I ask your advice on something?"

"Sure," you reply.

With a smile, Sam begins. "Okay. Well, I've finally been offered a consulate position overseas, and I have two options. Both posts are located in small, South Sea island states, which are a similar size, geology, and climate. The State of Reservitaria has strict laws which prohibit extra-marital sex, alcoholic drinks, recreational drugs, popular entertainments like movies, and even fine food. Reservitaria only permits what it considers to be the 'higher pleasures' of art and music, and it actually promotes them. It has a world-class symphony, opera, art galleries, and 'legitimate' stage theaters.

"On the other hand, the nearby State of Unreservitaria is an intellectual and cultural desert. However, it has excellent restaurants, a thriving comedy and cabaret circuit, and very liberal attitudes towards open lifestyles and recreational drug use." Sam pauses and grimaces. "I know you have your own beliefs about how a person should live, but a perfect day for me would combine good food, good wine, some high culture, and being a bit rowdy. I really don't know which consulate post I should choose. It seems like my private life is inseparably bound up with my professional life. What do you think I should do?"

ENGAGEMENT—What Do You Think?

Keeping in mind Sam's own preferences and his job, what advice would you give him? Would your advice be considered "ethical"? Why? If Sam takes your advice, would he be content? How could he explain his decision to the State Department?

Section 2.1 How Individuals Make Decisions

When making decisions, individuals usually analyze, or at least understand, what would be the "right" thing to do. This process is based on how an individual's **moral reasoning** has developed. (See Figure 2.2.) Individuals arrive at different levels of moral reasoning as they pass through different stages of development. In a seminal study of a person's developmental stages of moral reasoning, Lawrence Kohlberg identified six stages that can be divided into three

MORAL REASONING

For an individual, this means using a decision-making framework based on a belief system in order to determine right from wrong.

Figure 2.2 Development of Moral Reasoning
Source: Courtesy of Steven Lovett

CHALLENGE QUESTIONS:

Think about how you make many of your own decisions. What values motivate you? What do you consider to be an important "outcome" for most of your decisions? Financial success? Popularity? Happiness? Avoiding negative consequences?

levels[2]. During the first level, called the "preconventional level," an individual's decision-making is motivated by selfishness, that is, how that individual will benefit from a decision. A child does this when it decides to take a toy from a playmate. The child is simply thinking of how possessing the toy will benefit him, instead of how the decision may hurt the other child's feelings or might be considered as stealing. During the second level, called the "conventional level," an individual's decision-making takes into account how others might perceive the individual as a result of his or her decision. A young person might decide to share with a friend because a teacher or parent has complimented him or her for sharing in the past. During the third level, called the "postconventional level," an individual's decision-making is motivated (at least in part) by how a decision actually affects others, regardless of whether it may also result in any personal reward. An older individual might decide to give his or her sandwich to a hungry person even if it means going hungry him or herself.

ENGAGEMENT—What Do You Think?

Describe how you make most of your everyday decisions. Are they driven by what best suits you? Are they driven by concerns about your reputation? Are they driven by the needs of others? Are they driven by the needs or expectations of society at-large?

_____

_____

_____

_____

_____

_____

_____

_____

In the latter half of the 20th century, Kohlberg's concept of moral development was criticized as being gender-biased in favor of males. While this may be true (and is arguably a very supportable criticism), the point for our purposes is that individuals typically make decisions based on some level of moral reasoning—life lessons and perceptions that inform attitudes, beliefs, and opinions about the world around us.

Section 2.2 How Businesses Make Decisions

Businesses are comprised of individual people and are treated as a "person" in many instances (including in a legal sense). The "face" of a business is usually a person—an officer, or a public figure, or a representative spokesperson. Decisions within a business are most often made by individual people (versus automated or programmable "decisions"). Because of this, and because of a popular sense that an organization acts as a "moral agent" (and can even be held criminally accountable for illegal and/or immoral actions), most people tend to think business decisions are, or should be, formulated in the same way decisions are made by individuals.

© kdshutterman/Shutterstock.com

However, for obvious reasons, businesses don't have, and cannot rely on, the same **developmental experiences or internalized experiences** as individuals do. Corporate methodologies for decision-making are, therefore, many times haphazard or, if structured, follow policy guidelines or a broader, organizational culture. A business, itself, does not possess any core values, and it is dispassionate about the world around it. People within a business impart values, but because those values

DEVELOPMENTAL EXPERIENCES

For an individual, this means those personal experiences which occur throughout life.

are "borrowed" they are deferential to the business' overarching goal (or "value"), which is to *stay in business*—to be sustainable over the long term. For instance, a company might have as one of its "guiding principles," that is, values, the imperative that it is "environmentally friendly," but if organizational decisions were made which repeatedly and substantively put environmental concerns above profit, productivity, and growth, the business would be headed for decline and insolvency.

ENGAGEMENT—What Do You Think?

Why can't businesses make their decisions in the same way individuals make their decisions? Why do most people mistakenly think businesses make their decisions like an individual makes his or her decision?

_____

_____

_____

_____

_____

_____

Figure 2.3 How Individual Developmental Experiences are Borrowed by a Corporation
Source: Courtesy of Steven Lovett

On the other hand, successful businesses are well aware of the need to incorporate external, or nonbusiness, values into their decision-making processes. (See Figure 2.3.) If the welfare of resources is ignored, or if employees are marginalized, or if public opinion isn't considered, or if customers are discounted, a business will similarly be headed for decline and insolvency. The long-term picture of delivering value to the marketplace in a sustainable and responsible way is critical for the well-being of a business, but because businesses have uniquely different goals—and usually a much longer-term horizon and life cycle—than an individual human being, business decisions can often appear "immoral" or "unethical."

Section 2.3 Critical Thinking, Rationalizations, and Logical Fallacies

Becoming a part of the business world means that decisions, and decision-making frameworks, have a greater chance of effecting more people in more serious ways than they do when only making decisions as an individual. Participating in, owning, and/or operating a business requires that an enormous amount of decisions need to be made on an ongoing basis—many of which that do not have a clear "right" or "wrong" resolution. In the context of a business environment, every situation and every issue or dilemma is likely to be more complex than what is faced on an individual level. Moreover, those complexities can change and vary rapidly. The fourth-century Greek philosopher from Ephesus, Heraclitus, formed his philosophical theories on the shoulders of two major principles, one of which was characterized by the saying, "No man ever steps in the same river twice." He believed that change was a fundamental characteristic of the universe. Later, Greek philosophers, such as Socrates, Plato, and Aristotle, expanded on, and refined, various methods of analyzing, critiquing, and resolving problems, as well as challenging popular conceptions or personal opinions. The ability to objectively (or as objectively as possible) evaluate, appraise, and critique problems, decision-making processes, and actions is invaluable. Ethical paradigms provide the framework to accomplish these points of analysis, but everyone involved in a decision-making process should be actively engaged in applying each of these points of analysis in a constructive way. (See Figure 2.4.)

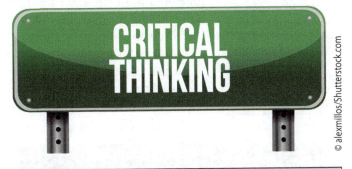

© alexmillos/Shutterstock.com

CHALLENGE QUESTIONS:

In your own words, describe why you think "critical thinking" is important for ethical decision-making. What did you identify as valuable about critical thinking? What, if anything, did you identify as a weakness with critical thinking?

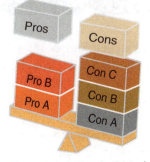

Figure 2.4 A Simple Critical Thinking Process
Source: Courtesy of Steven Lovett

Even though a morality-based decision-making framework may not be the most effective way to determine a company's ethics, a company's decision-making *can* be judged as "ethical" or "unethical." This is because ethics can be used as a systematic decision-making framework based on specific criteria. Those criteria are not, necessarily, the result of conflicting or meaningful values. This means that people and societies that may not share the same set of moral values would still be able to share a systematic set of decision-making criteria—ethics. Because of this, external observers can characterize business decisions as "ethical" or as "unethical" without resorting to incompatible moral codes. In order to do this, external observers, and those who are making the decisions on behalf of business organizations, have to use reflective, analytical thinking skills. It is imperative to train your mind, and to continuously practice, **critical thinking** skills. Answering the questions of "why" and

CRITICAL THINKING

The application of an objectified analysis and evaluation of a dilemma or issue in order to better inform a decision or judgment.

© Gajus/Shutterstock.com

© iQoncept/Shutterstock.com

RATIONALIZATION

The process of explaining or justifying behavior with reasons which appear substantive and appropriate; using a predetermined conclusion to develop supporting evidence.

"how" when faced with a dilemma and the various ways in which to resolve a dilemma will help to scrutinize your decision-making process, the stakeholders affected by your decisions, the rationale behind your motivations and objectives, and the impact your decisions will have on your business.

A temptation when critically thinking about a dilemma is to begin shoring-up a preferred solution with one or more "rationalizations." The use of **rationalizations**, in this sense, acts much like a defense mechanism, allowing preexisting feelings and behaviors to appear justified as logical or rational when, in fact, they are illogical and/or irrational. For instance, if a business person decides to refuse service to a customer because he or she doesn't "like" the customer, the business person might rationalize the decision by explaining that the customer would not have been "approved" for credit anyway in order to make the purchase.

Honest critical thinking can help to avoid rationalizations. Challenging the reasoning or rationale for a particular decision and for a decision-making framework can help alleviate the use of rationalizations. If, as an example, an employee considers taking home a ream of copy paper from work (i.e., theft of company resources) and rationalizes his or her decision by saying, "I see everyone else doing it," he or she can challenge that rationalization through critical thinking: Why do other employees take paper home? What policies are in place to address those actions? How am I expected to behave as a matter of company policy? What might be the consequences of my actions if I decide to take home a ream of paper?

Rationalizations are tricky because they look and smell like genuine justifications. The use and understanding of various ethical paradigms will help you identify whether a justification is genuine or whether it is a mere prop for an otherwise irrational or illogical feeling or behavior.

When in the process of analyzing a dilemma and a decision-making process, it is equally imperative that you avoid logical fallacies. A **logical fallacy** is a pattern of reasoning that is ultimately flawed (discredited) usually because of its structural assumptions. Sound confusing? A simple example of a logical fallacy might be the following: "I saw a picture of a penguin colony. All the penguins in the colony are black and white. Since all the penguins in the picture are black and white, *all penguins must be black and white*." Extrapolating a conclusion based on a limited set of data—especially when the data does not appear to be limited—can sometimes be a dangerous logical fallacy.

LOGICAL FALLACY

A pattern of reasoning which relies on flawed structural, or foundational, assumptions.

ENGAGEMENT—What Do You Think?

Discuss why you think people use rationalizations to justify their decisions. Why do they use logical fallacies to substantiate their conclusions or opinions?

_____

_____

_____

_____

_____

_____

_____

Logical fallacies are landmines when dealing with various ethical paradigms. For instance, if a person is processing a dilemma and a decision using Ethical Relativism, and decided a particular choice was beneficial because it had been beneficial in the past, he or she would need to understand that the absence of a negative result in the past does not, ipso facto, mean there will never be a negative result. If a person decided that transparency is always a positive attribute because of the Virtue Ethics paradigm, he or she would need to also understand that sometimes "transparency" might violate a legally enforceable fiduciary duty to keep certain information private, such as personnel records, customer financial data, trade secrets, and nonpublic information on which someone might make an investment decision (i.e., insider trading).

Ethical paradigms should not be, and are not designed to be, taken as "absolutes" in the same way moral beliefs and core values are. Ethical paradigms by their nature are flexible tools for processing information, critiquing those processes, analyzing solutions, and communicating justification for those solutions.

> **CHALLENGE QUESTIONS:**
>
> Why do you think businesses might use rationalizations when making decisions?
> Think of a situation when you experienced a temptation to rationalize an action, or when you relied on a logical fallacy to support a decision. Would critical thinking have helped you avoid those pitfalls? Why or why not?

Section 2.4 Ethical Frameworks and Philosophies

Many models for solving ethical dilemmas emerge from the field of ethics. Some of the models applied to business include those of Dr. Peter Drucker, management expert; Laura Nash, Harvard Divinity School; Ken Blanchard and Dr. Norman Vincent Peale, people experts and authors; and Warren Buffet, investor and philanthropist. Drucker's test is simple: "Above all do no harm." Intentionally making decisions that will not do harm will encourage ethical decision-making. Likewise, Buffet's simple front-page-of-the-paper

> **CHALLENGE QUESTIONS:**
>
> Describe your own "model" for solving ethical dilemmas. What are the values, issues, or concerns which your model addresses? Would your model be effective in a business situation? If so, why?

test supports critical thinking to envision how the decision may look on the front page of a paper before making the final decision. Blanchard and Peale subscribe to a three-question test: "Is it legal?" "Is it balanced?" and "How does it make me feel?" This method considers the law, society and the individual's conscience.

Ethical decision making is part of business. The intention of this section is to show that there is no one right theory or model; instead there are many tools available to assist in making business decisions.** The following is not intended to be an exhaustive list (or explanation) of every ethical paradigm. Instead, the purpose is to familiarize ourselves with the most common ethical theories and to gain a basic understanding of how they work.

Virtue Ethics

For Plato and Aristotle, resolving ethical dilemmas required developing virtue. Developing these virtues took place through training and knowledge acquisition. According to this theory, business decisions involve the application of one or more of the following virtues:

> Ability, Acceptance, Amiability, Articulateness, Attentiveness, Autonomy, Caring, Charisma, Compassion, Cool-headedness, Courage, Determination, Fairness, Generosity, Graciousness, Gratitude, Heroism, Honesty, Humility, Humor, Independence, Integrity, Justice, Loyalty, Pride, Prudence, Responsibility, Saintliness, Shame (capable of), Spirit, Toughness, Trust, Trustworthiness, Wittiness, and Zeal.

In a business setting, a company may adopt several or most of these attributes as its "corporate values." These values are then intended to be used as analytics for each of its decisions. In other words, are the company's decisions caring? Are they responsible? Are they trustworthy, and do they have integrity? Be aware of the fact that the contexts to each of these attributes may be significantly different,

Aristotle

Plato

or may have more limitations, than if they were applied to an individual. For example, a financial institution may make decisions which are trustworthy and have integrity even though they involve withholding critical financial data as a result of privacy laws.

CHALLENGE QUESTIONS:

What do you like, or don't like, about Virtue Ethics? Do you think this ethical perspective would be effective in a business situation? Why or why not?

Ethical Relativism

While this theory sounds especially cringeworthy from a moralist point of view, ethical relativism does not equate arbitrariness or randomness. Relativist decisions are justified based on specific circumstances coupled with subjective experiences and knowledge. Most often, decisions are based on experiences (shared or personal). "Relativism" usually carries with it a negative connotation (which may, or may not be, deserved), but for purposes of Ethical Relativism, the "relativist" part is the result of subjectively different experiences and perspectives. It is not, necessarily, intended to mean that a decision is "right just because I say it is." It is also not intended to mean that each company arbitrarily forms its own convictions about what is "right" or "wrong." Instead, Ethical Relativism means that a company's decisions are informed and guided by that particular company's experiences, its history, and the experiences it has adopted from other companies or entities. This is not an arbitrary process, although, when viewed from the outside, it can seem like it is.

© M-SUR/Shutterstock.com

CHALLENGE QUESTIONS:

What do you like, or don't like, about Ethical Relativism? Do you think this ethical perspective would be effective in a business situation? Why or why not?

© GlOck/Shutterstock.com

Immanuel Kant

Kantian Ethics (Deontology)

The ethical theory most people attempt to follow (or believe they are attempting to follow) relies on the concept of a "universal" law: The principle of universal law essentially means that an individual should make a decision in such a way that if the same decision was made over and over again, even by thousands or millions of other people, the result would still be viewed as fair and just. This concept was developed by the philosopher, Immanuel Kant (1724–1804).

Kant believed common knowledge about moral values could be translated into objective philosophical knowledge. He shunned the idea of using personal experience as a justification for decision-making and instead promoted the use of "reason." Kant's theory also relied on the concept of a "categorical imperative," meaning principles that are intrinsically (by themselves) valid or good should always be obeyed. This is a "bright-line" perspective; if humans are to be rational agents, a universal "law" (an absolute standard) should guide all decision-making. A simplistic example would be to say that telling a lie is always wrong, regardless of the consequences.

Jeremy Bentham

Utilitarian Ethics

The theory of utilitarianism seeks out the greatest good for the greatest number of people, even if a minority of people are harmed or disenfranchised by a decision.

This is known as applying a "cost-benefit-analysis" in which the cost (liability) of a decision is weighed against its benefit (gain). If a particular decision would result in a greater cost than benefit, it is not chosen. If a particular decision would result in a greater benefit than its cost, it is chosen.

However, just because the word, "benefit," is used does not mean the outcome is harmless. For instance, for the first time in history, the Ford Motor Company faced criminal charges in 1980 for reckless homicide as the result of a defective product—the infamous Ford Pinto. Ford had manufactured and sold the Pinto, even with known defects in the vehicle's fuel tank design, because Ford's cost-benefit analysis document showed that paying out millions in damages in lawsuits was more profitable than implementing design changes.

John Stuart Mill

This ethical perspective was articulated and championed by Jeremy Bentham (1748–1832) and John Stuart Mill (1806–1873).

Free Market Ethics

Free Market Ethics (or theory) uses the law as its limitation, or decision-making constraint, on business decisions. Milton Friedman has been recognized as the champion of Free Market Ethics, what is referred to as "shareholder theory."

Friedman's theory proposes that a business organization's pursuit of profit is paramount and should only be limited by two considerations: (1) all decisions should be lawful, and (2) all decisions should follow an "ethical custom" in the event the law does not provide useful boundaries. These considerations are flexible and not absolute—they may change as a result of time, national boundaries, and cultural differences. The two limitations are intended to act a check on decisions which might otherwise cause harm or violate social norms. In proposing this theory, Friedman posited that a business' primary responsibility was to its owners; the purpose of a business organization is to maximize its owners' financial gain as long as it does so within the permitted bounds of the law and social custom. Profitable individuals are then enabled to pursue charitable interests, but unelected business organizations should not be used to address social needs. Friedman believed that if businesses became surrogates for governmental responsibilities, it would lead to a state-controlled economy and a loss of individual freedoms. "Stakeholder Theory," which we'll address later on, directly contradicts Free Market Ethics.

© ChristianChan/Shutterstock.com

© Olivier Le Moal/Shutterstock.com

Egoist Ethics

In this theory, actions are grounded in self-interest. This does not mean Egoist Ethics ignore other interests, but the

CHALLENGE QUESTIONS:

What do you like, or don't like, about Free Market Ethics? Do you think this ethical perspective would be effective in a business situation? Why or why not?

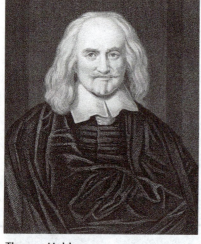

Thomas Hobbes

Adam Smith

overarching concern is: "how will this decision benefit me?" In business situations, this perspective is most often coupled with the idea of rational self-interest, which means an egoist decision looks at a much longer-term event horizon. For instance, a company might decide to spend an enormous amount of its capital reserves updating its manufacturing facilities to improve the working environment for its employees. On its face, this may look like a decision against its own self-interest, that is, spending money for the well-being and safety of one of its stakeholder groups; however, the company can make this decision because it projects that with improved manufacturing facilities, productivity will increase, employee retention will improve, and its public reputation will strengthen.

This ethical perspective was advanced by Thomas Hobbes (1588–1679) and Adam Smith (1723–1790).

CHALLENGE QUESTIONS:

What do you like, or don't like, about Egoist Ethics? Do you think this ethical perspective would be effective in a business situation? Why or why not?

Ethics of Care

A relatively new theory of ethics has been posited as an "Ethics of Care." In this theory, self-promoting decisions are seen as ethical as long as others are also helped by those decisions. Think of a particular decision being at the center of a Venn diagram. An ethical decision would be one in which all of the overlapping relations are being helped and/or improved, along with the decision-maker. This ethical perspective was primarily developed by Carol Gilligan (b. 1936), an ethicist, feminist, and psychologist, who studied developmental

CHALLENGE QUESTIONS:

What do you like, or don't like, about Ethics of Care? Do you think this ethical perspective would be effective in a business situation? Why or why not?

psychology under Lawrence Kohlberg. Ethics of Care is an ethical theory in response to, or in contrast to, Kohlberg's stages of moral development.

Ethical Justice

A social contract is the way to think about this theory. The guiding principle is that rational people will choose the most equitable and fairest result. Most often, "equity" and "fairness" are interpreted as "equality," and this ethical theory maintains that justice can only exist within the parameters of equality. This is a restatement of "distributive justice," which presupposes that goods, services, and overall benefits should be distributed among various stakeholder groups equally (or as equally as possible), even if this process might diminish the benefit to one (or more) of the stakeholder groups. For example, if a company's quarterly sales fell as a result of the poor performance of its salesforce, the company might decide to not only lay-off a certain number of sales people but also an equal number of manufacturing employees. This decision would be "unfair" to the manufacturing employees,

John Locke

but it would be a "just" decision because it distributed the effects of the company's loss among all its workers equally. In the same way, a company might pay both its sales people and its manufacturing employees a bonus, based on the sales generated by its marketing department. This might be "unfair" to the sales people, but it is a "just" decision because it distributed the company's profits among all its employees.

> **CHALLENGE QUESTIONS:**
>
> What do you like, or don't like, about Ethical Justice? Do you think this ethical perspective would be effective in a business situation? Why or why not?

This ethical perspective was articulated by John Locke (1632–1704) and John Rawls (1921–2002).

Teleological Ethics

Essentially, teleology can be explained by "the ends justify the means." In business, this is sometimes referred to as management by objectives. This does not mean stakeholders are not taken into account during a decision-making analysis, but it does mean that a decision can be

> **CHALLENGE QUESTIONS:**
>
> What do you like, or don't like, about Teleological Ethics? Do you think this ethical perspective would be effective in a business situation? Why or why not?

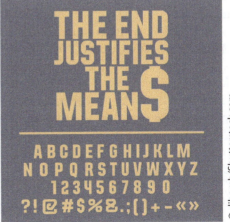

THE END JUSTIFIES THE MEANS

A B C D E F G H I J K L M
N O P Q R S T U V W X Y Z
1 2 3 4 5 6 7 8 9 0
? ! ✉ # $ % & . ; [ ] + – « »

considered "ethical" if an objective, a goal, or an outcome is accomplished as a result of the decision.

Section 2.5 Using Ethical Languages in the Decision-Making Process

While we have been referring to various ethical paradigms as "tools" (which seems like a helpful analogy when talking about "frameworks"), all the preceding ethical paradigms can also be understood as various "languages."

People within an organization, and indirect and direct stakeholders to an organization, are all motivated by, concerned with, and influenced by many different, sometimes conflicting, values. For instance, an employee may be motivated by concern for his or her personal safety. A shareholder may be motivated by growth and profit. A compliance officer may be motivated by adherence to applicable regulations. A member of the community may be motivated by controlling pollution and harm to the local environment. A company CEO may be motivated by earnings and productivity. All of these various stakeholders are likely to "speak a different language." If a dilemma came up concern-

Figure 2.5 Building an Ethical Decision
Source: Courtesy of Steven Lovett

ing whether or not to refurbish and modernize the company's manufacturing facility, it is likely that each of these various stakeholders would have different—if not conflicting—demands, expectations, and objectives about what would need to be done, how it should be done, and what should not be done. Ultimately, the company would have to make a decision. (See Figure 2.5.) Using morality to arrive at a decision would probably be too cumbersome (if not inapplicable), but even if the company formulated its decision, and communicated its decision, using a set of "core values," it is very likely that several, if not all, of the various stakeholders would feel shortchanged or marginalized or disengaged from the process. However, using different ethical paradigms as the "lingua franca"—the universal language—for this situation might cause there to be a much different outcome.

If a decision-maker was leaning toward the remodel of the manufacturing facility, he or she could critically analyze the decision and the decision-making process, as well as dialogue with each of the various stakeholders as follows:

- The employee—use *Ethics of Care* to show how modernizing the facility would make it safer
- The shareholder—use *Free Market Ethics* to show how modernizing the facility would ultimately lead to more growth and greater profitability

- The compliance officer—use *Kantian Ethics* to show how the plan for modernizing the facility would adhere to all applicable laws and regulations (i.e., safety, environment, local codes, etc.)

- The member of the community—use *Ethical Relativism* to show how modernized facilities in the past have decreased their carbon footprints and have economized the use of local resources

- The CEO—use *Utilitarian Ethics* to show how modernizing the facility would lead to an overall increase in productivity and earnings, even if there was a significant upfront cost and downtime in manufacturing

> **CHALLENGE QUESTIONS:**
>
> Which ethical paradigm(s) do you primarily use when making many of your own decisions?
>
> Think of a recent, important decision you made, and use an ethical paradigm which you normally would not use in order to explain your decision to someone else. Was this an effective process? Were you able to communicate effectively? Did your decision still make sense?

This is, admittedly, a simplified example of how ethical paradigms can act as tools—better yet, as languages—to effectively analyze and communicate a decision-making process and a decision to a wide variety of stakeholders.

This process is *not* cherry-picking between different ethical paradigms for the purpose of justifying or rationalizing an action simply to call the action "ethical." That would be just as disingenuous as selecting a single moral axiom, such as "all men are created equal," to improperly justify what a person might otherwise know to be immoral or wrong, such as "women are not men, so they are not equal to men."

Using various ethical paradigms as "languages" to address and critically analyze various motivations, concerns, and risks promotes transparency, communication, and constructive resolutions even when a dilemma appears complicated by unfavorable outcomes and conflicting interests. Language is a tool of communication, establishing credibility, reconciliation, learning, information transfer, and persuasion, so, in order to accomplish all these things, we need to find out what "language" we are speaking, AND what language other stakeholders are speaking. Successful businesses—*ethical* businesses—put this process into practice every day.

SELECTED READINGS

- Bowie, Norman E. *Business Ethics: A Kantian Perspective* (Oxford: Blackwell Publishers, 1999), 63–78.

- Kegan, Robert, and Lisa Laskow, Lahey. *How the Way We Talk Can Change the Way We Work: Seven Languages for Transformation.* Jossey-Bass, 2002.

- Keynes, John Maynard. *Essays in Persuasion*, New York: W.W. Norton & Co., 1963, pp. 358–373.

- Moore, Jennifer. *What is really unethical about insider trading?*, Journal of Business Ethics, 9 (March 1990).

- Russell, Bertrand. *The Conquest of Happiness* (New York: Viking 1936), pp. 36–40.

- Aristotle. *Politics*, trans. W.S. Ross (Oxford University Press, 1916).

- Kidder, Rushworth M. *How Good People Make Tough Choices Rev Ed: Resolving the Dilemmas of Ethical Living.* Rev Upd edition. Harper Perennial, 2009.

TAKE-AWAY QUESTIONS AND IDEAS

Does everyone use one or more ethical paradigms when making most decisions?
If so, why do you think that is? If not, then what do people use to help them reach a decision?

How is the framework of making a business decision distinctly different than the framework for making a personal decision?
Why do you think most people perceive businesses, and business ethics, as moral agents and as morally driven?

How do you think ethical paradigms can promote and facilitate constructive decision-making processes in business settings?

- Individuals typically make meaningful decisions based on their moral development and belief systems.

- Businesses should typically make meaningful decisions based on constructive organizational cultures and a long-term horizon oriented toward providing value in a sustainable way.

- Critical thinking is a crucial tool used to apply, analyze, understand, and communicate decision-making frameworks and decisions. Critical thinking can help to alleviate the risk of rationalization and logical fallacies within a decision-making process. This takes practice and objective awareness.

- Ethical frameworks act like "languages," allowing various stakeholders and people to communicate constructively with each other and assimilate disparate goals into an overall, positive outcome.

KEY TERMS

- Critical thinking
- Developmental experiences
- Ethical decisions
- Logical Fallacy

- Moral reasoning
- Moral temptation
- Rationalization

ENDNOTES

1. Kidder, R. M. (2009). *How good people make tough choices: resolving the dilemmas of ethical living.* New York: Harper.

2. Brandenberger, Jay W. "Moral development: Theory and applications." *Journal of Moral Education,* 44 (3), 2015, pp. 387–389. Kohlberg's study has since been criticized for its bias toward males. Our use of his theory is limited to its generic demonstration of how an individual might go through stages of developmental reasoning, not whether Kohlberg's stages are accurate or universal.

ENGAGEMENT—WHAT DO YOU THINK?

Write down your own thoughts about what you've learned in this chapter. Consider the differences between how individuals make decisions and how businesses make decisions. What are your thoughts about rationalizations and logical fallacies—why are they used and how can practicing critical thinking guard against them?

CHAPTER 3

THE MECHANICS OF DECISION-MAKING: INFLUENCES, VALUES, AND CONSEQUENCES

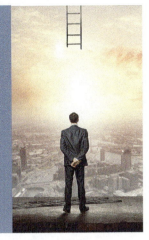

Mencius or "Master Meng" ("Mengzi" in Chinese) was born in the state of Zou in 372BCE, and was a disciple of Confucius who believed that all human beings were innately good, which could be acquired by education and self-discipline, or lost through neglect and negative influences, but always had the opportunity to return to the righteous path. One of Mencius' philosophies was his list of four cardinal virtues: benevolence, righteousness, wisdom, and propriety. Benevolence was the compassion one had for family, as well as for the suf-

© Attila JANDI/Shutterstock.com

fering of all humans and non-humans. So, a benevolent ruler will be cognizant of how policies affect those being ruled. Righteousness is not being disrespectful to others and serving one's parents. Propriety is respecting your elders and legitimate authority figures.[1] Propriety might mean spending more money on a particular chemical disposing process because it meets environmental regulations, even if it is highly unlikely anyone would find out if that particular chemical disposal process wasn't being used. The last virtue is wisdom, which involves the commitment to the other virtues. It is very much like Socrates' justice, which consisted of moderation, courage, wisdom, and justice, which was possessing the first three. In Mencius' virtual philosophy, possessing benevolence, righteousness, and propriety results in wisdom. One metaphorical example of his philosophy is being in the shoes of the person who's the recipient of your action. For example, you should not discharge a subordinate who has more expertise than you and could surpass you for a promotion as a result.[2]

As Mengzi realized, the concepts of "value," "influences," and "consequences" are all intertwined, and in order for "good" to occur, people must continuously educate themselves, discipline themselves, and avoid negative influences.

Figure 3.1 Decision-Making Influences
Source: Courtesy of Steven Lovett

The mechanics of decision-making—the nuts and bolts of how decision-making processes occur and how decisions are formulated—come from a cornucopia of individual factors, organizational factors, organizational structures, marketplace factors, and normative considerations. (See Figure 3.1.) Understanding these numerous influences, values, and consequences will help us to understand when, where, and how various ethical paradigms come into play and what makes one decision more "ethical" than another.

LEARNING OUTCOMES | OUTLINE

3.1 Business Ethics in the 21st Century

3.2 Values and Skills

3.3 Marketplace Influences and Consequences

3.4 Individual Factors in Business Ethics

3.5 Organizational Structure and Ethics

3.6 Organizational Factors and Normative Considerations

- Analyze business ethics as they are currently understood and have evolved in the 21st century.

- Describe the significance of, and difference between, "value" and "skill," especially as these concepts pertain to direct stakeholders, such as employees, managers, and executives.

- Understand the innumerable marketplace influences and consequences on running, growing, and sustaining an ongoing business interest.

- Understand how individual factors influence business ethics and decision-making processes.

- Understand how various organizational structures and power-relationships influence business ethics and decision-making processes.
- Understand how organizational factors and normative considerations influence business ethics and decision-making processes.

OPENING THOUGHT EXPERIMENT

You are an employee of a large, Fortune 500 company. Your salary isn't the highest in the industry, but it also isn't one of the lowest. Your company has excellent health care benefits and generous amounts of vacation time. One of your responsibilities is to monitor the use of company resources, especially the company's internet access and broadband usage. One day, you notice a significant amount of broadband usage is occurring from a single desktop terminal. You make note of it. For the next two weeks, you notice the same significant amount of broadband usage coming from the same desktop terminal. Every day, you log the unusual activity in your daily report.

After a short time, the Vice President of your department visits with you and other employees. He announces a new program which is being tested in your department. Employees in your department will all qualify for a "1-hour movie break" for every 20 work days. An employee can simply tell his or her supervisor that he or she wants to watch a movie for an hour, and then go to a new "theater" break room to enjoy a wide selection of movies. The VP tells everyone this new program is designed to provide a different kind of work incentive and to create a non-traditional benefit for employees.

Along with several of your coworkers, you sign up for your "movie hour" right away. When your turn comes, you enter the theater which has big, comfortable chairs and free popcorn. You pick up a tablet that allows you to scroll through hundreds of movie titles, but you gradually realize from the format of the movies most of them are pirated (illegal) downloads. Suddenly, it occurs to you maybe this was the cause of so much broadband usage from that one desktop terminal; however, you don't know whose desktop it was (you only have access to an item code designation for each computer). It could have been the VP; or it could have been a fellow coworker who was acting under instructions from the VP; or maybe the VP didn't know anything about how the movies were obtained.

You don't want to unnecessarily get anyone in trouble, but you aren't sure what to do. If these movies were the cause of the broadband usage, it was an abuse of company resources. Even if they weren't, they appear to be illegal downloads.

ENGAGEMENT—What Do You Think?

What should you do? Why? If you tell a supervisor, what do you think might happen? If you tell the Vice President, what do you think might happen? If you do nothing, what do you think might happen?

_____ .

_____ .

_____ .

_____ .

_____ .

_____ .

_____ .

Section 3.1 Business Ethics in the 21st Century

Business ethics in the 21st century has a progressive history that, for our purposes, can be addressed by looking at each decade since 1960.

The 1960s were a time in the United States when cultural values were changing. There was a heightened sense of individualism, but it was coupled with an equally heightened sense of social reform. Environmentalism, world peace, racial inequality, gender inequality, and sexual freedom were some of the issues that challenged the cultural status quo. Many businesses struggled with the noticeable change in the work ethic of their workforces and responded by expanding (or creating) human resource departments, establishing mission statements, and implementing codes of conduct. However, they also began to acknowledge the business community's role in effecting or advancing social issues and concerns. While most of the 1960s carried a guarded sense of optimism and positive change, the upsurge in the Vietnam War at the end of the decade ushered in the frustration and economic difficulties of the 1970s.

From a business perspective, the 1970s were a tumultuous time. A number of businesses in several different industries (especially defense contractors) suffered from, or participated in, various scandals. The national economy went through a recession and unemployment rose. The government imposed greater

© thodonal88/Shutterstock.com.

CHALLENGE QUESTIONS:

Why do you think ethical conduct is so important in the business world?

What do you think have been the most significant changes to business ethics in the past thirty years? Why?

Why do you think the world of business (domestically and internationally) continues to struggle with ethical decision-making? What do you think could effect lasting change?

regulations, including but not limited to the Federal Corrupt Practices Act (FCPA—designed primarily to prevent and penalize bribery when used to give a business an economic advantage) and popular management practices shifted from authoritarianism and rules-based management to increased collaboration and cooperation.

The 1980s experienced huge economic gains as the decade progressed, but those gains were hand-in-hand with a boom of fraudulent financial practices, illegal contracting, deceptive advertising, product liability issues, and bribery. Businesses began establishing ethics committees, ombudsmen programs, and ethics officers.

By the 1990s, environmental and healthcare issues were once again at the center of the stage of societal reform. Tobacco companies and junk food companies faced expensive litigation as a result of public health concerns. Petroleum companies and chemical processing companies also faced increased litigation and public outcry over environmental damage. Governmental regulations increased several-fold, and the Federal Sentencing Guidelines for Organizations began to be used as a yardstick for determining corporate complicity and liability for illegal or unethical activities. Businesses improved compliance programs and began to take a critical look at assessing corporate ethical wellness.

The first decade after the turn of the century was founded on fantastic economic growth driven, in large part, by the explosion of "dot-com" companies and excessive investment speculation. By 2002, the internet "bubble" had burst, and a vast number of internet-only businesses went under. The 2000s also saw a number of high-visibility corporate scandals mostly related to various methods of financial fraud. Because of the new internet economy, privacy issues, intellectual property infringement and theft, and cybercrime came to the forefront. More than ever, businesses operated within a global economy. International corruption, global debt, interrelated markets, and the advent of new and untested investment strategies, all suffering from a lack of meaningful governmental oversight, eventually led to the Great Recession from 2008 to 2012, a global recession as bad, if not worse, than the Great Depression of the 1930s. During this decade, and on into the 2010 decade, the U.S. government enacted a number of legislative measures and created new oversight agencies in an attempt to better manage financial services and investment markets. Businesses established ethics programs, implemented whistleblower protections, and looked for ways to improve their impact on, and involvement with, the communities in which they operated.

While the history of business ethics over the past fifty years exposes massive failures in private industry and in its relationship to society and the government, it also shows an immense amount of promise. Regulations, laws, organizations, recessions, public outcry, financial failure, and even social attitudes haven't been the magical elixir needed to permanently affix ethical decisions and ethical activity as part of the landscape for business. This does not mean these efforts have been entirely in vain. A lot has been accomplished and many things have changed, but we would be naïve to think that ethical decision-making can somehow be enduringly coerced through regulatory reform, or economic pressure, or public sentiment. Instead, we have to start with the *inside* and work our way out for there to be lasting change.

ENGAGEMENT—What Do You Think?

Historically, what do you think has been one of the greatest hurdles or challenges for businesses to overcome in order to make decisions that lead to greater prosperity? Why do you think this hurdle or challenge has been so difficult to overcome?

_____

_____

_____

_____

_____

_____

Section 3.2 Values and Skills

Business has a tendency to overwhelmingly focus on "skills" when hiring people, when trusting people, when promoting people, and when designating people as decision-makers. One major reason for this is because **skills** can be, for the most part, quantified. People can count how many years of education they've had. People can count and describe what kinds of degrees, or certificates, or licensures they have earned or possess. People can count how many years they've worked, and describe how many different positions they've held, and explain all of their various duties and responsibilities. Shareholders, executives, and managers can look at charts and graphs and see evidence of whether a person or

© garagestock/Shutterstock.com.

an organizational entity is "skilled" at delivering certain results. The public can hear about or read about various awards a company has earned or received and can assume the company is "skilled" at whatever it has accomplished. All of this may be true, and identifying skills and being skilled are certainly critical components to a business' long-term success and an individual's successful career. However, "skill"—even when it is impressive or obvious or exclusive—has far less to do with ethical decision-making than "value."

> **SKILLS**
>
> For an individual, this means the vocational or educational capacity to perform a task.

After taking our brief look at the most recent history of business ethics, especially in the United States, two things should become apparent as part of our current discussion:

1. The business world is full of people and companies with high levels of proficiency, expertise, ability, talent, cleverness, ambition, and persistence;

2. Even with all of that talent, drive, and *skill*, the business world seems to struggle with implementing and maintaining good ethical practices in spite of heavy doses of government regulation, economic failure, and reputational damage.

CHALLENGE QUESTIONS:

What are your own perceptions about the ethical bankruptcy, which continues to surface in the business world? What do you think causes ethical failure in business?

What are your thoughts about the concept of "value"? How do you think the use of ethical "languages" complements and encourages a focus on "value"?

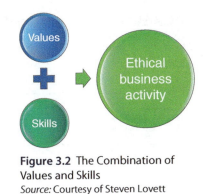

Figure 3.2 The Combination of Values and Skills
Source: Courtesy of Steven Lovett

ETHICAL BANKRUPTCY

For an organization, this means a lack of a constructive, sustainable decision-making process which leads to a more prosperous result.

VALUE

For an organization, this concept means the importance, worth, usefulness, and suitability in something or someone as that thing or person relates to an organization.

I would suggest that one of the major causes of **ethical bankruptcy** in the business world is because businesses place less emphasis on *value.* In this context, I want you to think of the word "**value**" in a multifaceted way: the value in *resources*, the value in *human capital*, the value in *beneficial products and services*, the value in *reputation*, the value in *transparency*, the value in *integrity and humility*, the value in *knowledge*, the value in *compliance and accountability*, and the value *customers.* "Value" implies that something is important, worthwhile, indispensable, respected, and advantageous.

It is insufficient (and a logical fallacy) to conclude business (yes, even capitalism) is "bad" because of the kind of ethical quandaries and failures the business world has caused and has brought upon itself. This is a self-serving misconception often perpetuated by those whose own agenda of collectivism or redistribution is at odds with free markets, entrepreneurship, and free enterprise. More importantly, this conclusion does little to address the problem because it misinterprets the symptoms.

The fact is, most businesses, and most business people, are trained to focus on the "skill"-side of the equation, instead of on the "value"-side of the equation. Ethical paradigms—especially those we discussed in the last chapter—foster an awareness of value through critical thinking, constructive challenges to decision-making processes and options, and more effective and more efficient communication among decision-makers and stakeholders. (See Figure 3.2.) By using ethical "languages" when confronting ethical dilemmas and an infinite number of different types of business decisions, there is a much greater likelihood that "value" in all of its multiple facets will play a much more prominent role.

ENGAGEMENT—What Do You Think?

Describe in your own words why you think the concept of "value" is a critical element of ethical decision-making for a business.

_____

_____

_____

_____

_____

_____

Section 3.3 Marketplace Influences and Consequences

MARKETPLACE

A word used to describe the general concept of where, how, and by whom "business" takes place, whether for-profit or not-for-profit.

An obvious influence on ethical conduct occurs in the marketplace. The **marketplace** represents the visible surface of the business world where sales are made, investments occur, relationships with external stakeholders transpire, and where society most visibly intersects with business. Like a ship on the ocean, businesses are constantly experiencing the movement and sometimes the beating of marketplace waves, and businesses are constantly trying to stay afloat in those waters, looking for smooth sailing and fair weather. Frequently, the greatest marketplace influence arises from sales, the nexus where a business provides its goods or services to an external consumer. This is a natural condition of a profit-seeking, competitive environment. However, while businesses attempt to cope with the vagaries of the marketplace, they must do so within the parameters of the law and within the larger social expectations that afford businesses their consumer base.

© MarkoV87/Shutterstock.com

© Iakov Filimonov/Shutterstock.com

The marketplace—existing within the rigid parameters of the law and within the highly dynamic notions of societal expectations—is a constantly changing environment. Businesses that remain static, as a matter of operations, finance, service, marketing, or products, are very likely to eventually succumb to the evolutions of the marketplace. The pace of change, and the force of marketplace influences, have increased exponentially over the past forty years.

The marketing era brought about change in focus to consumers and what they wanted. Marketing became a science with scientific studies on consumer buying behavior to determine how the buying

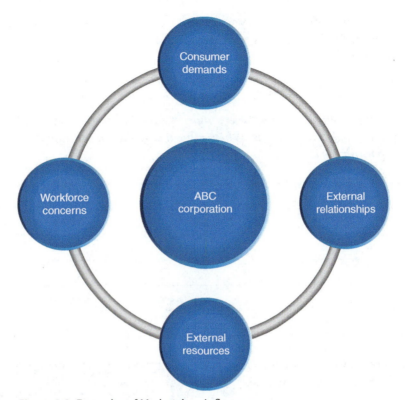

Figure 3.3 Examples of Marketplace Influences
Source: Courtesy of Steven Lovett

decision-making process works. Research has led to bright packaging, catchy television advertisements, product positioning in movies, paid "slotting fees" for special placement in stores, and any other technique to draw your attention away from competitors and on to a company's own products or services. The newest trends are to use the locating features on mobile phones and similar devices to provide real-time ad notices as you walk around in a mall or drive along a street. Using the Internet not only brings a wealth of information to you, it also provides a wealth of information to marketers about what interests you. This allows companies to download product information to you, which matches your search history.[3]

The relationship era is another change of focus. The intent in this era is to establish and maintain long-term, close relationships between suppliers, producers, transporters, and customers. You can hardly purchase anything anymore without being asked for your email address. The company

CHALLENGE QUESTIONS:

What do you think are the most damaging marketplace influences on a company's efforts to act ethically?

How do you think the use of ethical "languages" can help a company to cope with marketplace influences in a constructive and positive way? How important are marketplace influences and consequences on decisionmaking for a company?

doesn't just want to sell you something, they want to communicate with you as well. They want to get surveys done to find out if they are meeting your needs, and they want to correct any failings so they can generate repeat business.[4]

ENGAGEMENT—What Do You Think?

Describe a situation, hypothetical or real, where marketplace influences have had a direct and visible impact on how a business makes it decisions. Which ethical language or paradigm best describes that business' decision-making framework?

The "external forces" of the marketplace push against, challenge, and sometimes threaten to capsize (or *do* capsize) individual business concerns. Because of this, businesses can lose sight of the long-term horizon—the more far-reaching effects of unethical conduct and cultures—and focus instead on the "instant gratification" of day-to-day sales, minimizing costs, maximizing profits, high rates of growth, and keeping a "shiny" public image which may not be a very honest one. The influences, pressures, and consequences of the marketplace certainly cannot be ignored by a business, but

© Iakov Filimonov/Shutterstock.com

they need to be put into the proper context. As a business, and its people, reorient their focus on *value*, those external influences and pressures will be taken into account, but they'll be taken into account in a constructive, purposeful, appropriate, and *ethical* way.

Section 3.4 Individual Factors in Business Ethics

Organizations are comprised individuals. Because of this, factors and characteristics that influence individuals and their personal decision-making frameworks must be taken into account when discussing an organization's decision-making processes and frameworks. (See Figure 3.4.)

For the most part, individuals are able to make most of their decisions with very little critical analysis or reflective thinking. Individuals are largely creatures of opinion. A typical day is filled with decisions about relationships, hunger, sleep, clothing, shelter, financial responsibilities, transportation, entertainment, and relaxation that, for the most part, have very little effect on too many other people and, for the most part, are not burdened with the possibility of grave consequences. Individual decisions are many times disassociated from a broader worldview and are merely sufficient to satisfy

© bleakstar/Shutterstock.com

immediate goals without being optimal or efficient. Psychologists describe this kind of decision-making as using a "heuristic technique," an approach to problem-solving that uses a simplified strategy. Examples of this kind of simplified decision-making framework might include making an "educated guess," stereotyping, using "common sense," or applying a general "rule of thumb." Even though most individuals apply a certain level of rationality to most of their decisions, Herbert A. Simon, an interdisciplinary American professor of political science, management, psychology, and computer science, dubbed this as "bounded rationality" in his book, Models of Man. Simon asserted that an individual "behaves rationally with respect to [a simplified] model, and such behavior is not even approximately optimal with respect to the real world. To predict his behavior we must understand the way in which this simplified model is constructed."

When making a decision, and when influencing other people who are in the process of making decisions, several categorical factors manipulate how an individual decides to behave. These factors usually include age, socioeconomic status, past experiences, personal bias, thinking patterns based on generalizations and observations, and a personal perception about one's own self-worth or relevance. Some of these factors may result in irrationality, or limited rationality, when an individual makes a decision. These factors can also be part, or all, of the reason why an individual intentionally misbehaves or violates fundamental norms within an organization. While individual factors and influences may not be the primary contributor toward, or detractor from, ethical activity in the workplace, it is easy to see how personal development, personality traits, and personal biases do have a role to play in identification of ethical dilemmas, decision-making processes, and ethical conduct. Awareness and an appropriate level of attentiveness to individual factors and influences will go a long way toward preventing and dealing with ethical dilemmas in the workplace.

CHALLENGE QUESTIONS:

What are some of your own personal traits and influences that may lead to unethical conduct?

What are some of your own personal traits and influences that may help to maintain and encourage ethical conduct?

To what extent are you influenced by family? Friends? Social media? Income (or money)? A particular lifestyle? Your educational experiences?

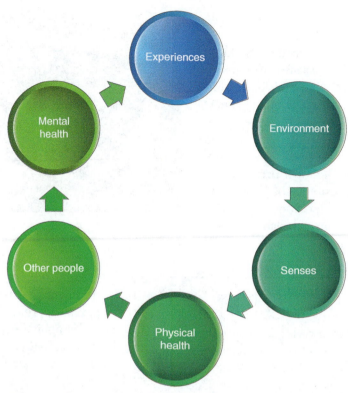

Figure 3.4 What Are Your Individual Influences?
Source: Courtesy of Steven Lovett

However, individual factors that influence personal decision-making can also be an advantage for organizational decision-making. Individual perspectives and biases can provide variety and an ultimate balance of diverse evaluations and viewpoints when analyzing an issue or dilemma.

ENGAGEMENT—What Do You Think?

At this point in your life, how (in what way) do you think you—as an individual—would influence an employer's decision-making? How do you think your own set of personal influences might affect your interaction or performance as an employee?

Section 3.5 Organizational Structure and Ethics

Organizational structure—distinguishable from organizational culture—is any system, formal or informal, used by a definable group of people to define hierarchy within that group. Ideally, a good organizational structure will identify and describe titles, authorities, functions, reporting lines, and formal relationships, and it will do so in such a way as to provide a clear configuration of expectations, responsibilities, and obligations for every person who participates in the operation of the organization at every level. Just as an organization's structure influences its strategies and its management systems, structure also influences the mechanics of decision-making within the organization.[5]

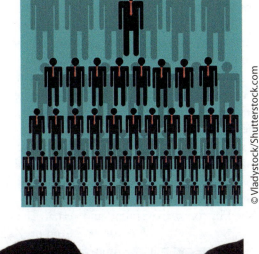

While there has been and still is a vigorous focus on *individuals* and on organizational *systems* (such as ethics programs) that address an individual's level of ethical decision-making judgment, an equal amount of attention should be paid to how an organization's formal *structure* (versus culture) effects the ethical decision-making and behavior of individuals within an organization, either for the better or for the worse.

[M]anagerial efforts should first build on an examination of the organization's formal structure because of the direct affect it has on employee behavior and because it is directly controllable by business managers.[6]

© Vladystock/Shutterstock.com

© BeeBright/Shutterstock.com

DECENTRALIZED

When most of an organization's decisions are made by mid-level or low-level employees, usually resulting in a horizontal organizational structure with less emphasis on formal policy.

The quality of influence on ethical decision-making that is influenced, if not directed by, organizational structure can be illustrated in part through the following findings published in *The American Economic Review*:

Our three main results are:

(i) absent communication, horizontal firms with static decision procedure based on averaging proposals are more ethical … than both vertical firms and consensus-based horizontal firms;

(ii) comparing structures with communication, vertical firms are more ethical than consensus-based firms;

(iii) communication significantly improves ethical outcomes in vertical firms.

While there are a variety of organizational structures, for the purpose of our discussion about the mechanics of decision-making, we will take a look at two primary categories: decentralized and centralized.

Decentralized organizations delegate decision-making authority as far down the chain-of-command as possible. Usually, there aren't too many formal rules or policies to guide the decision-making process. Coordination, communication, and control are also informal. These characteristics allow for greater adaptability and flexibility, and they tend to empower employees. However, decentralized organizations have more difficulty responding to policy changes established by top management, and certain centers or divisions or groups within the organization might easily deviate from organizational goals. In decentralized organizational structures, it is imperative that all employees and managers regularly receive the same kind of training in ethical issue identification, ethical decision-making processes, acceptable and unacceptable conduct, and remediation or reporting controls.

> **CHALLENGE QUESTIONS:**
>
> In your own words, explain how an organization's structure influences ethical conduct and decision-making processes. Why do you think structure plays such an important, even if unobvious, role?
>
> What do you think matters more: organizational structure or frequent and comprehensive training?

CENTRALIZED

When most of an organization's decisions are made by highlevel managers or executives, usually resulting in a vertical organizational structure with more emphasis on formal policy.

Centralized organizations exert more control and influence over their employees and lower-level management, and they typically have a core set of policies, procedures, and codes which predetermine decision-making processes, decision-making authority, controls, and consequences for unethical conduct. However, much like a heavily regulated marketplace, an abundance of policies and procedures does not automatically ensure ethical conduct. In centralized organizational structures, it is still imperative that all employees and managers regularly receive the same kind of ethical training, and it is perhaps even more an imperative than in a decentralized structure that ethical languages and open communication channels are well-known, utilized, encouraged, and protected.

ENGAGEMENT—What Do You Think?

What kind of organizational structure do you think would be more likely to encourage organization-wide ethical decision-making? Does an organization's structure matter? If so, in what way?

_____

_____

_____

_____

_____

_____

_____

Section 3.6 Organizational Factors and Normative Considerations

The influence managers and owners have over the behaviors and decision-making of employees is usually significant. Leadership is most often the key to identifying ethical issues, dilemmas, and actions. We'll spend some time in Chapter 5 discussing individual leadership and leadership styles, but for now, it is important to

POWER BASE
A source of influence, authority, support, or pressure.

note that leadership—being "in charge" in any substantive way—is one of the determinative organizational factors which influence decision-making processes and ethical activity.

© deviyanth79/Shutterstock.com.

This is a result of a **power base**. Exerting power—which is sometimes a very subtle activity—is one meaningful way in which management of a business organization can encourage, model, and compel ethical conduct within an organization. The way in which that power is exerted—similar to the way in which ethical issues are identified and discussed through different ethical paradigms—forecasts how influential a manager or owner might be in any given situation. There are five commonly recognized power bases:

- *Expert Power*—This arises from a person's knowledge (or perception of knowledge) about a particular issue. Power usually comes from credibility (deserved or not), which can be abused when it is used to unfairly manipulate others or to gain an unfair advantage.

- *Referent Power*—This exists when one person believes he or she shares a common goal(s) with another person or entity.

- *Coercive Power*—This punishes a person for his or her actions or behavior. Typically, this power base is most effective in the short-term.

- *Reward Power*—This is the opposite of Coercive Power. Influence is exerted by rewarding people for beneficial or constructive actions or behavior. The reward may be money, status, position, or reputation. This power base is typically more effective over the long term.

- *Legitimate Power*—This is the result of a person's belief that another person has the "right" to exert influence and that others have the "obligation" to accept that influence. This power base is usually held by figures in authority by title, position, or responsibility.

Power, in itself, is not ethical or unethical. Instead, it acts as a critical factor in influencing ethical or unethical behavior and decision-making. The exercise (or the lack of) power usually establishes organizational norms—standardized behavior. This is different than behavior guidelines which is directed

---

CHALLENGE QUESTIONS:

Which power base do you think might be most effective for guiding and implementing an ethically oriented culture in an organization? Why?

What kind of power base would you most likely respond positively to over the long term? Why?

Why do you think "groups" are able to exert so much influence over their members? If you were a manager, how would you engage with your company's various groups in order to encourage ethical norms?

© Rawpixel.com/Shutterstock.com.

NORMS

This refers to wide-spread practices, informal customs and processes, which become part of an organization's habitual expectations.

by corporate culture (which we'll discuss in Chapter 5). **Norms** refers to the kind of behavior that members of a group informally expect from other members.

Depending on the size of a business organization, it may or may not be comprised of many different "groups." These groups can be defined by any number of common characteristics, such as shared work functions, job titles, common responsibilities, income levels, and organizational roles. What is important to understand is that these groups will exert standards of behavior on their members; most often, this is very informal and is usually in the form of some type of peer pressure. These pressures can result in strong degrees of conformity among group members, even if conformity conflicts with the greater culture and direction of the organization as a whole. Because of this, it is essential for managers, owners, and other leaders within an organization (and within each group!) to prescribe values and rules within these groups which reflect and advance the organization's culture. Ethical "languages" are a great tool for accomplishing this task. Like individuals, groups will possess motivations, concerns, and interests, which may be competing against (or, hopefully, parallel to) other groups and the organization at-large. Using the verbiage and perspectives of the appropriate ethical paradigm can draw together and align those distinct points of view.

Power is a factor with a "vertical" (or hierarchical) effect. Group norms are a factor with a more "horizontal" effect. Together, these factors and considerations can have a far-reaching impact on ethical issue identification, decision-making processes, ethical activities, and controls.

SELECTED READINGS

- Carr, Albert. *Is Business Bluffing Ethical?* Harvard Business Review, January-February 1968.
- Bowie, Norman E., and Beauchamp, Thomas. *Business Ethics* (Englewood Cliffs, NJ: Prentice Hall, 1988).
- Hochshild, Arlie. *The Managed Heart* (Berkeley: University of California Press, 1983), pp. 3–9.
- Burlingham, Bo. *Small Giants: Companies That Choose to Be Great Instead of Big.* Updated edition. Portfolio, 2007.
- Stack, Jack, and Burlingham, Bo. *The Great Game of Business, Expanded and Updated: The Only Sensible Way to Run a Company.* Revised, 20th Anniversary edition. New York: Crown Business, 2013.

TAKE-AWAY QUESTIONS AND IDEAS

What keys ways can the business world begin to change from the inside-out, ethically speaking? Why do you think so many businesses struggle with recognizing, implementing, and maintaining ethically constructive and positive practices?

How is a "value-based" approach related to ethically constructive and positive practices?

How can businesses ethically cope with marketplace influences? Individual influences? Organizational factors?

Why is understanding power bases and group norms so important to learning about, and eventually acting on, ethically constructive and positive practices?

- Businesses have long struggled with recognizing, implementing, and maintaining ethically constructive and positive practices. Rarely can a business (much like a person) be *forced* to consistently act in a way in which it does not fundamentally believe it should act. In part, this pattern of ethical failure is because businesses spend more energy, time, and resources focusing on "skill" rather than on "value."

- "Value" implies that something is important, worthwhile, indispensable, respected, and advantageous. By using ethical "languages" when confronting ethical dilemmas and an infinite number of different types of business decisions, there is a much greater likelihood that "value" in all of its multiple facets will play a much more prominent role.

- Individuals are influenced by a wide variety of prompts—some developmental, some characteristic, and some environmental. They bring these with them into the workplace, and while individual influences may not result in systemic ethical failure, these influences can make it vastly more difficult to foster and maintain ethically constructive and positive practices.

- Similar to individual influences, but much more pervasive, organizational factors, structure, and normative considerations can many times inspire or discourage ethically positive decision-making and outcomes. These factors and considerations can have a far-reaching impact on ethical issue identification, decision-making processes, ethical activities, and controls.

KEY TERMS

- centralized
- Decentralized
- ethical bankruptcy
- marketplace

- Norms
- power base
- skills
- value

ENDNOTES

1. From *Conducting Business Ethically: A Philosophical Approach*, 2/E by Martin J. Lecker, Ed.D. Copyright © 2015 by Kendall Hunt Publishing Company. Reprinted by Permission.

2. From *Conducting Business Ethically: A Philosophical Approach*, 2/E by Martin J. Lecker, Ed.D. Copyright © 2015 by Kendall Hunt Publishing Company. Reprinted by permission.

3. From *Open for Business* by Brock Williams and Dane Galden. Copyright © 2015 By Kendall Hunt Publishing Company. Reprinted by Permission.

4. From *Open for Business* by Brock Williams and Dane Galden. Copyright © 2015 By Kendall Hunt Publishing Company. Reprinted by Permission.

5. James, Harvey S. "Reinforcing Ethical Decision Making Through Organizational Structure." *Journal of Business Ethics* 28, no. 1 (November 1, 2000): 43–58, at p. 44.

6. Ellman, Matthew, and Paul Pezanis-Christou. "Organizational Structure, Communication, and Group Ethics." *The American Economic Review* 100, no. 5 (2010): 2478–491, at p. 2479.

ENGAGEMENT—WHAT DO YOU THINK?

Write down your own thoughts about what you've learned in this chapter. Consider the previous discussions about values and skills, marketplace influences, individual factors, organizational structures, power bases, and norms. In your own words, describe how you think these various factors affect decision-making processes within an organization. If it helps, look back at the Opening Thought Experiment; how would these factors affect the answers you gave?

_____

_____

_____

_____

_____

_____

_____

_____

_____

_____

_____

_____

UNIT TWO

THE ROLE OF ETHICS IN BUSINESS

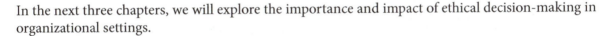

In the next three chapters, we will explore the importance and impact of ethical decision-making in organizational settings.

Chapter 4 will look at the various relationships a business creates and maintains while conducting its business. We will explore expectations, needs, and misapprehensions throughout those relationships. This includes an examination of current theories about ethical conduct in business and why those theories are impractical in real-world contexts. This sets up a conversation about a business' accountability beyond what is mandated.

Chapter 5 discusses how a business should conduct itself culturally. This explores the benefits of ethical conduct, the advantages of values over compliance, and the impact of various leadership styles on an organization's decision-making frameworks.

Chapter 6 introduces a new concept called the "prosperity opportunity" and how ethical decision-making can maximize that opportunity. We will look at the way in which expectations should be set within an organization and how actions and decisions can be constructively vetted and improved over time.

This second unit is intended to introduce and demonstrate the role ethical decision-making has in an organizational setting—how it can improve relationships, create and maintain constructive cultures, and maximize the possibility of prosperous outcomes over time.

CHAPTER 4

VESTED INTERESTS: ORGANIZATIONAL MOTIVATIONS, RESPONSIBILITIES, AND RELATIONSHIPS WITH AFFECTED PARTIES

As obvious as it might sound to say it, a business' purpose is to remain "in business." The practical mechanisms which promote this single purpose are comprised of dozens of activities, and operational and administrative categories, such as sales, advertising, human resources, logistics, manufacturing, finances and accounting, public relations, information systems, compliance, labor, management, licensing, procurement, vendor relations, shareholder relations, and reporting. But what ties all of these things together—as disparate and as distinct as they might be—is a business' objective to *earn a profit* (or, for a not-for-profit enterprise, to continue satisfying a consumer demand for its service or product).

Unfortunately, "earning a profit" has, in many corners, received a bad rap. Instead of it sounding ambitious and admirable, it more often is disparaged as something cold, dispassionate, elitist, and ruthless. Admittedly, the business world hasn't been a very good shepherd of its own image—we saw this when we took a look at the last forty years of business ethics—but we have also learned this lackluster image does not automatically mean business, or "doing business" (earning a profit) is, therefore, a bad thing. In fact, for a business, earning a profit is not only its primary, long-term objective, but it is a very, very good thing.

Andrew Flew (1923–2010), an English philosopher, pointedly took issue with the notion that earning a profit might be thought to be an immoral, or selfish, thing. Flew said that profit was an essential trait of capitalism. He said that no one should simply assume that an effort to make a profit was, in and of itself, a selfish or disreputable aspiration. Insightfully, Flew noted that selfish actions are, inherently and always, driven by a specific interest, but it does not therefore follow that every action with an "interest" was inherently "selfish." His argument underscored the fact that

© PILart/Shutterstock.com

any particular economic system (such as capitalism) cannot be arbitrarily dismissed simply on the basis that it relies largely on people pursuing their own self-interests, or that it relies on people pursuing a profit because of specific interests.

Flew also took issue with the idea that the pursuit of a profit—selling goods and services in the open market—created some kind of a zero-sum, or unfair, relationship between a merchant and the merchant's customer (or another stakeholder who "needed" something of value from the merchant). He said that any transaction in the marketplace is the result of a mutual relationship. He also said the relationship, and the transaction, are voluntary actions. By its nature, a marketplace transaction is not a coerced transaction—it doesn't happen as a matter of force.

The fact is successful businesses actually have deeply vested interests in their relationships with stakeholders. Businesses need those relationships to be meaningful, constructive, valuable (there's that word "value" again), and mutually beneficial. Ethical paradigms ("languages!") will allow a business to better understand each stakeholder's needs and concerns; a business will be able to better communicate with each stakeholder; a business will be able to be more thoughtfully and constructively work through each dilemma; a business will be able to improve its decision-making process; and a business will be able to begin, and to continue, aligning various and different goals and interests.

It is imperative, in order to manage those relationships in a constructive and positive way, that we first begin by understanding the context of each relationship and then take a look at how a business should handle its responsibilities and obligations (and expectations) to those various stakeholders.

LEARNING OUTCOMES | OUTLINE

4.1 Advancing the Business Purpose

4.2 The Marketplace and Society

4.3 The Marketplace and Government

4.4 Corporate Social Responsibility

4.5 Stakeholder Theory versus Shareholder Theory

4.6 Core Practices and Voluntary Accountability

4.7 The Significance of Organizational Trust

- Understand the overarching purpose of business relationships and how those relationships should be constructively and positively managed.
- Understand the relationship between the marketplace and society at-large, and how society perceives business.

- Understand the relationship between the marketplace and the government, and the government's most constructive role in business relationships.
- Describe ideal core practices and what purpose they serve in managing business relationships in a constructive and positive way.
- Describe voluntary accountability in business relationships and its purpose in managing those relationships in a constructive and positive way.
- Understand "Stakeholder Theory" and how it affects long-term business purposes.
- Understand "Shareholder Theory" and how it affects long-term business purposes.
- Describe the significance of organizational trust when managing business relationships in a constructive and positive way.

OPENING THOUGHT EXPERIMENT

As you're settling into your Thursday night routine of popcorn and a scary movie, you receive a message from one of your long-time friends, Scarlett. Earlier in the day, you'd seen her posts of her and her hubby on their vacation to the Bahamas, but you didn't expect to actually hear from her. As you read Scarlett's message, you put your popcorn down and turn off the television. You lean back and let out a long sigh. *What should I tell her? . . .*

. . . Scarlett could not believe her luck. For as long as she could remember, Brad Depp had been her heart-throb. Now, amazingly, she had stumbled across his secluded holiday home in the Bahamas, which not even the paparazzi knew about.

© sharpshutter/Shutterstock.com

What is more, when Brad saw the solitary walker on the beach, he had offered her a drink, and as they talked, he turned out to be as charming as she had imagined. And then, because of his lifestyle, he admitted he got a bit lonely. After revealing this to her, Brad leaned over to kiss Scarlett, but she quickly hopped up and excused herself to the bathroom.

Scarlett stared at herself in the mirror. She wanted so badly to let Brad kiss her, but there was one major problem: Scarlett was married to a man she loved very much. *But what you don't know, can't hurt you*, she thought, and he would never know. She would have an evening of fantasy, and Brad would get a little comfort. Everyone would either be as they were or (supposedly) richer for the experience. No one would suffer. However, if she refused Brad's advances, she might regret it, and Brad would still be lonely. On the other hand, she would also know she'd been unfaithful to her husband. With so much to gain or lose, Scarlett stood there, tapping her nails against the porcelain sink. *What should I do?*, she kept repeating to herself.

Suddenly, she reached inside her clutch and pulled out her phone. As fast as she could, she began typing out a message to one of her old friends.

ENGAGEMENT—What Do You Think?

What would you tell her to do? Should Scarlett give in to her temptations with Brad?
Depending on what advice you would give Scarlett, what do you think her future looks like? How will she feel? What will her relationship be like with her husband? What will her relationship be like with Brad?

_____

_____

_____

_____

_____

_____

_____

Section 4.1 Advancing the Business Purpose

In the final analysis, business is driven by, succeeds by, and is sustainable through, its relationships. Businesses, almost without exception, have a number of critical, overlapping, and sometimes delicate relationships with a large number of **stakeholders**, who are directly, and indirectly, affected by what the business does, how it does what it does, and what the consequences are. Establishing, managing, and sometimes ending, all of these different kinds of relationships can be a very difficult and complex challenge, even though it can also be rewarding and very valuable to an ongoing business concern.

> **STAKEHOLDER**
>
> In organizations, this is any person or entity, internal or external, who has an interest, whether or not financial, in the success of a company.

Temptations in business are much like temptations in our private lives, and those temptations are motivated by factors such as instant gratification, long-term success, satisfaction (i.e., happiness or contentment), competition (or sometimes retaliation), likes and dislikes, basic needs, pride and reputation, duty and obligation, and goodwill. Ethical considerations and decision-making processes are bound up in all of these factors and are provoked, inspired, or encouraged by all of these factors. At the end of the day, however, a business' relationships with its stakeholders must (or should) be managed so as to advance the business' purpose—to remain in business, to grow, to prosper, and to be sustainable over time. That purpose, and its aligned goals, must always be taken into account when making decisions about those relationships.

© Constantin Stanciu/Shutterstock.com

> **CHALLENGE QUESTIONS:**
>
> What do you think is the "purpose of business"? Why?
> How do you think a business could advance or further its purpose through its relationships with other persons or entities or organizations?

(Although, as in Scarlett's situation, merely taking into account certain goals doesn't automatically provide an easy answer as to what should be done... That's where ethical "languages" and value step in to help out and provide the "right" compass point!)

ENGAGEMENT—What Do You Think?

Describe in your own words why the primary purpose of every business must be to make a profit—or better yet—to increase "prosperity."

_____

_____

_____

_____

_____

_____

_____

Knowing this, and in order to better understand how to establish, and constructively and positively manage, those relationships, we need to take a look at where various stakeholders come from, how they interact, and how their interests intersect or diverge.

Section 4.2 The Marketplace and Society

In the previous chapter, we talked a bit about marketplace influences and consequences, and how those affected business decision-making frameworks and outcomes. The "marketplace," which we'll use as shorthand for the "business world," is most often where a business interacts with, and establishes relationships with, society at-large. This is where goods and services are bought, sold, and licensed. This is where so many of our society's financial and lifestyle expectations are supplied, such as health benefits, personal income, retirement plans, investment income, and our careers (which, for so many people, is part of their identity and which absorbs most of their time and energy). Many businesses, of course, have a physical presence within communities and certainly interact with local "societies" through those physical footprints, but even those physical locations are the result of the business *being*

in business, that is, advertising and selling its services and goods to a consuming market. . . out there in the larger society.

Based on our historical review of business ethics in the last chapter, it would be easy to conclude that the marketplace has repeatedly chosen to "cheat on its spouse," most often thinking no one would find out or (like Scarlett imagined) "no one will get hurt." Eventually though, as Shakespeare scripted in *The Merchant of Venice*, "truth will out," and the marketplace has had to sit in the hot seat as society has suffered from its unethical conduct, judged its actions, and been compelled

© Rawpixel.com/Shutterstock.com

to impose new rules and restraints (laws and regulations) on the marketplace. Instead of businesses taking the lead to properly establish and manage this significant relationship, society has been the one (like a jilted spouse) to pick up the pieces, endure the damage, and then, even if in a very gun-shy way, insist that the relationship continue.

On the other hand, the marketplace's poor conduct should not be overly demonized. Society has often imposed unrealistic expectations and ultimatums on the marketplace, looking to the business world to provide the kind of lifestyle, safety, security, and happiness it wants and expects. Society has often demanded more jobs, higher pay, better benefits, more economic growth, more and better products, faster results, and greater returns on investments. Society has often unfairly criticized the marketplace for doing what it's supposed to do (make a profit, provide goods and services, etc.), while at the same time, demanding the marketplace do what it's supposed to do at a faster pace and with better outcomes.

(For instance, many people would be quick to criticize mortgage providers for creating high-risk mortgages prior to the last recession, but many people would be equally critical of mortgage providers who have refused to lend to "high-risk" customers, especially if that customer happens to be the person doing the complaining.)

> **CHALLENGE QUESTIONS:**
>
> In the relationship between the marketplace and society, what do you think are each side's obligations to the other? How do you think those obligations should inform a business' decision-making processes?
>
> Thinking about this relationship, what do you believe would be reasonable expectations for businesses? What would be reasonable expectations for society? How are those expectations mutually beneficial?

The relationship between the marketplace and society, and all of the resulting chaos, harm, and benefit, is the perfect backdrop to better appreciate the concept of "value" we discussed in Chapter 3. For a business to constructively and positively manage its relationship with society, *value* must remain at the center of its analyses, decision-making objectives, and its aimed-for outcomes. (See Figure 4.1.) Arguably, the burden is on the marketplace to properly establish and maintain this relationship. While businesses cannot control the whims and vagaries of society, they can hold themselves accountable, act with integrity, and create value while still advancing every business' purpose—to remain in business, to grow, to prosper, and to be sustainable over time.

Figure 4.1 The Relationship Between the Marketplace and Society
Source: Courtesy of Steven Lovett

ENGAGEMENT—What Do You Think?

What should society be doing or asking in order to bring "value" to the marketplace? What should the marketplace be doing or asking in order to bring "value" to society?

_____

_____

_____

_____

_____

_____

_____

Section 4.3 The Marketplace and Government

The law and subsequent regulations are where the marketplace and the government (local, state, and federal) intersect. Laws are a series of rules and regulations designed to express the needs of people, provide a sense of right and wrong, and guide behavior. The relationship between the marketplace and the government is usually more formalized, much like a renter might have with his

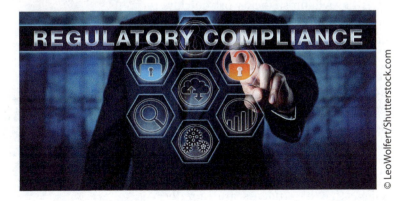

© LeoWolfert/Shutterstock.com

or her landlord. Roles, responsibilities, obligations, and consequences are much more likely to be spelled out. This is a "rule-based" relationship; one which has spanned an entire cottage industry of "compliance"—something that has, like a shoe which is a little too small, been shoved on many business' feet as "ethics," which has unfortunately led to far too many missteps and misconceptions (don't worry, we'll address this in Chapter 5). But just like a rental contract, even rules and obligations which are "spelled out" can be confusing, onerous, or lead to unfair results.

The relationship between the marketplace and the government (one which the government views itself in a "custodial" or "parental" role) can be confusing, unbalanced, and easily derailed. From the government's perspective, the answer to this has often been to add even more rules. Sometimes, this approach has led to improvements—rules, after all, are excellent tools for setting boundaries, imposing particular expectations, and compelling particular actions. For instance, this side of the relationship has led to better working conditions for employees, increased transparency with financial reporting and investments, improved safety, and enlarged consumer protections. But it is perhaps just as obvious that new compliance standards, laws, and regulations have not actually ensured more ethical behavior. (See Figure 4.2.)

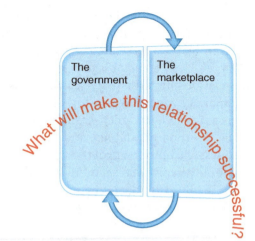

Figure 4.2 The Relationship Between the Marketplace and Government
Source: Courtesy of Steven Lovett

Imagine two, similar classroom settings where each student's primary objective is to paint a picture. All of the "normal" etiquette expectations exist in both classrooms, such as no rudeness, no fighting, and so on. In classroom "A," all of the students understand that if they act constructively and positively (i.e., sharing paints, being polite, concentrating on their own work, and making every effort to paint as good of a picture as each of them possibly can), they will finish their work quickly, receive high marks, and have an early recess.

However, in classroom "B," the students are different. They believe the goal is to paint the best picture each of them can *at any cost*. In fact, they have been taught that their goal is an inherently selfish goal, therefore, pursuing it is an inherently selfish pursuit. People outside classroom B believe that its students are morally bankrupt, and a proctor is placed in

© Billion Photos/Shutterstock.com

CHALLENGE QUESTIONS:

When or where do you think government regulations are appropriate? How do you think government regulation and laws affect the marketplace?

How do you think the marketplace—businesses—can improve, and better manage, its relationship with government at every level?

the room. The proctor hands each of the students a thick rulebook, containing all kinds of rules and requirements, which are intended to force each student to behave. The students in classroom B, try to paint their paintings, but they spend a lot of time trying to make sure they aren't breaking any rules, being penalized when they do break rules, and engaging with the proctor in an attempt to work out compromises when they are in trouble or when their paintings end up being abysmal failures.

As with any analogy or allegory, there are gaps in the application, but hopefully the point is clear: ethical conduct in the marketplace will never be the result of rules, regulations, or laws. In fact, those things have more of a tendency to hamper and impede a business' long-term success. Instead, constructive and positive conduct and ethical decision-making must come from the inside-out (which is what this course is all about). In the relationship between the marketplace and government, rules are reactive, attempting to make sure that whatever fell apart in the past won't fall apart again (at least in the same way) in the future. Because this relationship is typically so rigid, so reactive, and so punitive, it should *ideally* be relatively diminished or light-handed.

As Milton Friedman once cautioned, business persons, while extremely astute in matters which are internal to their respective businesses, can be imprudent when it comes to issues outside of their own companies. Friedman pointed to examples of business persons calling for wage and price controls, or regulatory policies affecting corporate income. Friedman said these absurdities would destroy the free marketplace and replace it with a centralized, and administrative, system.

ENGAGEMENT—What Do You Think?

What should government be doing or asking in order to bring "value" to the marketplace? What should the marketplace be doing or asking in order to bring "value" to the government?

_____

_____

_____

_____

_____

_____

_____

The marketplace can vastly improve its relationship with government by setting out to improve its core practices and to be voluntarily accountable (two concepts we'll discuss shortly) for its decisions and subsequent consequences. With "value" acting as the North Star, the marketplace can change its relationship dynamic with government from a classroom "B" setting to a classroom "A" setting.

© garagestock/Shutterstock.com

Section 4.4 Corporate Social Responsibility

The idea of businesses having the responsibility to improve relationships between society and the marketplace, and government and the marketplace, is (relatively speaking) a universally agreed upon conclusion. The concept of business ethics can be broken out (very roughly) into two camps: one in which business ethics should arise from companies focusing on, and delivering, value; and one in which business ethics should arise from companies focusing on acting as "moral agents" to improve society and the environment. Both camps believe businesses should act ethically, but how a business

© garagestock/Shutterstock.com

gets there, and what "acting ethically" means, can be two, very different things.

Within the past several decades, a growing point of critique has become part of the marketplace environment: the perceived duty of an organization to further some social good beyond what is required by law and even beyond what may be required to operate the organization. Although there is no institutionally determinative definition, this perceived "duty" has been called **corporate social responsibility**, or CSR. Consumers, and society at-large, have progressively become more and more concerned with ecological issues, social reform and social justice issues, and economic issues that relate to, or appear to relate to,

CORPORATE SOCIAL RESPONSIBILITY (CSR)

Refers to business practices which are primarily intended to benefit society-at-large usually focused on three general areas of concern: ecological, social, and economic.

socioeconomic status and/or quality of life. Popular culture has adopted, or been infused with, the broad concept of sustainability—roughly defined as the ability to meet present needs without weakening the ability of a future generation to meet its needs. CSR has become the champion theory for advancing the concept of sustainability within the business world.[1]

The development of CSR as a theory reflects the shaping of several other theories, such as institutional theory (a focus on deeper and more enduring aspects of social structure), agency theory (managers acting as agents of owners may act in such a way as to cause a less than maximized shareholder return for the sake of promoting the interests of the organizational entity), stewardship theory (when left to act on their own, managers will act as good custodians of the assets in their control), and stakeholder theory (actions of an organization should take into account a variety of stakeholder interests other than just ownership interests). However, a firm formulation and application of the theory of CSR has had difficulty finding authentic traction among academics and business people alike. (See Figure 4.3.)

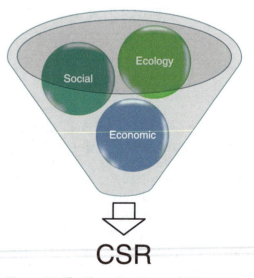

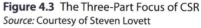

Figure 4.3 The Three-Part Focus of CSR
Source: Courtesy of Steven Lovett

The best conceptualizations remain in their—to use a strong word—embryonic stages, and prescribed approaches to CSR seem perplexing to theorists and completely elude practitioners. This state of affairs probably impedes a full understanding among managers of what CSR should comprise and hinders further theoretical development of CSR.[2]

Additionally, because the idea of CSR relies on vague concepts of furthering some social good, the theory has increasingly been appropriated as a tool by political-ideological interests of, for the most part, social activists.[3] For businesses that recognize the possibility of obtaining a competitive edge by overtly addressing the populist demand for "socially responsible" actions, or for businesses that genuinely want to "make a difference" in the long term, there are not any other fashionable or widespread theories on which to rely except for CSR.

As Milton Friedman said in a very straightforward manner,

> The discussions of the "social responsibilities of business" are notable for their analytical looseness and lack of rigor. What does it mean to say that "business" has responsibilities? Only people can have responsibilities. A corporation is an artificial person and in this sense may have artificial responsibilities, but "business" as a whole cannot be said to have responsibilities, even in this vague sense....This is the basic reason why the doctrine of "social responsibility" involves the acceptance of the socialist view that political mechanisms, not market mechanisms, are the appropriate way to determine the allocation of scarce resources to alternative uses....[T]he doctrine of "social responsibility" taken seriously would extend the scope of the political mechanism to every human activity. It does not differ in philosophy from the most explicitly collectivist doctrine. It differs only by professing to believe that collectivist ends can be attained without collectivist means.

Friedman also commented on the absurdity of insisting on the absolutism of "social responsibility" when prosperity is best achieved by an organization having the liberty to identify and deliver true value, thereby aspire to achieve prosperity and to advance the prosperity of this various stakeholders. "A major source of objection to a free economy is precisely that it...gives people what they want instead of what a particular group thinks they ought to want."

At this point, it would seem that CSR is the way to go, but it is very important to realize that something subtle, yet extraordinarily potent and damaging, is going on with the move toward CSR. The clarion call of CSR *changes the fundamental reason* why businesses should act in constructive and positive ways. CSR essentially says that a business should act responsibly because it has an *obligation* to act responsibly. This is rule-based thinking, and it's thinking which we don't even apply to individuals in our society. We might *want* individuals in our society to act responsibly (ethically), but we only *obligate* them to act lawfully (within the bounds of the law).

Ironically, we have already seen how decades of increasing laws, regulations, and rules have not stamped out unethical conduct in the marketplace. Why then would

> **CHALLENGE QUESTIONS:**
>
> Why do you think CSR is such a popular theory? What kind of corporate conduct is important to you?
>
> How, or why, do you think a business could best address your concerns, while at the same time, achieve its own primary objective?

© Krasimira Nevenova/
Shutterstock.com

we believe that yet another "rule," some kind of socially generated moral rule, would better accomplish what a multitude of laws cannot? Furthermore, isn't this exactly like the kind of intolerance we abhor in our society today—for one person or group to impose their set of morals onto another?

In our earlier discussion about "value" (which we'll continue in the chapters to come), we have learned about a far more effective and genuine fundamental reason why businesses should act responsibly: by focusing on, and delivering, *value*, a company's decision-making and conduct will lead to increased profits (a company's primary objective) and to prosperity for a business' stakeholders. *Value* doesn't obligate a company to act in a certain way as a result of some other person's, or entity's, expectations or agenda. (This is classroom "B.") Value encourages and inspires a business—from the inside-out—to conduct itself in a constructive and positive manner in order to achieve prosperity for itself and for its stakeholders. (This is classroom "A.") The concepts of *value* and *prosperity* constructively align a business' interests, and its goal to "earn a profit," with society's interests in furthering the common good, well beyond what is required by law.

CSR, as appealing as it first looks on the surface, does not actually establish or encourage the kind of permanent and authentic improvements we, as a society and as business people, want in the relationship between the marketplace and society, or the relationship between the marketplace and government. CSR ignores the variety of ethical "languages" which are the frameworks for decision-making and for identifying concerns, interests, and goals. In short, CSR is just another rule developed in classroom "B."

ENGAGEMENT—What Do You Think?

What do you think would ultimately happen if businesses were required to make CSR their primary objective—to frame each business decision based on external consequences?

_____

_____

_____

_____

_____

_____

_____

_____

Section 4.5 Stakeholder Theory *versus* Shareholder Theory

Close in-hand with CSR is **stakeholder theory**. This theory was conceptualized by R. Edward Freeman in the book *Strategic Management: A Stakeholder Approach*. A stakeholder "in an organization is (by definition) any group or individual who can affect or is affected by the achievement of the organization's objectives."[4] Accordingly, stakeholders may include customers and clients, employees, vendors, owners, regulators, lenders, and all of the persons and entities who comprise the community within which an organization operates. In favor of this theory, Freeman argued that.

> **STAKEHOLDER THEORY**
>
> A framework of organizational management which proposes that business decisions, as a primary concern, should take into account the interests of all affected stakeholders.

We need to understand the complex interconnections between economic and social forces. Isolating "social issues" as separate from the economic impact which they have, and conversely isolating economic issues as if they had no social effect, misses the mark both managerially and intellectually. Actions aimed at one side will not address the concerns of the other. Processes, techniques and theories that do not consider all of these forces will fail to describe and predict the business world as it really is.[5]

By considering a variety of stakeholder interests, an organization should be able to better avoid exploiting one stakeholder in favor of another. However, the challenge is to be able to accurately and adequately understand, valuate, and prioritize all of the variable interests of a multitude of, sometimes changing, stakeholders.

This problem has led to the idea of separating stakeholders into two groups: a "primary" group and a "secondary" group, although there are a wide variety of opinions as to which stakeholder fits into which group. This has further resulted in the normative theory of stakeholder identification (which stakeholder belongs where) and the descriptive theory of stakeholder salience (how stakeholders are "seen and heard").

CHALLENGE QUESTIONS:

Why do you think stakeholder theory has become so popular? Do you think stakeholder theory is "ego-centric"—placing stakeholders ahead of the business with which they have a relationship? Why or why not?

If a business placed its stakeholders' interests first, how could it explain this to its shareholders (owners) without risking being found liable (responsible) for breaching its fiduciary duty to its shareholders?

Once again, as with CSR, the stakeholder theory of corporate "responsibility" appears productive on the surface. But in reality, stakeholder theory also redirects a business' focus away from its primary objective of earning a profit—delivering value and concentrating on prosperity—to *obligating* a business to account for its stakeholders. This change in a business' *fundamental reason why* businesses should act in constructive and positive way is another rule-based approach, and it shifts the interests of stakeholders (to whom a business does not owe a legal obligation) onto a business—suddenly a company is responsible for whether its stakeholders are satisfied, happy, successful, and gratified. (See Figure 4.4.)

Figure 4.4 Stakeholder Theory
Source: Courtesy of Steven Lovett

SHAREHOLDER	**SHAREHOLDER VALUE MODEL**
Any person or entity who owns all or any part of a business enterprise.	A model of business management that equates a business' success with the extent to which it financially enriches its owners.

Instead of a nebulous stakeholder-orientation, a business should be clearly oriented toward its **shareholders**—its owners. (This, in fact, is actually a duty imposed by law—a *fiduciary* obligation.) This is not necessarily what has been termed as the "**shareholder value model**," which implies that a business is only successful if it enriches its shareholders. Earning a profit, sustainably and constructively, means that profit is earned by delivering true value and promoting prosperity.

This is much more than simply adding another dollar into a shareholder's pocket. By constructively and positively managing its various stakeholder relationships (*not* "focusing" on those relationships, but managing them in order to maximize value and to promote prosperity), a business will be fulfilling its primary objective of earning a profit in a sustainable, positive way. This, in turn, is what ultimately enriches a company's shareholders.

ENGAGEMENT—What Do You Think?

There are some positive aspects to Shareholder Theory—a business should be concerned about those persons and entities affected by its decisions. Describe a situation, real or hypothetical, in which a business makes its decisions based primarily on its own business objective while also considering the interests of various stakeholders.

Section 4.6 Core Practices and Voluntary Accountability

Interposed in our discussion about relationships between the business world, society, government, other stakeholders, and its shareholders are the concepts of "voluntary accountability" and "core practices." Simply put, these concepts represent the means by which a business can achieve its primary objective (earning a profit) by constructively and positively managing its relationships with all of its stakeholders.

© Boris15/Shutterstock.com

MANDATED BOUNDARIES

For all organizations, this describes externally imposed processes and actions based on laws, regulations, and other compulsory conventions.

VOLUNTARY ACCOUNTABILITY

In organizations, this describes practices that includes beliefs, values, and voluntary contractual obligations which are not otherwise required by law or industry-wide practices.

All businesses are subject to **mandated boundaries** that impose processes and actions as a matter of law. But beyond these "outer markers" of how to manage a business, there are far more effective ways in which a company can implement and enjoy the benefits of constructive, sustainable decisions which lead to more prosperous outcomes.

"**Voluntary accountability**" is, essentially, self-regulation (but not the kind imposed by CSR). This type of accountability is first and foremost an internal mechanism, established, maintained, and monitored inside a business. This is when every person and every component of a business shares in well-known and well-distributed communication channels, oversight functions, and challenge processes. Decision-making frameworks are based on shared, and understood, ethical paradigms, where roles and responsibilities are clearly set, and where everyone (from the top to the bottom) has a positive sense of "ownership" in decision-making and its outcomes.

This self-regulation is akin to a person *choosing* to adhere to a healthy diet and an exercise regimen (which results in long-lasting, positive lifestyle changes), instead of being forced to diet and exercise (which might work in the short term for participation in high school or college sports, a term of military enlistment, or while simply at a summer camp). If the "self-regulation" is forced externally, the change is very likely to be temporal and artificial. But if the voluntary accountability is systemic from within, the change is likely to be long-lasting and genuine. From this primary layer of voluntary accountability can then come the kind of "accountability" popularly sought after in society and government: transparency, environmental or resource responsibility, social responsibility, and financial responsibility. These areas of corporate accountability, as important and as highly publicized as they might be, are truly residual to a business' internal, voluntary accountability.

© Vmaster/Shutterstock.com

This voluntary accountability also leads to, and is simultaneously supported by, a set of "**core practices**." These are the set of practices—methodologies, procedures, measures, systems, and techniques—utilized by a business to inform, monitor, analyze, and advance its voluntary accountability. We'll talk more about core practices when we discuss value-based cultures in Chapter 5 and the tools of ethics management in Chapter 6.

Voluntary accountability and core practices create a business environment—internally—which is in a perfect position to advance the business purpose (to earn a profit) while doing so in a way which also establishes and manages relationships with affected parties (society, government, and other stakeholders) in a constructive and positive way. As is the case with any positive relationship, all of this only works productively if a business also insists on, and maintains, organizational *trust* (in much the same way as the law expects it to do as a fiduciary).

CORE PRACTICES

In organizations, this describes appropriate and common (usually industry-wide) practices that ensure compliance with legal requirements and societal expectations; sometimes described as "best practices."

ENGAGEMENT—What Do You Think?

Describe a business decision, real or hypothetical, which illustrates mandated boundaries, core practices, and voluntary accountability.

_____

_____

_____

_____

_____

_____

_____

Section 4.7 The Significance of Organizational Trust

Because we've spent this chapter talking about a business' relationships and how a business can best manage and maintain those relationships in a constructive and positive manner, we need to spend a few uncomfortable minutes also talking about the greatest act of violence on any such relationship—deception. Unfortunately, lying—an ultimate betrayal of trust—is a phenomenon that continues to be an endemic problem among individuals, whether in their personal lives or at work. In fact, "60% of people lie during a typical 10-minute conversation and that they

average two to three lies during that short timeframe."[6] Ironically, it can sometimes be the "good" qualities of a workplace that actually tempt employees and managers to lie. An employee who lies might be trying to avoid disappointing others within an organization with high expectations and high standards. An employee might lie in order to impress other people at work who have a venerable and admired status. No matter what the reason, lying is deception; it is the antithesis of trust. It can be passive through omission or active through commission. First, lying damages the ability to make a free, rational choice; and second, lies rob others of their freedom to choose rationally.

"Trust" is a belief that something is truthful or reliable. Trust is created and preserved through integrity, a sense of dependability, and

CHALLENGE QUESTIONS:

From a theoretical standpoint, deception may be "ethical" for certain ethical paradigms, but if that point of view was put into practical use, what do you think the impact would be on a business' long-term sustainability?

How do you think a business can establish and maintain "organizational trust"?

fairness and honesty. Remember the students in classroom "A"? That situation could only work because the students could be *trusted* to understand what their goal was and to understand how acting in a constructive and value-based way could help achieve their goal. Those students were free to act, and saw the benefit in acting, with integrity. This may seem to dip into a sense of morality (which I'm not opposed to), but it doesn't have to for our purposes. Instead, this concept of trust and integrity in a business setting means that all interested parties should be able to depend on, rely on, and make decisions on, an open and fair (an *honest*) understanding of the circumstances and features as they are conveyed and exhibited by the business. For instance, if a government agency is going to have a constructive and positive relationship with a business, it should be able to rely on that business' representation and description about whatever it is the government agency possesses oversight. Otherwise, the business has not taken the necessary steps to maintain and manage a constructive and positive—a prosperous—relationship with the agency; something which is bound to impede its ability over the long run to "earn a profit."

Organizational trust, internally and externally, is an essential element of each ethical "language" used by a business and its stakeholders. It is not a philosophical toy to be tinkered with through theoretical and academic debate. Organizational trust is a critical component—perhaps *the* critical component—to advancing the primary purpose of every business and to establishing and managing a business' relationships in a constructive and positive way.

SELECTED READINGS

- Carr, Albert H. Zolotoff. *Business as a Game*. Littlehampton Book Services Ltd, 1971.

- Peppers, Don, and Martha Rogers. *Extreme Trust: Turning Proactive Honesty and Flawless Execution into Long-Term Profits, Revised Edition*. New York: Portfolio, 2016.

- Johnson, Larry, and Bob Phillips. *Absolute Honesty: Building a Corporate Culture That Values Straight Talk and Rewards Integrity*. AMACOM, 2003.

- Solomon, Robert C. *A Better Way to Think About Business: How Personal Integrity Leads to Corporate Success*. First edition. Oxford University Press, 2003.

TAKE-AWAY QUESTIONS AND IDEAS

What do you think is the most important thing a business can do in order to advance its business purpose? Why? In what way should businesses (the marketplace) work to improve and better manage its relationship with society? In what way should businesses (the marketplace) work to improve and better manage its relationship with government?

If a business focuses on value and on prosperity, how can this improve the effect it has on the environment? How can this improve the effect it has on the common good? How can this improve the effect it has on the larger economy?

Why is a focus on shareholders (its owners), above other stakeholders, so important to a business? Who should ultimately be responsible for other stakeholders' success, happiness, gratification, and sustainability? Why?

- Businesses are in business to "earn a profit." Advancing that business purpose must be at the core of how a business conducts itself.

- The marketplace has had an often contentious relationship with society and with government. Businesses have to accept the responsibility to establish and maintain those relationships in a constructive and positive way in order to achieve a business' primary purpose over the long term.

- The fundamental reason why businesses should act responsibly toward their various stakeholder relationships is because this is the best way to achieve prosperity over the long term. Value is the linchpin to successful relationships.

- Trust, inside and outside of an organization, is imperative if a business' relationships with its stakeholders are going to be profitable and mutually beneficial over the long term.

KEY TERMS

- Core Practices
- Corporate Social Responsibility (CSR)
- Mandated Boundaries
- Shareholder
- Shareholder Value Model
- Stakeholder
- Stakeholder Theory
- Voluntary Accountability

ENDNOTES

1. Baumgartner, Rupert J. "Managing Corporate Sustainability and CSR: A Conceptual Framework Combining Values, Strategies and Instruments Contributing to Sustainable Development." *Corporate Social Responsibility and Environmental Management* 21, no. 5 (September 1, 2014): 258–71.

2. Lindgreen, Adam, and Valérie Swaen. "Corporate Social Responsibility." *International Journal of Management Reviews* 12, no. 1 (March 1, 2010): 1–7, at p. 1.

3. Orlitzky, Marc. "The Politics of Corporate Social Responsibility or: Why Milton Friedman Has Been Right All Along." *Annals in Social Responsibility* 1 (June 8, 2015): 5–29.

4. Freeman, R. Edward. *Strategic Management: A Stakeholder Approach.* Cambridge New York Melbourne Madrid Cape Town Singapore: Cambridge University Press, 2010, at p. 46.

5. Freeman, R. Edward. *Strategic Management: A Stakeholder Approach.* Cambridge New York Melbourne Madrid Cape Town Singapore: Cambridge University Press, 2010, at p. 40

6. Bradberry, Dr Travis. "Sixty Percent of Your Colleagues Are Lying to You." *Huffington Post* (blog), February 14, 2016. https://www.huffingtonpost.com/drtravis-bradberry/sixty-percent-of-yourcol_b_9044758.html.

ENGAGEMENT—WHAT DO YOU THINK?

Write down your own thoughts about what you've learned in this chapter. Consider the previous discussions about a business' primary purpose, the relationships between the marketplace and society and government, the interplay between social concerns, stakeholder concerns, and shareholder interests, and the idea of voluntary accountability. In your own words, describe the role you think these various factors have in decision-making processes within an organization—is it easy to organize these factors based on their importance? Their influence?

CHAPTER 5

CORPORATE CULTURES: THE ROLES AND IMPACT OF LEADERSHIP AND GOVERNANCE

Definitions of "culture" vary greatly, but the essential elements remain fairly consistent:

- a culture is shared among individuals who identify themselves as belonging to a particular group;
- an established culture actually takes some time to mature; and
- a mature culture is relatively unchanging.

In the marketplace in particular, corporate culture is a shared belief among a business' leaders and managers about how they should conduct the business' activities and manage its relationships. (See Figure 5.1.) A number of influences and factors inform a company's culture: among the most important are its history and its procedures, both written and unwritten. These cultural "habits" forecast how a company resolves disputes, how it handles day-to-day concerns, how it treats its employees and how its employees treat each other, how it handles criticism, how it plans for various contingencies, how it manages risk, how it reacts under stress (economic, political, reputational, and litigious), and how it prepares for the future. Cultural habits reflect whether a company

Corporate Identity

© Rawpixel.com/Shutterstock.com

© Prachaya Roekdeethaweesab/Shutterstock.com

believes in, and insists upon, value in its products and services, and whether it delivers that value to its consumers.

[Culture drives governance, and governance drives culture. Leadership—*purposeful* leadership—establishes, models, fosters, and oversees both.]

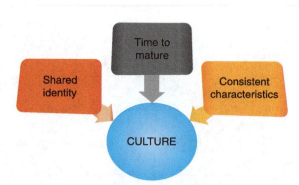

Figure 5.1 Essential Elements of a Culture
Source: Courtesy of Steven Lovett

LEARNING OUTCOMES | OUTLINE

5.1 The Concept of Corporate Culture

5.2 Benefits of Ethical Practices

5.3 Compliance versus Value-Based Cultures

5.4 Corporate Governance

5.5 Individual Leadership and Leadership Styles

- Describe the concept of culture as it relates to businesses by understanding its influences, factors, and impact.
- Understand the benefits of constructive and positive practices within a business as they relate to employees, investors, and consumers.
- Analyze the differences between compliance- and value-based cultures, and understand the limitations to compliance-based cultures.
- Describe corporate governance and basic responsibilities and roles of governance.
- Analyze the impact of positive leadership and various leadership styles, and how those styles work in relation to a business setting.

OPENING THOUGHT EXPERIMENT

The dinner party had gone extremely well . . . mostly. After a long 5-year of planning and working yourself to the bone, you and the company you helped to launch had finally hit a major earnings' benchmark. Sales for the trailing 3 years had exceeded 50% growth per year. To celebrate and to attract your next round of capital investment, you and your partners had decided to throw a lavish dinner party. You invited several deep-pocket investors, all of whom showed up and appeared to have a great time.

One man in particular, however, Mr. Darkside, had approached you with an unsettling proposition.

"Well done!" Mr. Darkside said, slapping you on the shoulder. "I didn't think you could pull it off, but you and your partners are well on your way to long-term success."

"Yeah, it's been a long road to get here, but it was a team effort."

Mr. Darkside winks knowingly. "Speaking of 'team,' I hear you've been looking for a new Chief Operations Officer. I think I might know the perfect candidate."

"Who?" you ask, a little bothered by his remark. The search for a new COO was supposed to be confidential. The former COO was leaving unexpectedly, and no one wanted the change in leadership to upset investor confidence.

"Well," Mr. Darkside said smugly, "he shares my same last name. He's my son."

"Oh." You try not to sound unfriendly. You've heard of Mr. Darkside's son, and actually, what you've heard has mostly been good. He graduated from a well-known business school back east, and he had recently received a lot of favorable press because of his management style and results. He might be a good candidate, but something about Mr. Darkside's tone sounded strange.

© Civil/Shutterstock.com

He continues. "Yes, I thought he might be a good fit. I'm sure you've heard of his track record. By the way, I want you to know I'm thinking of making a large stock purchase. I think your company has a lot of potential, and it makes sense for me to put my money where my mouth is."

You stand there not sure what to say. The wheels in your mind are spinning. Did Mr. Darkside just somehow attempt to bribe you? Legally, it wouldn't violate any laws for your company to hire his son whether or not Mr. Darkside invested a lot of money in your company, but it didn't feel right. You couldn't think of any company policy that would be a problem either, but. . . what kind of message would this send? Would some kind of precedent be set for "selling" executive positions? On the other hand, the current Chief Information Officer was the brother of one of your company's biggest shareholders. Their relationship hadn't seemed like a big deal at the time. Additionally, Mr. Darkside's son had a good reputation and would likely be a great asset to your company. What should you do?

ENGAGEMENT—What Do You Think?

A company's culture is something which is created over time by a series of decisions, repeated practices, and seasoned experiences. While culture remains relatively stable, it doesn't always provide a clear-cut way by which to resolve dilemmas. In fact, dilemmas can be the things which challenge cultural norms and expectations. What would you do in this situation? What kind of culture would your decision encourage? Why would you make a particular decision—what about your company might support your decision?

_____

_____

_____

_____

_____

_____

_____

Section 5.1 The Concept of Corporate Culture

The concept of a "**corporate culture**" is not a difficult one. Organizations (to use a loose analogy) are micro-societies. They develop, advocate, allow, and adhere to various values and behaviors that create a unique environment—physical, psychological, and social—within the organization. A number of factors contribute to corporate culture, including but not limited to, a company's history, industry, management style, corporate structure, strategy, product(s) or service(s), types of employees, and geographical location(s). A company's culture is typically demonstrated through its vision statement, its mission statement, its policies and procedures (formal and informal), its systems, its symbols, its language, and its norms.

It is tempting (and popular) to speak of "culture" as if it's a stand-alone consciousness or component of a business, but, in fact, culture is only the outcome of (and therefore only the evidence of) a collection of factors and influences. Within the recent past, businesses have been characterized as "**moral agents**" as if a non-entity could be moral or immoral, distinct from individuals who perceive it, or individuals who are involved with it. A lot of debate (and philosophical and academic hot air) has gone into this particular debate, but what is critical for you to keep in mind is that a business cannot, and does not, in any way act independent of its collective parts—independent of its culture.

Manuel Velasquez, has argued that "corporate organization lacks the kind of causal powers and intentionality that an entity must possess to be morally responsible for what it does."[1] According to Velasquez, to speak of a corporation as having intentions is only a metaphor, and nothing in the corporate internal decision structure can "transform a metaphorical intention into a real one," nor can it "create group mental states nor group minds in any literal sense." Human intentions, he has argued, are mental in character and can only occur within a conscious human mind. To talk about corporate "intentions" in a literal sense would mean that a corporation has a unified conscious mind, which is absurd.[2]

But perhaps more dangerous than any absurdity is the consequence of shifting "moral" or "ethical" responsibility onto an unconscious, inanimate "culture"; in the final analysis, such a shift of responsibility would eliminate, or go a long way toward eliminating, moral and ethical responsibility from the individuals who comprise the micro-societies of the business world. Therefore, it is critical to remember

> **CORPORATE CULTURE**
>
> This describes an amalgamation of behaviors, standards, values, and routines generally shared throughout an organization.

> **MORAL AGENT**
>
> As applied to an organization, this means an entity has the ability, and the responsibility, to make moral decisions, decisions which are accountable for being "right" or "wrong."

© Gustavo Frazao/Shutterstock.com

CHALLENGE QUESTIONS:

How important do you think a particular "culture" is to a business? What does a corporate culture accomplish? What are its benefits? What are its risks?

What kind of corporate culture do you think would advance a business' primary objective of earning a profit in a sustainable way? Why?

that the culture of a company, in whatever condition it may be, is the responsibility of those individuals who comprise the company. When that responsibility is met through "voluntary accountability," the need for compliance (outside of what the law may currently require) begins to diminish significantly.

This responsibility is best met by establishing effective, well-maintained compliance and ethics programs, and by imparting, at every level, the benefits of ethical—value-delivering—practices and decision-making.

ENGAGEMENT—What Do You Think?

Do you think corporate entities should be treated as "moral agents?" If so, what moral framework should they follow? Who decides whether a decision is moral or immoral? If organizations shouldn't be treated as moral agents, what kind of framework should guide its decision-making?

_____

_____

_____

_____

_____

_____

_____

Section 5.2 Benefits of Ethical Practices

There are at least three, crucial ways in which ethical practices (value-delivering and sustainable) promote a business' primary objective of earning a profit: the stimulation of employee commitment and loyalty, the encouragement of investment and investor loyalty, and the enhancement of consumer satisfaction and loyalty. (See Figure 5.2.)

Employees at every level of a company, who work in an environment—a *culture*— of ethically oriented practices are more likely to be creative, satisfied, and loyal. This isn't, as one might say, "rocket science." If a person knows he or she is valued, and if a person knows decision-making processes are trustworthy and fair (remember the significance of "organizational trust"), that person is much more likely to be satisfied with his or her employment, be loyal to the needs and goals of the organization, and be more likely to think creatively as a problem-solver. When a company focused on creating value, and stays transparently true to its primary objective, employees are more likely to feel good about what they do and feel good about their future, that is, their job security.

© bfk/Shutterstock.com

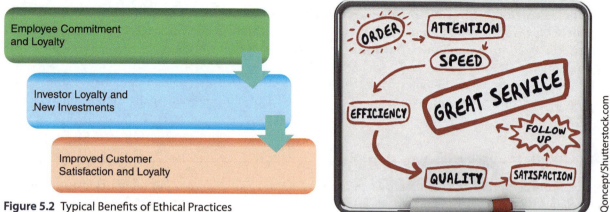

Figure 5.2 Typical Benefits of Ethical Practices
Source: Courtesy of Steven Lovett

Investors are also likely to feel good about investing (and reinvesting) their money and resources into a company which they perceive to be ethically oriented. As with employees, this appeals to a psychological sense of trustworthiness and security. Investors perceive (and rightly so) this kind of an organization as supplying a foundation for productivity, efficiency, effective risk management, and profits. Investor confidence, in turn, provides a business with stability, especially over the long term, and fosters relationships which the public at large interprets as healthy for the marketplace and for the economy.

Perhaps the most visible result of ethical decision-making and practices is the enhancement of consumer satisfaction and loyalty. In a marketplace where consumers are the ultimate arbiters of which companies survive and which companies fail; this benefit of ethical practices cannot be overstated. Enduring relationships built on respect, trust, and integrity are a goldmine of repeat business, free advertising, and sustainability. In these situations, consumers experience an emotional identification with a business, which fosters brand loyalty. This kind of relationship is mutually beneficial: one in which the consumer is provided a valuable service or product, and one in which a business receives the long-term loyalty and profit it needs to thrive in a competitive marketplace.

Ethical practices and decision-making cultivate and ultimately reap enormous rewards in the marketplace. This occurs as a result of a corporate culture, which focuses on value-creation and prosperity for itself ("earning a profit") and its stakeholders.

CHALLENGE QUESTIONS:

If you were an investor, what kinds of practices and what kind of culture would you like to see in a company?

If you were an employee, what kind of environment would you like to work in? How would the environment you've described result in value for a consumer? Would it be a sustainable environment over the long term? Why or why not?

ENGAGEMENT—What Do You Think?

What might be other benefits to ethical practices? How do all of the benefits reflect the concept of "value?"

_____

_____

_____

_____

_____

_____

_____

Section 5.3 Compliance versus Value-Based Cultures

In a nutshell, "**compliance**" refers to a company's ability and willingness to conform to, and satisfy, all applicable legal and regulatory requirements. Over the past 40 years, the marketplace has experienced an exponential blitzkrieg of statutory and regulatory demands. Many of these new rules and expectations are the result of corporate failures and an effort by the government to set boundaries and improve standards.

> **COMPLIANCE**
>
> This refers to an organization's obedience to, or a fulfillment of, laws and rules that apply to its industry and business practices.

The net effect from a practical standpoint is that "compliance" has become its own cottage industry. Many companies have, and/or are required to have, designated compliance officers whose job is to make sure that the company has in place the procedures and controls to meet its legal and regulatory obligations. This is, in part, an area of risk management. Along with a multitude of government-imposed mandates comes a multitude of potential, sometimes devastating, punitive measures if those mandates are not satisfactorily met. Moreover, businesses can also face criminal liability for violations of criminal statutes at both the federal and

state level. All of these obligations, and the potential downside, should lead a responsible business to develop plans and procedures for ensuring its compliance and for protecting itself from, or swiftly remediating, unlawful or criminal activity.

Taking into account the practical realization that organizations convicted of committing federal crimes could not be punished or censured the same way in which an individual could be, the United States Sentencing Commission provided guidelines for federal

© Wright Studio/Shutterstock.com

sentencing judges to use when levying punishment against organizational offenders. Those guidelines were framed by four general principles:

1. Making every attempt to remedy the harm that had been caused;
2. Setting fines commensurate with the level an organization focused its purpose or operations toward committing a crime(s);
3. Setting fines commensurate with the severity of the committed crime(s); and
4. Allowing probation of an organization in order to ensure additional sanctions if needed or to act as motivation for the organization to take steps that will "reduce the likelihood of future criminal conduct."[3]

The creation of the Federal Sentencing Guidelines for the Sentencing of Organizations (FSGO), codified in Chapter Eight of the U.S. Sentencing Commission Guidelines for the Sentencing of Organizations (Section 8AI.2/K)[4] created an institutionalized "buffer to prevent legal violations in organizations."[5] Organizations began adopting the guidelines as a framework for internal compliance and ethics programs; by doing so, organizations could expect to receive reduced penalties in the event of criminal misconduct. The FSGO outline seven criteria for establishing an "effective compliance program."[6]

- The provision of oversight by high-level personnel.
- Efforts to take due care in delegating substantial discretionary authority.
- The use of effective communication among all levels of employees.
- The provision of reasonable steps to achieve compliance that would include systems for monitoring, auditing, and reporting suspected wrongdoing without fear of retaliation.
- The consistent enforcement of compliance standards, including disciplinary mechanisms.

> **CHALLENGE QUESTIONS:**
>
> In your own words, describe why you think "compliance" is important for a business and the business' stakeholders. Why do you think many companies struggle with compliance issues?
>
> How do you see "compliance" and the concept of "value" complementing each other? How does "value" improve upon a business' efforts to comply with the law?

- The provision of reasonable steps to respond to and prevent further similar offenses upon the detection of a violation.[7]

While these seven guidelines are just that—*guidelines*—they provide an excellent baseline for compliance programs within any business. They are centered on risk avoidance and risk remediation. However, these guidelines are much like *rules*, which drift more in the direction of lawful duties rather than in the direction of voluntary accountability. Even if all eight guidelines are developed into an excellent compliance program—and there is good reason they should be—compliance programs are best designed to keep businesses in line with the law; they aren't, by their nature, designed to promote and deliver *value*. (See Figure 5.3.) That's where ethics program come into play.

Many ethics textbooks will discuss "values"—upstanding principles or morals to which a business should adhere (usually based on a Virtue Ethics framework)—but somehow be light-footed with "value"—the significance of delivering real benefits to consumers and prosperity to itself and to other stakeholders. Upstanding principles, such as integrity, trustworthiness, and humility (which we discussed in Chapter 4) are essential; they establish and maintain organizational trust and result in constructive and positive business relationships. However, the concept of *value*, as a matter of prizing resources, human capital, beneficial products and service, reputation, transparency, as well as integrity and accountability, is the cornerstone of highly principled conduct (just as we discussed in Chapter 3).

A *value*-based culture is not, necessarily (or even legally), a substitute for a compliance regimen, but instead it is layered on top of applicable compliance requirements and compliance procedures. Compliance should act as a *baseline*, not a finish line. Constantly working to deliver value should be the ultimate goal.

With this in mind, a **value-based culture** is typically focused on accomplishing a purposeful mission statement—its overarching aim to deliver value with integrity, which then prescribes how relationships with employees, consumers, and investors are to be managed and perceived. A value-based culture engenders a strong commitment to positive core practices, constructive behavior, and integrity throughout the organization. This kind of corporate culture arises out of a set of shared (acknowledged and understood) ethical "languages," which is modeled by, and personally invested in, by the organization's leadership and management.

A value-based business will possess a shared set of principles by which it, and stakeholders connected with it, achieves genuine prosperity.

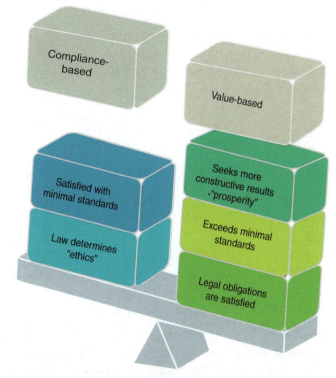

Figure 5.3 Compliance vs. Value
Source: Courtesy of Steven Lovett

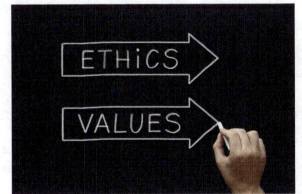

© Ivelin Radkov/Shutterstock.com

VALUE-BASED CULTURE

This refers to an organization's shared practices, routines, and beliefs that aim to repeatedly and sustainably achieve positive results ("prosperity"); typically, a value-based culture focuses on an organization's mission and ideals.

ENGAGEMENT—What Do You Think?

Compliance is extremely important for every organization but so is the concept of value. Describe a situation, real or hypothetical, in which a company has remained compliant (met its lawful obligations) but has also focused on a more robust vision of prosperity (made repeatable, sustainable decisions which have created value).

_____

_____

_____

_____

_____

_____

_____

Section 5.4 Corporate Governance

Governance is a deeper concern than corporate responsibility, or mission statements, or public relations campaigns (although they are all derived from how a business is run). "**Corporate governance**" is literally how a corporation goes about governing—supervising and monitoring—all of its affairs.

The governance of a company involves its board of directors, its shareholders, and its officers and managers. Corporate governance involves the policies, goals, and actions or decisions, taken by a company's decision-makers. The roles of governance—both monitoring and supervisory—come with legal or compliance and ethical duties. To a greater extent, board members wear the bull's-eye of blame when the duty to properly run a company comes into question, but because the bulk of governance's legal responsibilities lay with a company's board, the placement of the bull's-eye makes sense. In a practical

> **CORPORATE GOVERNANCE**
>
> This describes a structure of practices, procedures, and policies by which an organization is directed, managed, and evaluated; usually applies industry standards, or "best practices," in addition to lawful obligations and duties.

> **CHALLENGE QUESTIONS:**
>
> How do you think frontline employees affect and influence corporate governance?
>
> Based on what you've learned so far, what do you think is the key to successful corporate governance? Why?

© zsirosistvan/Shutterstock.com

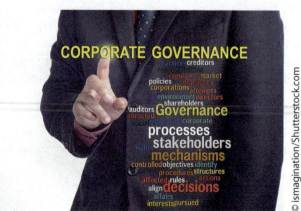

© ismagination/Shutterstock.com

sense, a board's governance activities involve maximizing returns, protecting assets, looking after the company's share price, increasing efficiency, promoting integrity and fairness, requiring transparent reporting, properly managing risk and liability exposure, and retaining public trust and confidence.

LEADERSHIP

For organizations, this refers to how directors, executives, managers, and employees behave when faced with ethical dilemmas, conflict, and business challenges.

Section 5.5 Individual Leadership and Leadership Styles

Leadership has been a heavily discussed and highly publicized topic in business for a number of years. The purpose of this section is not to revisit the broader conversation about leadership but to focus on how leadership, and its various styles, impact and interrelate to, ethical conduct within an organization. **Leadership**, for our purposes, looks at how a leader should behave when faced with an ethical decision and what a leader should not do to make ethical decisions.

© ProStockStudio/Shutterstock.com

Our first step will be to take a look at a way in which a leader—at *any* level within an organization—should behave when faced with an ethical dilemma. Here is a simple step-by-step sequence. A person should:

- *Look* at the problem from the position of the other person(s) affected by a decision.
- *Try* to determine what virtuous response is expected.
- *Ask* yourself—
  a. How would it feel for the decision to be disclosed to a wide audience?
  b. Is the decision consistent with organizational goals?
- *Act* in a way that is right and just for another other person in a similar situation and good for the organization.

Now let's talk about what a decision-maker should not do when faced with an ethical dilemma. Specifically, a leader should not be motivated by selfish gains or take selfish actions, bluff or lie, depend on principles easily explained to one's peers, and take undue advantage of a situation, even if law or social practices permit it. Leaders know almost reflexively what to do or what not to do. However, it is those situations that they don't know clearly and readily what to do where help is needed. It is those dilemmas that are not reducible to common methods of decision analysis, that exist outside clearly defined systems of corporate ethics, that need a step-by-step procedure, something practical and concrete in nature. If not, we are relying on the leader's integrity and character to make the right decision. Of course, that may be enough.

CHALLENGE QUESTIONS:

What kind of a leader do you think you are? Why?

Which kind of a leader do you think would be likely to encourage and model principled conduct? Why?

Why do you think it is important for every person in an organization to act as a leader? What does being a "leader" really mean?

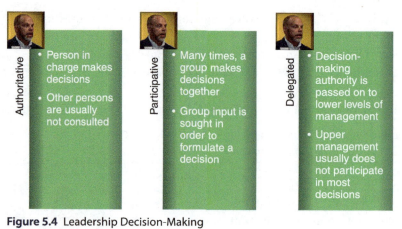

Figure 5.4 Leadership Decision-Making
Source: Courtesy of Steven Lovett

Some criteria to help ensure appropriate ethical considerations should be incorporated into the decision-making process. For example, compliance, promoting good and reducing harm, responsibility, respecting and preserving rights, promoting trust, and building reputation. Two recommendations for navigating through an ethical gray area also need consideration. First, after you make the decision are you able to sleep well, or are you tossing and turning, constantly replaying the decision or the consequences of the decision; second, if you were to face the final roll call and die tomorrow, will you be comfortable explaining your actions in this final accounting? There is no substitute for the ability to make good decisions, even in the gray zone.[8]

Many leaders have particular styles of leadership. We can divide those styles into several categories, although it is important to remember that no particular style of leadership is necessarily right or wrong or the best for a particular situation. (See Figure 5.4.)

Some leaders follow an *authoritative* style of leadership; that is, one in which the leader makes the decision, with or without checking with anyone. Many of the most successful and famous leaders use this style. Authoritarian leaders are very confident with both their leadership and with their decision-making. These leaders naturally assume that they know what to do and how to go about it. Authoritative leaders may check with others and gather information, but when it is time to make a decision, this style of leader does so by themselves. Authoritative leadership is particularly effective when there are time constraints or when subordinates are not trained to participate or do not have the necessary information to participate in the decision-making.

Participative leadership, also known as democratic leadership, is a style that employs group input and sometimes group decision-making. In this style, a leader asks for input and debate. Decisions are made by a group or at least with substantial input from a group of knowledgeable people. Participative leadership is able to draw on the expertise of the group and frequently leads to not only better answers and decisions but also better buy-in by the employees. Participative leadership tends to be a better style when there is plenty of time and the answer is complex and needs to be made with careful consideration.

Figure 5.5 Leadership Styles
Source: Courtesy of Steven Lovett

Delegated leadership, also known as Laissez-Faire or free-rein leadership, is a style that moves the decision-making and leadership down the levels of management. This style is sometimes viewed as non-participating because the upper management is not participating in the decision-making. However, this style is very effective in an organization that is geographically spread out, communication is difficult, or people at all levels are well trained and able to make clear decisions. Delegated leadership is less effective if people making the decisions are not aware of all the factors that impact issue, but much more so if there are local issues of which the senior leadership is not aware.

Another way to look at leadership styles is to consider transactional versus transformational leadership. (See Figure 5.5.)

Transactional leadership is said to be more mission-oriented. The transactional leader recognizes the task at hand and the skills of the people involved. This type of leader attempts to get the job done primarily by using the risk versus reward system. This leadership style focuses on the job and expects people to accomplish the job because they are supposed to and are paid to. Although not ignoring people's needs, they are secondary to the mission.

Transformational leadership is more focused on the people and their motives and desires. This style of leadership tries to inspire people to go beyond just the job, but to be accountable for getting the job done with less need for supervision. Transformational leaders look beyond the immediate mission

and to the bigger picture, trying to create a workforce that in a sense has less need for a leader. The transformational leader is more focused on the people and what they can do, than on the individual project.

Situational or *Fluid leadership*, also sometimes known as adaptive leadership, is a style of leadership that depends on the situation at the time. Although most leaders adopt a style that best suits their personality, training, or environment, some are able to adjust their leadership style as the situation changes.[9]

Regardless of the methodology a leader uses to address an ethical dilemma, and regardless of the leadership style, which he or she uses, the crux of leadership in a business situation is that a leader *thinks critically* and *acts in a principled way* in order to *advance the business' purpose.*

SELECTED READINGS

- Edmonds, S. Chris. *The Culture Engine: A Framework for Driving Results, Inspiring Your Employees, and Transforming Your Workplace.* 1st edition. Hoboken, New Jersey: Wiley, 2014.

- Rönnegard, David. *The Fallacy of Corporate Moral Agency.* 2015 edition. New York, NY: Springer, 2015.

- Johnson, Craig E. *Meeting the Ethical Challenges of Leadership: Casting Light or Shadow.* 5th edition. Los Angeles: SAGE Publications, Inc, 2013.

- Linsky, Martin, and Ronald A. Heifetz. *Leadership on the Line: Staying Alive through the Dangers of Leading.* 1st edition. Boston, Mass: Harvard Business Review Press, 2002.

TAKE-AWAY QUESTIONS AND IDEAS

How is a "corporate culture" formed within an organization? Who is responsible for maintaining a business' culture? How does a business' culture affect its relationships and its long-term success?

What are some of the key benefits to ethical conduct for a business? Why are these "benefits" important to a business' long-term success?

What is a "value-based" culture? How is this distinct from a "compliance-based" culture? Why is this distinction important?

What does "leadership" mean as it relates to principled conduct in an organizational setting?

- Businesses form their own "micro-society" cultures based on a number of factors and influences, such as history, structure, strategy, and the kinds of employees who work for it. A business' culture is relatively static and can strongly influence the success and sustainability of its relationships.

- Conduct and decision-making, which are constructive, positive, and principled results in a number of advantages to a business. These advantages—benefits—are crucial elements for long-term success and prosperity.

- Compliance is an extremely important component of running a successful and low-risk business, but compliance policies, procedures, and plans should act as a company's baseline for how it, and its employees, managers, and owners, conduct themselves. A corporate culture based on "value" is directed toward delivering genuine benefit to consumers, and in the process, contributes heavily to a company's long-term success and prosperity, as well as the prosperity of its stakeholders.

- Leadership, regardless of its style, directly affects ethical conduct and decision-making.

KEY TERMS

- Compliance
- Corporate Culture
- Corporate Governance

- Leadership
- Moral Agent
- Value-Based Culture

ENDNOTES

1. Velasquez, M. (2003). *Debunking corporate moral responsibility*. Business Ethics Quarterly, 13, 531–562.

2. From *Introduction to Business Ethics* by James Fieser and Alexander Moseley. Copyright © 2013 by Kendall Hunt Publishing Company. Reprinted by permission.

3. "2015 Chapter 8." United States Sentencing Commission, August 11, 2015. https://www.ussc.gov/guidelines/2015-guidelines-manual/2015-chapter-8.

4. The FSGO have since been revised when the Revised Federal Sentencing Guidelines for Organizations (2004) were adopted.

5. The Federal Sentencing Guidelines for Organizations: A Framework for Ethical Compliance." *Journal of Business Ethics* 17, no. 4 (March 1, 1998): 353–63, abstract.

6. Quoted from "An Overview of the Organizational Guidelines," Paula Desio, Deputy General Counsel, United States Sentencing Commission, "Organizational Guidelines." United States Sentencing Commission, November 1, 2013. https://www.ussc.gov/guidelines/organizational-guidelines.

7. From *Ethics in the World of Business* by Phillip Lewis. Copyright © 2014 by Kendall Hunt Publishing Company. Reprinted by permission.

8. From *Ethics in the World of Business* by Phillip Lewis. Copyright © 2014 by Kendall Hunt Publishing Company. Reprinted by permission.

9. From *Open for Business* by Brock Williams and Dane Galden. Copyright © 2015 by Kendall Hunt Publishing Company. Reprinted by permission.

ENGAGEMENT—WHAT DO YOU THINK?

Write down your own thoughts about what you've learned in this chapter. Consider the previous discussions about the concept of "culture," compliance- versus value-based organizations, the benefits of ethical practices, and various leadership practices. In your own words, describe how you think these factors affect decision-making processes within an organization.

CHAPTER 6

THE CREATIVE DESTRUCTION OF BUSINESS ETHICS

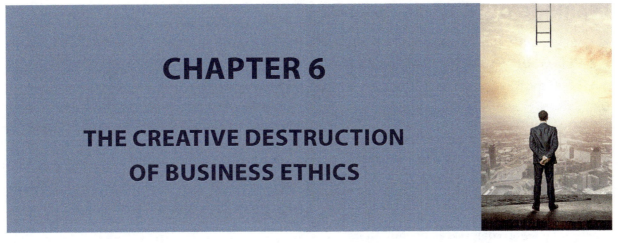

The Austrian American economist Joseph Schumpeter is credited with articulating a theory of economic innovation commonly called "creative destruction." Schumpeter hypothesized that "industrial mutation"[1] continuously developed, or transformed, the economic structure of the marketplace, each industry, and even each business by destroying (outdating) the old structure and creating (updating) a new one. The theory has undergone various iterations and applications, even enjoying popularity within free-market economics—for instance, the idea of downsizing (a "destructive" action) can cause an increase in efficiency (a "creative" outcome). Thankfully, we can leave economic theory to the economists and political theory to the political philosophers; however, we *can* use the lens of creative destruction to better understand the role ethics and ethical decision-making play in the overall and long-term success of a business.

© file404/Shutterstock.com

© BSWei/Shutterstock.com

LEARNING OUTCOMES | OUTLINE

6.1 Maximizing the "Prosperity Opportunity"

6.2 Voluntary Cooperation and Setting Expectations

6.3 Challenge Processes and Driving Constructive Change

6.4 Value Creation and Measures

- Recognize the role "creative destruction" plays in ethical decision-making processes by understanding how loss (cost) can be an integral part of gain (prosperity).
- Describe the significance of identifying a "prosperity opportunity" as part of an ethical decision-making process.
- Analyze what practices create and encourage voluntary cooperation among individuals who comprise an organization.
- Analyze the importance of challenge processes when critiquing the efficacy of alternative decisions; how constructive criticism and knowledge-sharing can lead to more prosperous outcomes.
- Recognize the usefulness of qualitative measures for determining value-creation.

OPENING THOUGHT EXPERIMENT

The holidays have finally arrived! Having had a very successful year and a bank account now flush with a year-end performance bonus, you're feeling very generous. Maybe too generous. It's gift-giving season, and this year, you plan on going big.

Foremost in your mind are your three nephews Bob, Bill, and Buster. Your sister and her husband always do their best to treat the boys as equally as possible, and out of respect for their parenting style, you decide to spend exactly $500 on each of your nephews. Once you make that decision, figuring out what gifts to give them seems fairly easy. Each of the boys loves to fish, but all they have is one 30-year-old, no-name, cast-and-reel rod they all have to share. You head over to the local sporting goods store with an idea in mind. In the fishing section, you find what you're looking for: a "CastOff F7X" casting rod with a "Aberdeen 2-RL Baitcast Reel." Each boy's rod and reel will cost $500. You load up your cart with three rods and reels, and you head to the check-out counter feeling really good about your decision. But before you make it to the front of the store, you pass a big sign announcing a springtime special: "Receive one FREE 'Aberdeen 2-RL Baitcast Reel' with the purchase of two, top-of-the-line 'Aberdeen 3-RL Baitcast Reels'!" You realize if you buy two of the "3-RL" series reels, you'll get one "2-RL" series reel for free, and you'll spend exactly what you would otherwise be spending if you buy three of the "2-RL" series reels.

The worst form of inequality is to try to make unequal things equal.

Aristotle

"What a deal!" you say aloud and turn around to go get two "3-RL" series reels. Wait a second, you suddenly realize. If I buy two "3-RL" series reels and get one "2-RL" series, one of my nephews is going to be getting a reel of lower quality. On the other hand, if I take advantage of the special, none of the boys are going to receive a worse gift than what they would have gotten, and two of the boys are actually going to receive a better gift than what I originally planned. In fact, if I don't take advantage of the special, two of the boys will be worse off than they otherwise would be.

"Why does my sister want all of them to be treated the same," you ask aloud in exasperation. "What if being 'equal' means they're worse off?"

ENGAGEMENT—What Do You Think?

The idea of equality is usually perceived as being positive; it's a concept we value in our society sometimes to the point we incorporate it into our laws. Equality, however, can also have a negative, even if unintended, consequence. It can mean that something else, or someone else, who would otherwise excel or improve or progress might be held back. Both equality and improvement are, generally, desirable outcomes, but one might have to sometimes give way in order for the other to realize its potential. Businesses struggle with this kind of a paradox all the time. What would you do in this situation? Would you stick with your original purchase or would you elect to go with the special? Why? How, if at all, does your decision lead to a "better" outcome?

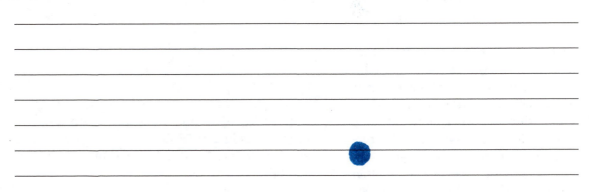

Section 6.1 Maximizing the "Prosperity Opportunity"

In Chapter 1, we introduced the idea of "prosperity." We observed the following:

> Prosperity means value. It means growth. It means resiliency and sustainability. When those kinds of results are helping to steer business decisions—decisions which are already being vetted through an ethical paradigm—then it helps eliminate outcomes which ultimately cause harm over the long-term, and it provides a consistent value-baseline.[1]

One of the roles ethical decision-making plays in an organizational setting is to help identify and develop an outcome that leads to prosperity. (See Figure 6.1.) An ethical approach to decision-making—*regardless* of which ethical paradigm or language is used as a framework—should consistently introduce the question: Depending on which decision is made in this instance, *will it lead to a more prosperous outcome?* That's a big question, one loaded with words which need explanations influenced by the specific circumstances and issued raised by a particular dilemma.

The concept of "prosperity" (remember the "compass" we identified in Chapter 1) can be a tricky measure even if it is one of the more important measures for whether a decision is a "good" one—a

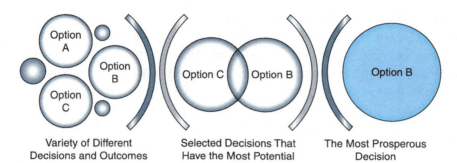

Variety of Different
Decisions and Outcomes

Selected Decisions That
Have the Most Potential

The Most Prosperous
Decision

Figure 6.1 Evaluating Alternatives to Maximize the Opportunity for Prosperity
Source: Courtesy of Steven Lovett

successful one. Prosperity can be viewed through a short-term lens, or a long-term lens, or a financial lens, or a "growth" lens. It could potentially be defined any number of ways, but hopefully we've come to understand that, no matter how it is defined for a specific circumstance, it needs to always be within the context of improving a business' overall position. In other words, an ethical decision is going to be one that leads to a better situation for the business overall, even if in the short-term, the long-term, the profit-and-loss statement, or the market-share percentage, there are specific sacrifices to be made.

> **CREATIVE DESTRUCTION**
>
> As an economic theory, this refers to continuous product and service innovation that constantly replaces and outdates current and past innovations.

Herein lies the intersection of the concepts of "**creative destruction**" and ethical decision-making. Sometimes—many times, in fact—an ethical business decision (one which leads to a more improved overall situation) involves the "destruction" of an existing interest, or an otherwise expected short-term goal, or another metric of growth, etc. Think of it this way: A person who is trying to make a decision between going to college and joining the workforce full-time might ultimately make the decision to go to school. This decision might be made through the use of Utilitarianism (a "cost-benefit-analysis"). This decision to attend school instead of working is likely to involve temporarily choosing debt, a lower quality of life, and delaying the start of a family (all of which could be deemed to be sacrifices— "destructive"). But the long-term effect of this decision is likely to lead to a higher income, more professional opportunities, a higher standard of living, and a content family life (all of which could be deemed to be overall improvements—"creative" prosperity). In this situation, a person who has decided to go

> **CHALLENGE QUESTIONS:**
>
> How do you think the concept of creative destruction can be applied to ethical decision-making?
>
> How would creative destruction help an organization identify a "prosperity opportunity" within an ethical dilemma?

© Rawpixel.com/Shutterstock.com

to school—a decision that comes with certain hardships—has identified how to maximize the opportunity to have a more prosperous life.

Most ethical decisions in business follow a similar analysis: accepting (and identifying!) the existence of destruction for the sake of overall improved circumstances. The question of whether a particular decision will lead to "a more prosperous outcome" is really asking: *Where is the "prosperity opportunity?"*

ENGAGEMENT—What Do You Think?

Describe an example, whether real or hypothetical, in which a destructive process is necessary in order to accomplish a creative process. What are your thoughts about "creative destruction?" In your own words, discuss how you thing ethical decision-making—decisions which lead to prosperous outcomes—often includes creative destruction.

_____

_____

_____

_____

_____

_____

_____

Section 6.2 Voluntary Cooperation and Setting Expectations

In Chapter 5, we discussed the concept of, and influences on, corporate culture. A successful, prosperous culture of a business organization—of *any* organization—is not only going to establish and encourage an environment centered on "value," but also it is going to procreate the right incentives for all of its "people-parts" to individually, as well as collectively, make ethical decisions. This is where we can really see how financial success, individually and corporately, is insufficient by itself to create an ethical culture.

When a business establishes an environment centered on the concept of value-creation, it is using the compass of prosperity to drive its decision-making. This, naturally, should lead to greater economic profits, but very importantly, it also leads to a "ricocheting" effect of "self-value." *What does this mean?*

Let's look at a lemonade stand as a simple illustration.

On a bright May morning, Sally decides it's finally time to set up a lemonade stand next to the sidewalk in front of her house. She actually has been diligently planning this event for some time,

© Nadia Leskovskaya/Shutterstock.com

saving her money to purchase cups, fresh lemons, a bag of sugar, a large pitcher, and a cooler for ice. Sally has researched recipes for lemonade and tried out a few until she settled on the mix she thought most people would really like—she not only wants to sell lemonade to make money for summer camp, but she also wants people to actually enjoy what they're drinking. Because Sally knew she'd need an actual "stand" from which to sell her lemonade, Sally asked her big sister, Lucy, if she would like to be part of Sally's new venture—if so, would Lucy please help her to build her lemonade stand? Lucy mused that she would like to be part of her sister's enterprise; she can see that Sally has planned ahead, and with the warm spring weather, her idea is likely to make some money. Sally offers to share profits with Lucy, but she also tells her big sister this:

"Long before anyone tastes my lemonade, they're going to see the lemonade stand you build. Just think of it, Lucy. Anybody can sell lemonade, but our customers are going to know we sell the best even before they taste it because they'll see how much care we've put into building a nice lemonade stand."

Lucy agrees to partner with Sally—she likes the idea of money, but now she feels good about what she's doing. She can see how her work will add value, and *that* gives her a sense of value. The girls build the nicest lemonade stand they can. And on that bright May day, when people are lining-up to buy lemonade, Lucy knows the money she and her sister are receiving is confirmation of their commitment to value.

Ethical decision-making leads to, and then perpetuates, **voluntary cooperation** from an organization's "people-parts"—those, like employees, who work to advance the primary business purpose. Ethical decision-making gives people a sense of value, a sense of positive impact, on the overall outcome. Aligning financial reward—things like bonuses and pay—with the value a person delivers is certainly a common and natural way to incentivize ethical decision-making. Where the incentive of financial compensation falls short is when it is only tied to the financial performance of a business; this is because it sends a message to individuals that "prosperity" is only defined by economic success, not by overall value-creation. If prosperity is only defined economically, individuals within an organization will begin to shape their decisions to maximize financial gain—a pattern that can perpetuate greed, unhealthy competition, cutting corners, selfishness, and, worst of all, unlawful conduct. This situation—a very common one—tells individuals they are only as valuable as the money they generate; and it doesn't matter if the money being generated is the result of providing consumers with improved products or services.

On the other hand, imagine a company that aligns financial incentives with actual value-creation. Bonuses or increased pay (or other incentives)

> ## VOLUNTARY COOPERATION
>
> In reference to an organizational setting, this refers to individuals within an organization willingly choosing to seek value-creation options or decisions because those individuals understand their own role, and their own value, in that process

> ## CHALLENGE QUESTIONS:
>
> Why is it so important to convey a sense of "self-value" to individuals within an organization?
>
> Why aren't financial incentives alone sufficient motivators to encourage and create an environment of ethical decision-making?

© Nadia Leskovskaya/Shutterstock.com

might be tied to economic gain, but they are also tied to good ideas—employee-generated ideas that improve morale, improve efficiency, help with conflict resolution, improve interdepartmental communication, and improve customer loyalty. These things would lead to an overall better, more improved, situation for the company—prosperity. In this kind of business environment, employees would look for solutions, and would make decisions, that would add value, *overall value*. They would look for the "prosperity opportunity." A business that centers its decision-making on value-creation thereby creates a "ricocheting" effect of "self-value" for its people-parts. They see themselves—whether they work in a back-office occupation or a frontline sales position—as *value-creators*, capable of making a positive, sustainable impact on the business' overall situation.

Sally set the expectation for Lucy. Lucy realized the positive impact her efforts would make. And by the end of that bright May day, Sally, Lucy, and their little venture were far better off than they would have been if they had simply said, "Nothing else matters; we just want to sell as many cups of lemonade as we can."

ENGAGEMENT—What Do You Think?

Describe an experience, in which you discovered a sense of value in what you were doing—in who you were—apart from any financial gain. How important was that experience to you? What kind of motivation does the idea of "value" have for you? Are there expectations set by stakeholders in your own life which encourage a sense of "self-value" in you?

_____

_____

_____

_____

_____

_____

_____

Section 6.3 Challenge Processes and Driving Constructive Change

In order for value-creation to occur, and in order for ethical decision-making to drive constructive change, there needs to be some kind of mechanism in place that helps to answer the question: *Where is the prosperity opportunity?* The mechanism, in whatever specific form it may take, involves a process of "challenging" the proposed decision.

Critical thinking (recall our earlier discussion in Chapter 2) can move decision-makers through the weeds and dead-ends of rationalizations and logical fallacies, but it can also provide a means by which knowledge can be shared and tested. The willingness to think critically about a dilemma and the proposed solutions to a dilemma results in decisions that are fairly vetted and that reflect the overarching corporate goal of value-creation. This mechanism—the process of exchanging information and critically evaluating decision-making—can only thrive in an environment of *trust* (go back and reread Section 4.7). If the road beneath your feet is falling away (destruction), you have to be able to trust those around you to help you build a new path (creation through critical thinking).

© ImageFlow/Shutterstock.com

The people-parts of an organization have to trust that the process of challenging decision-making arises as a result of the organization's commitment to value-creation, not because of selfish interests, negative motivations, or disparagement. Prosperous ethical decision-making, regardless of the ethical paradigm or language being used, should welcome constructive criticism of its proposed decision(s). Within this process is where crucial information can be shared between individuals or departments, where various outcomes can be hypothesized and discussed, and where a collage of influencing variables can be put together in order to better understand a decision's impact on different stakeholders.

This kind of challenge process drives constructive change. It creates a cultural environment of **constructive criticism** and testing in order to maximize the prosperity opportunity in any given situation. It perpetuates a corporate culture of intellectual honesty and decision-making aimed at achieving a more prosperous result. This kind of challenge process invites individuals with different perspectives, different kinds of knowledge, and (ideally) with different roles, responsibilities, and positions to engage each other, learn from each other, and drive each other to come up with the "best" solution possible to an ethical dilemma or issue.

CHALLENGE QUESTIONS:

Why do you think a "challenge process" is such an important part of ethical decision-making?

How can challenges to proposed decisions be delivered or stated in such a way as to be constructive instead of negative? How could ethical "languages" help with this process?

Why is the concept of organizational trust so important in order for challenge processes to work effectively?

CONSTRUCTIVE CRITICISM

This describes a form of analytical evaluation that offers positive feedback based on positive and/or negative observations; typically, this kind of evaluation is intended to improve the subject of its criticism.

ENGAGEMENT—What Do You Think?

If you were to apply a "challenge process" to Sally and Lucy's lemonade stand, what questions would you ask? What information would you, could you, share with them about their business venture? What specific talents, knowledge, or expertise could you offer?

_____

_____

_____

_____

_____

_____

_____

Section 6.4 Value Creation and Measures

The idea of "measures" in business is most often applied to **economic profitability**. In this sense, measures help identify the stimuli—variable components—that cause something to be economically profitable. The concept of measures, however, can also be applied to ethical decision-making and value-creation. To do this, we must accept that measurement data for ethical decision-making and value-creation is likely to be much more **qualitative** and approximate than it would be for data that shows what drives economic profitability. Indeed, identifying what kind of measures—what kind of data to capture—in order to identify and isolate causes of value-creation is likely to be a creative undertaking.

> **ECONOMIC PROFITABILITY**
>
> While there are formulaic descriptions of this term, it generally refers to the specific financial gain experienced after costs and investments are accounted for.

> **QUALITATIVE**
>
> This refers to the measure of something according to its attributes or characteristics, instead of its numerical extent.

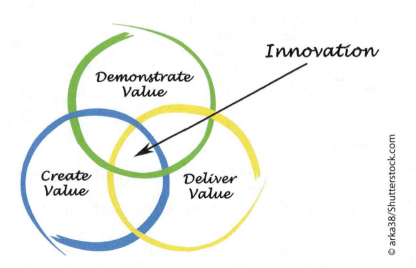

© arka38/Shutterstock.com

For the purpose of ethical decision-making, measures that reveal prosperous decisions might, in part, focus on **opportunity cost**, eliminating waste, and economic profitability, but they might equally focus on increased customer loyalty, improved employee loyalty and talent retention, escalating investor loyalty (and requests from people who want to invest), enhanced reputation, declining litigation risk, and less internal conflict. Some of this would involve quantitative data (numbers), but an organization must also pay just as close attention to qualitative data (opinions, experiences, and attitudes). To develop useful measures, business leadership at every level should be asking things like:

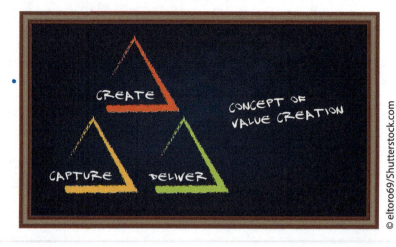

- *Where does the "prosperity opportunity" lie?*
- *Is our cultural setting the right expectations for value-creation?*
- *Are we encouraging or rewarding voluntary cooperation?*
- *What are we doing that we could be doing better?*
- *Are we missing something?*
- *What decisions in the past have resulted in improved overall circumstances?*

OPPORTUNITY COST

This refers to the loss of potential gain from other alternatives or options when one particular alternative or option is chosen; what could have been gained if another option had been chosen?

True value-creation that is the result of constructive, sustainable decisions which lead to prosperity includes a destructive element as part of its process. Loss might be a part of gain. Criticism might be a part of creativeness.

Ethical decision-making is interwoven with the concept of value-creation, and prosperity is the result of that orientation. This is why a principal role of ethical decision-making in organizational environments is to create *value*: this leads to long-term, positive improvements—prosperity. (See Figure 6.2.)

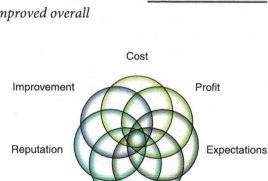

Figure 6.2 The Interrelation Between Different Measures of Value-Creation
Source: Courtesy of Steven Lovett

SELECTED READINGS

- Koch, Charles G. *Good Profit: How Creating Value for Others Built One of the World's Most Successful Companies*. New York: Crown Business, 2015.
- Madden, Bartley, J. *Value Creation Thinking*. Naperville, Illinois: LearningWhatWorks, 2016.

- Zenger, Todd. *Beyond Competitive Advantage: How to Solve the Puzzle of Sustaining Growth While Creating Value.* Boston: Harvard Business Review Press, 2016.
- Conard, Edward. *The Upside of Inequality: How Good Intentions Undermine the Middle Class.* New York: Penguin Random House, 2016.
- Woodbury, Lance. *The Enduring Legacy: Essential Family Business Values.* Life Stories, Inc., 2012.

TAKE-AWAY QUESTIONS AND IDEAS

What is it about ethical decision-making that can make it a "destructively" creative concept?

Why should ethical decision-making focus on the "prosperity opportunity"? How can ethical paradigms or languages provide frameworks to effectively identify a "prosperity opportunity?"

How can a business effectively create an environment that sets expectations of value-creation?

How can a business encourage voluntary cooperation from its people-parts?

Why is a challenge process critical to ethical decision-making? How does this part of the process of decision-making lead to more prosperous results?

What kinds of "measures" should an organization be looking for in order to determine what drives prosperity? Why are those measures important?

- One of the roles ethical decision-making plays in an organizational setting is to help identify and develop an outcome that leads to prosperity.
- An ethical approach to decision-making—*regardless* of which ethical paradigm or language is used as a framework—should consistently introduce the question: <u>Depending on which decision is made in this instance,</u> *will it lead to a more prosperous outcome?*
- Sometimes—many times, in fact—an ethical business decision (one which leads to a more improved overall situation) involves the "destruction" of an existing interest, or an otherwise expected short-term goal, or another metric of growth, etc.
- The question of whether a particular decision will lead to "a more prosperous outcome" is really asking: *Where is the "prosperity opportunity?"*
- Ethical decision-making leads to, and then perpetuates, voluntary cooperation from an organization's "people-parts" by giving people a sense of value, a sense of positive impact, on the overall outcome.
- The willingness to think critically about a dilemma and the proposed solutions to a dilemma results in decisions that are fairly vetted and that reflect the overarching corporate goal of value-creation.
- For the purpose of ethical decision-making, measures that reveal prosperous decisions might focus on increased customer loyalty, improved employee loyalty and talent retention, escalating investor loyalty (and requests from people who want to invest), enhanced reputation, declining litigation risk, and less internal conflict.

KEY TERMS

- Constructive criticism
- Creative destruction
- Economic profitability
- Opportunity cost
- Qualitative
- Voluntary cooperation

ENDNOTES

1. Schumpeter, Joseph A. *Capitalism, Socialism and Democracy.* New York: Harper & Brothers, 1947.

2. Chapter 1, Section 1.4.

ENGAGEMENT—WHAT DO YOU THINK?

Write down your own thoughts about what you've learned in this chapter. Consider the previous discussions about maximizing the "prosperity opportunity," perpetuating voluntary cooperation through the expectation of value-creation, the mechanism of constructively challenging decision-making, and how to measure value-creation. In your own words, describe the role you think these various factors have in the ethical decision-making processes within an organization.

UNIT THREE

THE APPLICATION OF ETHICS IN BUSINESS

In the next three chapters, we will explore how ethical decision-making advances the primary purpose of businesses and how it can lead to improved outcomes over the long term for society at-large.

Chapter 7 takes a look at Ethics' Programs, how ethical issues and dilemmas can be identified and analyzed practically in order to arrive at an optimal outcome. Tools of ethical management—experimentation, observation, and evaluation—will be introduced, as well as the concept of "managing self."

Chapter 8 challenges the popular idea of "sustainable development" and introduces the practical concept of "resilient prosperity." We will examine how businesses, through the application of ethical decision-making, preserve resources, acknowledge their responsibility to their communities, improve efficiency, and encourage constructive creativity.

Chapter 9 ties ethical decision-making together with the common good—a realistic objective for every business organization. We will identify how the common good provides a universal measure for "ethicalness" and how resilient prosperity leads to improved and prosperous outcomes for external stakeholders.

This third unit is intended to take the meaning of ethics in business, and the role of ethics in business, and demonstrate how they can be practically and beneficially applied in real-world contexts. This unit looks beyond the limitations of the current theory and challenges us to remain faithful to a business' primary purpose in order to achieve prosperous outcomes over time.

19th April
Exam B

CHAPTER 7

ETHICS PROGRAMS: KNOWLEDGE PROCESSES AND DECISION RIGHTS

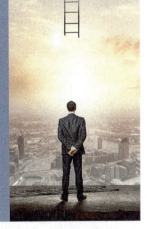

A business *does* its business based on the decisions it *makes*—the decisions its employees, managers, owners, and agents make on behalf. Those decisions have a lasting effect on a business' success, reputation, growth, and long-term sustainability. Those decisions are not made in a vacuum, and they are usually the result of some kind of decision-making matrix— a process for receiving information, reflecting on or analyzing that information, and finally choosing how or when to act on that information. This process may be applied to nothing more complex than an office supervisor deciding which of three catering companies will be hired

© Rawpixel.com/Shutterstock.com

to provide an employee barbecue. Or it may be applied to very complex situations, such as when an international conglomerate is deciding whether its domestic headquarters' team should make pricing decisions for all vendor bids submitted to the conglomerate's international subsidiaries. Regardless of the situation, however, a successful business must have in place a *reliable*, *repeatable*, and *constructive* framework by which its personnel can make business decisions.

Most theorists, and many businesses, relegate the framework for decision-making to compliance programs—programs fundamentally designed to satisfy legally imposed obligations and expectations, the "mandatory boundaries." Compliance programs are, however, insufficient frameworks for most, daily business decisions; once the legal "boxes have been checked," compliance programs offer little assistance to decision-makers. Recognizing this shortcoming, some companies enmesh their "corporate ethos" into the body of their compliance programs, but this most often results in compliance programs simply littered with generalized statements about virtuous characteristics and expectations, for example, "treat everyone with respect," "the customer is always right," and "uphold a high standard of integrity and honesty." Beyond this, some companies have "**Codes of Conduct**" geared more toward behavioral guidelines than actual decision-making, for example, employees are expected to "act responsibly," "set examples," "use their best judgment," and "report violations."

With these tools, an employee or manager might know what is considered lawful, what is considered "virtuous," and what is considered acceptable conduct, but they are still unlikely to have a working methodology—a *useable framework*—for making "good" business decisions.

A business' decision-making framework—its *Ethics' Program*—should be the tool an employee or manager can use to make most business decisions and to address the majority of dilemmas that arise on a daily basis. To fulfill this purpose, an effective Ethics' Program needs to provide guidance for identifying ethical dilemmas, analyzing how those dilemmas can be resolved, setting expectations, encouraging a challenge process (remember Chapter 6), and requiring accountability . . . all while remaining flexible!

Creating and implementing such a program should be a very individualistic task for every business; a program's provisions should reflect a business' culture, values, stakeholders, environment, industry, and vision. Ultimately, however, the construct of *every* Ethics' Program should be responsive to the survivalist instinct *every* business has to make constructive, sustainable decisions that lead to prosperous outcomes.

> **CODE OF CONDUCT**
>
> A set of rules and guidelines stating the norms, expectations, responsibilities, and behavioral practices of individuals within an organization

© Rawpixel.com/Shutterstock.com

© Vmaster/Shutterstock.com

LEARNING OUTCOMES | OUTLINE

7.1 The Case and Construct for an Ethics' Program

7.2 Identifying Ethical Issues and Dilemmas

7.3 Dissecting Ethical Dilemmas

7.4 Tools of Ethics' Management: Experiment, Observe, and Evaluate

7.5 Managing Self

- Identify the need for Ethics' Programs in businesses.
- Recognize how such programs should be structured.
- Describe the benefits of a well-designed and consistently implemented Ethics' Program.
- Describe ways in which ethical issues and dilemmas can be identified in business situations.
- Describe ways in which ethical issues and dilemmas in business situations should be analyzed for the purpose of addressing or constructively resolving them.
- Analyze different "tools" of managing ethical decision-making processes through the use of experimentation, observation, and analysis.
- Analyze how an individual can supervise and assess his or her own ability to identify, diagnose, and resolve ethical issues and dilemmas in a business setting.

OPENING THOUGHT EXPERIMENT

One sunny, spring morning, you decide to ask a good friend of yours, Dr. Donoharm, to join you for a round of golf. You haven't seen your old friend in awhile, and you decide a relaxing round of golf will give you a chance to have a good chat.

Dr. Donoharm agrees and meets you at your favorite course, Plato's Golf Club. After trading a few jokes and driving the cart out to the first tee box, Dr. Donoharm suddenly says, "I had a really interesting case this past week. I know you're interested in ethics, so you might find it interesting."

"Tee it up," you respond with a smile.

"Well, I've been treating one particular patient for a long time. She has struggled with a chronic pain disorder as the result of some head trauma she suffered years ago. I've done my best to help her with pain management, but most of the time she is miserable and lives in agony. It's a really terrible situation."

"My gosh," you say. "That sounds awful."

"Yeah, I can't imagine living like that." Dr. Donoharm swings, and you watch enviously as his golf ball sails down the middle of the fairway. "So here's the thing," he continues as he walks back to the golf cart, "she came in to see me this past week and said, 'Doc, you've got to help me. I can't deal with this pain anymore. I've decided I want to die, but I don't think I can kill myself.' I was shocked, but I tried to remain calm. I believe in a person's 'right to die,' but it's illegal in this state, and this is the first time any patient has ever approached me about it."

"Wow!" you say, shaking your head. You walk up to the tee box and take your first golf swing. It ends up spinning wildly off to the left and into a line of hedges on the side of the fairway. You slowly climb into the golf cart trying to imagine what kind of physical pain your friend's patient must have been enduring to want to end her own life. "What did you do?"

"I asked her if she was suggesting that I administer a very high dose of painkillers, which would cause her to lose consciousness and then die. She

© Andrei_R/Shutterstock.com

immediately said, 'Yes! That's exactly what I want. Please help me.' But I told her I couldn't do that because helping her to kill herself is illegal." Dr. Donoharm steps on the cart's accelerator and explains, "However, I then offered to prescribe a very powerful painkiller. I explained that the medicine could pose a lethal risk—if she took twice the recommended dose, she would peacefully lose consciousness and die a few moments later."

Feeling troubled, you ask, "What did she say when you told her that?"

"She said she definitely wanted the prescription."

You can't help but look puzzled. "I don't think I understand. Didn't you say you couldn't help her kill herself because it's against the law?"

Dr. Donoharm looks at you surprised. "I thought you'd understand right away. I've described two, very different scenarios. In the first one, I would have been administering drugs to my patient in order to kill her—that *is* illegal, and I said I couldn't do that. But in the second scenario, I will be administering drugs in order to relieve her pain—that is legal, and I can do that."

"Yeah, but either way, she ends up dead."

"Yes," says Dr. Donoharm, "but I haven't done anything illegal."

ENGAGEMENT—What Do You Think?

What do you think? What dilemma does Dr. Donoharm's story pose? Could this dilemma be characterized as an ethical dilemma? If so, how or why?

If Dr. Donoharm asked for your advice (not as a lawyer, but as an ethicist), what would you say? Why? Which ethical paradigm(s) would support your advice?

_____

_____

_____

_____

_____

_____

Section 7.1 The Case and Construct for an Ethics' Program

This chapter's opening remarks hopefully made the case for why an Ethics' Program—a framework designed to provide a decision-making processes—is a much better structure than a compliance program or even a code of conduct. However, because compliance programs and codes of conduct certainly have their place in business, and because they seem to provide information and instruction that overlaps with what an Ethics' Program provides, it is fair to ask a few questions:

1. *Why have a distinct Ethics' Program?*
2. *What additional value will an Ethics' Program deliver?*
3. *What should be the core goals of an Ethics' Program?*

Because every business organization is unique, answers to these basic questions might be near-infinite. There are, however, answers with underpinnings shared by all organizations. The most straightforward way in which to discuss those answers

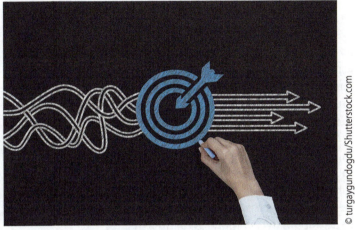

© turgaygundogdu/Shutterstock.com

> **CHALLENGE QUESTIONS:**
>
> Based on what you've learned so far, why do you think an ethics' program is a necessary tool for successful businesses to have in place?
>
> How would you create an effective Ethics' Program? What would it need to include? How would you enforce it—positive or negative mechanisms?

might be to compose conditional statements; this will provide us working hypotheses and conclusions.

1. Why have a distinct Ethic's Program?

IF businesses compete for investment dollars, employees, and market share . . . *and*

IF ethical dilemmas are so common in business settings . . . *and*

IF effective Ethics' Programs can lead to constructive, sustainable, and prosperous business decisions . . . *and*

IF constructive, sustainable, and prosperous decisions make businesses more competitive and successful over the long-term . . . *then*

A business that intends to be successful and competitive should create and carry out an Ethics' Program apart from its compliance program and/or its code of conduct. Ethics' Programs are the best mechanisms for helping employees and managers identify ethical dilemmas (i.e., issues not resolved by applicable law or policy), evaluate those dilemmas, and resolve them in such a way as to result in more prosperous outcomes.

2. What additional value will an Ethics' Program deliver?

IF businesses are more competitive and successful when employees and managers make constructive or productive decisions . . . *and*

IF businesses need constructive or positive decisions to be made on a regular and long-term basis . . . *and*

IF businesses need decisions which result in better outcomes, that is, lead to prosperity, . . . *and*

IF an effective Ethics' Program provides a framework for constructive, sustainable decision-making that leads to prosperity . . . *then*

An effective Ethics' Program can deliver value above and beyond what is delivered by a compliance program and/or a code of conduct. Ethics' Programs provide benchmarks for self-evaluation, foster high standards of practice, encourage critical thinking and challenge processes, favor an exchange of knowledge, promote deliberation about the potential impact of alternative decisions, and support decision-making by the person(s) with the greatest expertise or experience.

3. *What should be the core goals of an Ethics' Program?*

IF higher expectations are best established by focusing on "value-creation" . . . *and*

IF previous decisions can set standards for future decisions . . . *and*

IF decisions should lead to constructive and prosperous outcomes . . . *and*

IF decision-making processes should also remain flexible and responsive to shared knowledge, innovation, and constructive criticism . . . *then*

An effective Ethics' Program should be constructed around goals which advance the business' primary purpose over the long term. Ethics' Programs are frameworks that aspire to set standards, encourage challenge processes, promote the exchange of knowledge, remain adaptable, and advance the primary business purpose. Effective Ethics' Programs emphasize critical thinking and challenge processes among those individuals who are primarily responsible for a business' decision-making—employees and managers who are thoughtful, prudent, supportive, competitive, and loyal.

There isn't any perfect "template" for creating an effective Ethics' Program. They come in a vast number of shapes and sizes. Many resemble stock policies, but they can also be imaginatively assembled and implemented. The key is to keep them on-point: to establish clear expectations built around value-creation, to lead by example, and to emphasize communication and critical thinking. Figure 7.1 uses a "grocery list" approach to how an effective Ethics' Program might be developed. (See Figure 7.1.)

ENGAGEMENT—What Do You Think?

Describe how you would create an Ethics' Program for your own company. What goals would you identify? What standards would you expect of decisions made by others within your company? How would you encourage people to share their expertise—their knowledge—with each other? What processes would you put in place to evaluate your company's decision-making?

_____

_____

_____

_____

_____

_____

_____

Figure 7.1 Development of an Effective Ethics' Program
Source: Courtesy of Steven Lovett

Section 7.2 Identifying Ethical Issues and Dilemmas

Identifying what constitutes an ethical issue or dilemma seems like a simple task at first. And, in many instances, it is. For instance, if a question arises regarding the full disclosure of potential litigation risks to an errors and omissions underwriter (to an insurance provider) when applying for an E&O ("errors and omissions" policy), it shouldn't take a legal expert to identify the existence of possible consequences if all known, or reasonably anticipated, litigation risks aren't fairly disclosed. If an issue arises where an employee has been caught using company resources for personal reasons, it shouldn't take a law enforcement, or a forensic accounting, expert to identify the consequences of allowing an employee to waste or destroy corporate resources. These might be easy ethical issues or dilemmas for most people to identify. Most people would be able to agree on the standards of conduct (acceptable, or unacceptable, behavior) related to these kinds of easily identifiable ethical dilemmas.

However, real difficulties arise when an issue is not easily identified as an ethical dilemma. (This difficulty harkens back to our discussion in Chapter 1 about the impracticality of using a moral standard as an ethical framework.) People don't always agree on what constitutes "right" or a "wrong" when underlying issues aren't overtly tied to applicable laws, regulations, policies, or a well-known and accepted standards of behavior.

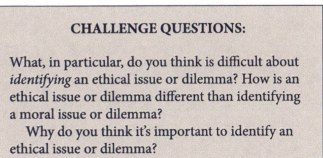

CHALLENGE QUESTIONS:

What, in particular, do you think is difficult about *identifying* an ethical issue or dilemma? How is an ethical issue or dilemma different than identifying a moral issue or dilemma?

Why do you think it's important to identify an ethical issue or dilemma?

Even though employees and managers who work together might possess a basic agreement about certain standards of conduct (i.e., stealing is unacceptable behavior), there is unlikely to be a foregone consensus about which ethical paradigm(s) to apply in situations where the presence of an issue or a dilemma is unclear or is debatable. Most textbooks about ethics spend a lot of time talking about standards of conduct and behavior that most people would recognize as posing "ethical dilemmas": lying, cheating, stealing, abusing company resources, abusing raw resources, permitting (actively or passively) an unsafe work environment to exist, mistreating employees, mistreating customers, misleading investors, misleading regulators, and causing harm to, or taking advantage of, consumers. Unfortunately, all of these dilemmas and behaviors do exist in the marketplace, and they should be addressed and not tolerated. But identifying those actions is unlikely to present much of a challenge (i.e., either abuse is occurring or it's not); in fact, setting standards of behavior that proscribe those activities might best be addressed through a "Code of Conduct."

© ra2studio/Shutterstock.com.

On the other hand, identifying the need to constructively make ethical decisions about actions or circumstances that don't obviously conflict with a basic, shared sense of acceptable standards of conduct, is where an effective Ethics' Program can create a framework for issue-spotting and constructive decision-making to take place. Remember the Opening Thought Experiment in Chapter 1? Because Marsha's situation doesn't pose any overt conflict with any law, regulation, or widely accepted social norm, it is difficult to identify whether an ethical dilemma exists, and if one does, how it can be resolved. This is the nature of most dilemmas in business.

There isn't a one-size-fits-all answer to identifying ethical dilemmas. Each person has his or her own perspective about what may, or may not, constitute a constructive decision when an issue or dilemma isn't clearly defined, or answered, by an underlying moral belief system. We can, however, apply a few simple questions to help us determine whether an ethical issue or dilemma exists. These few questions can act as a "litmus test" of sorts, assessing a few variables and conditions in order to have a clearer picture of what might be going on or what could be going on. To help us illustrate an application, we'll use Marsha's situation as our example.

On the left-hand side of the table are the questions you can apply to almost any situation in order to determine if an ethical issue or dilemma exists. On the right-hand side, we'll answer the questions using Marsha's circumstances.

| #1 Is this issue likely to cause harm to someone in some way?

If "no," then this is unlikely to be an ethical issue or dilemma.

If "yes," go to #2. | *Yes*; either the interests of Marsha's existing employees and the domestic economy (even if it's local) would be harmed, or the interests of the new investors and Marsha would be harmed. |

#2 Is this issue addressed by any applicable law or regulation? If "no," go to #3. If "yes," use the applicable law or regulation to resolve the issue.	*No*; there aren't any laws or regulations which would compel Marsha to make a decision one way or the other. (There are likely to be laws—such as corporate tax laws—which influence her situation, but they're not forcing her to stay in the United States or to go abroad.)
#3 Is this issue addressed by any applicable company policy or procedure? If "no," go to #4. If "yes," use the applicable policy or procedure to resolve the issue.	*No*; there aren't any company policies or procedures (that we know of) which would compel Marsha to make a decision one way or the other. (There are likely to be policies—such as Marsha's mission statement—which might influence her situation, but they would be unlikely to compel her to stay in the United States or to go abroad.)
#4 What if the "whole world" made the decision I'm contemplating? Would this lead to global disaster? If "no," then this may not be an ethical issue or dilemma, or it may not have a high level of intensity or severity. If "yes," then go to #5.	*Yes*; if everyone else decided to move their companies overseas, the U.S. economy would collapse and millions of citizens would be out of work. (This question is intended to be exaggeration, but its exaggeration is what allows it to bring some clarity to the issue being considered.)
#5 What would be in the "best interests" of the business purpose—is there a decision which would clearly advance the long-term growth and sustainability of the company while delivering improved value to consumers and to the majority of the company's stakeholders? If "no," then this may not be an ethical issue or dilemma, or it may not have a high level of intensity or severity. If "yes," then this is very likely to be an ethical issue or dilemma, which needs diagnosing (analyzing) and thoughtful, purposeful resolving.	*Yes*; there is a greater likelihood that moving Marsha's company abroad would result in significantly more growth and long-term sustainability, while delivering greater value to the company's consumers. Taking her company overseas may still not be the "correct" answer, but we now know Marsha's problem represents a legitimate ethical issue or dilemma, which needs some thorough analysis and a framework (i.e., an ethical paradigm or a corporate framework) to resolve.

Now that we have a better handle (or a not-so-slippery handle) on how to *identify* an ethical issue or dilemma, let's discuss how to *dissect or analyze* the issue or dilemma.

ENGAGEMENT—What Do You Think?

Think of a situation in your own life—or a situation you observed—which might have benefited from this process of identification. If you were to apply these steps to that situation, describe what answers you would have developed. Would those answers have clarified the dilemma? Would they have provided a clearer picture as to how to resolve the dilemma?

_____.

_____.

_____.

_____.

_____.

_____.

_____.

Section 7.3 Dissecting Ethical Dilemmas

Analyzing, or dissecting, ethical issues and dilemmas can be as vexing as identifying them in the first place. But if part of a leader's job is to train others (or to model for others) how to *handle* ethical dilemmas in a constructive way, then it must also be part of the job to *dissect* ethical dilemmas. Vexing or not, understanding what an ethical dilemma could mean to the prosperity of the organization is a critical part of ethics management (a term we'll get to later in this chapter). In other words, if you know an ethical dilemma exists, you have to ask: *What does the existence of this ethical dilemma potentially mean?*

Steps for diagnosing an ethical dilemma do not come in neatly packaged boxes, and they're not necessarily hierarchical or sequential. Those variables depend largely on the specific situation in which they're identified. However, for our purposes, let's look at a representative way in which an ethical issue or dilemma might be constructively and effectively dissected.

Most ethical issues and dilemmas arise in the context of *relationships* (keep in mind our discussions from Chapter 4). A good <u>first step</u> would be to

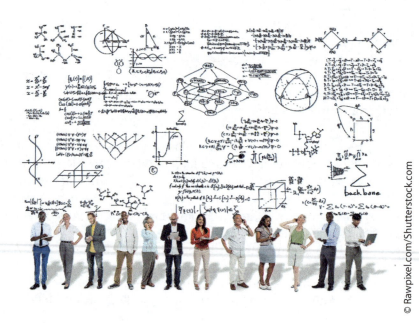

make sure you understand several, fundamental aspects about the affected relationship(s). Ask yourself the following questions:

- *<u>Who</u> is involved in this (or these) relationship(s)?*
- *<u>Who</u> are the (typical) <u>decision-makers</u> in this (or these) relationship(s)?*
- *<u>What</u> <u>advantages or benefits</u> does this (or these) relationship(s) bring to the business?*
- *<u>What</u> <u>value</u> does the business bring to this (or these) relationship(s)?*
- *<u>What</u>, if any, are the "<u>boundaries</u>" of this (or these) relationship(s)?*
- *<u>What problems</u>, if any, are there, or have there been, with this (or these) relationship(s)?*

Having now asked, and hopefully answered, these essential questions about the involved relationship(s), as a <u>second step</u>, ask a few more, but broader, questions.

- *<u>Who</u> are all of the <u>stakeholders</u> affected by this particular ethical issue or dilemma?*
- *<u>How</u> are they affected?*
- *What are their <u>interests</u> or concerns as they relate to this particular ethical issue or <u>dilemma</u>?*
- *<u>How</u> do these stakeholders bring <u>advantages or benefits</u> to the business?*
- *<u>What</u> <u>value</u> does the business bring to these stakeholders?*

You should now have a good idea of the persons, entities, stakeholders, and issues involved in the relationship(s) involved in the ethical issue or dilemma. For your third step, turn to the specific ethical issue or dilemma and ask a few more pointed questions.

© Biehler Michael/Shutterstock.com

- *How does this ethical issue or dilemma affect the business purpose?*
- *What, or who, are all of the business entities (division, sections, groups, etc.), which might be affected by this ethical issue or dilemma? How will they be affected?*
- *What are the possible risks for the business in this particular ethical issue or dilemma? What is the litigation risk, if any? What is the reputational risk, if any? What is the operational risk, if any?*
- *What are the possible advantages to the business posed by this particular ethical issue or dilemma?*
- *What business resources, if any, does this particular ethical issue or dilemma affect? How does it affect these resources?*
- *What experiments, if any, have been tried in the past to address this ethical issue or dilemma, or one very similar to it?*
- *What in the past has been learned about this particular ethical issue or dilemma? How, if at all, do those experiences inform the current situation?*

Finally, now having a much clearer picture of *who* is affected by the ethical issue or dilemma, *what* the ethical issue or dilemma affects, and *how* the ethical issue or dilemma affects those things, move to your <u>fourth</u> step. Determine which ethical paradigm(s) might provide the best (most constructive) guidance and most sound reasoning, which would advance the business purpose have the most constructive, positive, and *value*-based outcome. (If it helps, take a look back at Chapter 2.)

Treat these four steps of dissection flexible, and if the situation compels it,

> ### CHALLENGE QUESTIONS:
>
> Out of the four steps we just discussed, which step do you think is the most important or indispensable? Why?
>
> What do you think you should do if you can't answer one or more of the suggested questions? Who would you want to involve in this process? Why?
>
> What do you think you can do, or should do, to keep this four-step process free from bias?

dive deeper on any one of the analytical questions posed above. The element of *time* will almost always pressure you for a quick, half-thought-out conclusion. Whenever possible, don't give into this pressure. By the very nature of most ethical issues and dilemmas, the outcome is worth the time–cost it takes to come up with the most constructive answer. If you simply can't discount the clock, then be as thorough as you can be.

Having taken these steps, and having done your best to answer these questions, you should have a fairly good dissection of the ethical issue or dilemma at-hand.

ENGAGEMENT—What Do You Think?

Keeping in mind the experience you used in the "engagement" piece of the previous section, apply the dissection questions we've now discussed. How would answering these dissection questions have helped you arrive at a more constructive, prosperous solution?

_____

_____

_____

_____

_____

_____

Section 7.4 Tools of Ethics' Management: Experiment, Observe, and Evaluate

We've spent time discussing corporate cultures, organizational structure and influences, and how a person and organization might go about identifying ethical dilemmas, and dissecting those dilemmas. All of these topics tie into the end result: "**ethics management**."

This isn't a sub-discipline within the Management discipline (but maybe it should be), and this isn't a suggestion for a management rubric within a company

> **ETHICS MANAGEMENT**
>
> This refers to how ethical decision-making can be incentivized, monitored, and used in order to create an environment of constructive and repeatable processes that lead to prosperous outcomes

(although it could be—especially if it were embedded with an ethics program). Instead, the idea of "ethics management" addresses the general question of how ethical decision-making processes can be managed—procreated, encouraged, and incentivized—within an organization, regardless of the specifics of a company's ethics program or its management style (with a few qualifications). Ethics management is about overseeing (and not necessarily from a formal, management point-of-view) the process and characteristics of principled decision-making.

Experiment

The first working component is to urge and nurture *experimentation*. An enormous advantage to our marketplace—and an even more robust advantage in a free market economy—is the inspiration and ability to experiment. Businesses experiment all the time with new products, new services, new marketing campaigns, and various ventures. Investors experiment all the time with new portfolio choices, varied dollar-amounts, and a variety of investment vehicles. Consumers experiment all the time with new purchases, new brands, new products and services, and changing opinions. This "spirit of experimentation" should be one of the key tools used in ethics management. Employees and managers should be emboldened to experiment when faced with an ethical dilemma or issue. They should look for alternatives, to think outside the box, to literally try different options (when practical) or walk through different possibilities, without the fear of discipline or a negative outcome.

This attitude will encourage a willingness to find the best solution, a more efficient solution, and a more adaptive solution to accomplish the business purpose, while having accounted for the consequences to various other stakeholders. Experimentation is *not* a license or an excuse for poor judgment or unacceptable behavior. It is *not* an excuse for working outside the boundaries of a company's mission statement or its compliance or ethics program. But it *is* a license to propose a reasonable initiative or option, and to work toward a resolution in a constructive and positive

manner, even if the initiative or option is untested or "off the beaten path." In this chapter's Opening Thought Experiment, perhaps Dr. Donoharm could have suggested a third, or fourth, or fifth option to his patient. Perhaps what she *really* wanted was for the pain to end, not to end up dead. Maybe there would have been a homeopathic option or another non-traditional treatment option. Perhaps even a psychosomatic option—finding the right kind of therapy group or therapist to try out coping and cathartic methods. And even if his patient really *did* want to actually die, maybe there were other options, too. The point is, when a dilemma arises, it usually isn't enough to simply follow a regulation or to even follow an established procedure. Typically, a dilemma is a dilemma because there isn't any clear answer; there aren't any clear procedures or rules. This is when experimentation may reap significant rewards.

Observe

The second working component to ethics management is to be willing to, and be disciplined to, *observe*. In our fast-paced, frenetic world, it can be difficult to genuinely observe what's going on around us. We are all assaulted with a ton of information and data every day, and every day we "observe" it in that it registers with one or more of our senses. But what most of us do far less often is to genuinely observe—to take note of something, and to think about what we've taken note of, in order to use that examination as information by which we can formulate a subsequent action.

Observation is data collection, but its meaningful data collection. What information is likely to be significant? Why? What information is likely to better inform a decision? Does the information contemplate possible harm? Possible advantages? The right stakeholder interests? Is the information built around arriving at the overarching business purpose?

<table>
<tr><td>

CHALLENGE QUESTIONS:

In your own words, describe the concepts of experimentation, observation, and analysis. Why is each of these concepts important to ethics management?

If these concepts were applied to Marsha's problem, described in Chapter 1, how do you think she could best manage that ethical dilemma? Why?

</td></tr>
</table>

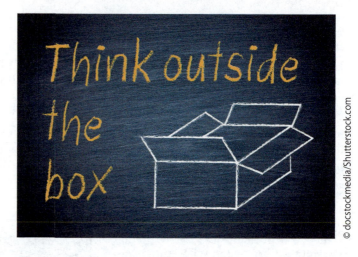

© docstockmedia/Shutterstock.com

Analyze

The third working component to ethics management is taking the initiative and time to *analyze* the data which has been collected and articulating what that data might mean. Do the answers to the questions posed above provide a clearer picture of the dilemma and its resolution? When an analysis is performed, there needs to be a meaningful review of risk exposures, opportunities, weaknesses, and strengths.

A common way of framing an effective and thorough analysis is to perform a SWOT Analysis. SWOT or Strengths, Weaknesses, Opportunities, and Threats are a formal means of doing that evaluation.

Strengths are areas where the company is strong or better than the competition. The strengths of an enterprise might be its highly trained staff or existing market share. Perhaps the organization has strong supply partners or long-term contracts. Maybe the company owns patents or copyrights that give it a competitive advantage. Understanding the strengths is important so those can be leveraged for gain in the future.

Weaknesses are those areas where the company is suffering or perhaps is at a dis-advantage to competitors in the industry. Weaknesses need to be realistically identified so they can be dealt with. It is easy to underestimate weaknesses. If a company is not willing to acknowledge them, it will be difficult to correct them. Weaknesses might be clients that are leaving due to poor customer service or an inexperienced sales staff that is not closing sales at the necessary rate. Weaknesses could be dated technology or operating in an area with restrictive regulations or excessive taxes.

Opportunities represent areas a company can take advantage of a new or changing situation. A new area might be opening up that will offer potential growth chances. Customer dissatisfaction with a competitor may give your company the opportunity to grow its market share.

Threats are areas in which there is potential danger to the firm. A new competitor opening up, or changing technologies that will leave your company behind are certainly threats. Changes in the local laws or regulations can also bring threats to the company. An SWOT analysis should be done regularly to keep the company aware of the results. A careful appraisal of the elements of the analysis can help reduce the tendency to act on intuition and instead act on facts. Fact- or evidence-based decision making is far superior to deciding based on opinion or feelings.[1]

ENGAGEMENT—What Do You Think?

If you were to apply the Experiment–Observe–Analyze approach to the experience you used in the "engagement" pieces of the previous sections, what might have happened? What would you now do differently, if anything? How would your decisions or actions been different? How could you take the lessons learned from that experience and use them in the future?

_____

_____

_____

_____

_____

_____

_____

Section 7.5 Managing Self

Especially in the previous section, the pronoun "you" was used very liberally. The assumption is (and the reality is) that you'll be personally involved in a myriad of ethical issues and dilemmas as you work your way through your professional career. You may be a frontline employee. You may be a mid-level manager. You may be a senior manager, or an executive. Or you may be a director or shareholder. You may be *the* decision-maker, or you may just be part of the decision-making process. Whatever your role, and whatever your normal responsibilities, you'll have the ultimate responsibility of doing—or helping others to do—whatever is the most constructive, positive, and beneficial to the business purpose for the long term. Because of this, it is worth a few moments to discuss *you* as one of the variables in the process of how to identify, diagnose, and manage ethical issues and dilemmas.

You must accept the fact that you are responsible for our own integrity. Your inner self, not your outer self, determines your future. You must understand your

© KAIZEN 333/Shutterstock.com

CHALLENGE QUESTIONS:

How do you view yourself? What experiences have you had resolving ethical issues or dilemmas?

What would make you feel more comfortable as a decision-maker when facing an ethical issue or dilemma? Do you feel well-equipped to handle ethical dilemmas? Why or why not?

How would you describe your own "sense of integrity?" What does it mean to you?

self-concept, how you perceive yourself. You must recognize your motivations and learn how to be true to yourself, how to keep yourself intact and incorruptible. The concept of self has two aspects: (1) *the existential self*—the most basic part of the self-scheme or self-concept and the sense of being separate and distinct from others, and (2) *the categorical self*—the realization that you exist as a separate experiencing being and an awareness that you are an object in the world that can be experienced and has properties.

The self-concept has also been described as having three different components: (1) the view you have of yourself (self-image), (2) how much value you place on yourself (self-esteem or self-worth), and (3) what you wish you were really like (ideal self). The self is the awareness of your being and functioning and plays an important role in perception. The "real self" is what you perceive yourself to be; the "ideal self" is what you would like to be. If your ideal self and real self mirror each other, you are said to be adjusted, mature, and fully functioning.

Your sense and perception of integrity may be defined in terms of the commitments or obligations that others identify you as keeping. It could hinge on your professionalism, trustworthiness, keeping an open mind, or being respectful. Or it could have something to do with your ethical treatment of coworkers, business meeting etiquette, admiration for efficient and accurate communication, or effective time management. Perhaps you are opportunistic about searching for dishonesty and deception. Whatever it is that causes people to see you as a person of integrity enhances your career. Continue to model that behavior.[2] And while you're modeling that behavior, don't forget to keep a keen eye toward the influences and factors which inspire or pressure you personally.

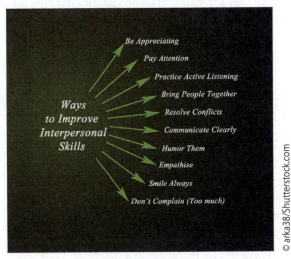

SELECTED READINGS

- Kegan, Robert, and Lisa Laskow Lahey. *Immunity to Change: How to Overcome It and Unlock the Potential in Yourself and Your Organization.* 1st edition. Boston, Mass: Harvard Business Review Press, 2009.
- Seglin, Jeffrey L. *The Good, the Bad, and Your Business: Choosing Right When Ethical Dilemmas Pull You Apart.* New York: Seapoint Books and Music, 2007.
- Kegan, Robert, and Lisa Laskow Lahey. *How the Way We Talk Can Change the Way We Work: Seven Languages for Transformation.* San Francisco: Jossey-Bass, 2002.
- Kidder, Rushworth M. *How Good People Make Tough Choices: Resolving the Dilemmas of Ethical Living.* 1st edition. New York: Fireside, 1996.

TAKE-AWAY QUESTIONS AND IDEAS

Why do businesses need ethics' programs?
What value should an ethics' program deliver to a business?
What can cause a particular situation to be difficult to identify as an ethical issue or dilemma? Why are ethical issues and dilemmas significant? Why is it critical to be able to identify them.

What are a few "universal" steps for diagnosing an ethical dilemma? What is the point to diagnosing an ethical dilemma?
Why are "you" a critical component to analyzing and resolving ethical dilemmas?
What kinds of tools and practices might be available to help you assess and resolve an ethical issue or dilemma?

- When discussing the creation and implementation of ethics programs, many companies lose sight of the need to combine their primary concern (i.e., making a profit) with advancing the values and principles by which they want to do business.

- Dilemmas which are addressed by laws, regulations, policies, or best practices are not as difficult as those dilemmas which materialize out of situations where there are little, to no, guidelines on which you can depend. This leads to the need for an ethics' program—a company-wide framework for decision-making, acceptable behaviors, and constructive actions.

- Because most dilemmas facing a business person are unlikely to have clear, moral parameters, it can be difficult to identify when an ethical issue or dilemma exists. Being able to identify an ethical issue or dilemma is crucial to further advancing the business purpose of long-term, sustainable prosperity.

- Diagnosing an ethical issue or dilemma can be a simple process, but it requires thoughtfulness and careful consideration. By asking a few "universal" questions, you can determine the intensity of an issue and begin to formulate what might be likely options to resolving the issue.

- "You" are almost always a "variable" when identifying and analyzing ethical issues and dilemmas. How you manage yourself, and how you see yourself, can forecast how you might approach and resolve ethical dilemmas, and whether your approach is likely to further the overarching business goal.

- Frameworks and tools for managing ethical issues and dilemmas require purposefulness. There isn't a single "turn-key" approach or set of tools, but by making sure ethical issues and dilemmas receive a thorough and consistent evaluation, based on informative data, they can be much more effectively and successfully managed.

KEY TERMS

- Codes of Conduct
- Ethics management

ENDNOTES

1. From *Open for Business* by Brock Williams and Dane Galden. Copyright © 2015 by Kendall Hunt Publishing Company.

2. From *Ethics in the World of Business* by Phillip Lewis. Copyright © 2014 by Kendall Hunt Publishing Company. Reprinted by permission.

ENGAGEMENT—WHAT DO YOU THINK?

Write down your own thoughts about what you've learned in this chapter. Consider the previous discussions about why Ethics' Programs are necessary, how they add value, how you can identify ethical dilemmas, how you can dissect those dilemmas, how you can manage the decision-making process, and how you can manage yourself. In your own words, describe the role you think these various factors have in ethical decision-making processes within an organization.

CHAPTER 8

PRACTICAL SUSTAINABILITY: ETHICS AND RESILIENT PROSPERITY

"Sustainability" is one of those words that comes loaded with social implications. Those social implications are largely derived from the use of the term in ecology. In an ecological context, sustainability is the property of a biological system to produce (or reproduce) indefinitely and to remain productively diverse. This ecological observation about biological systems made for a simple framework when, in 1987, the World Commission on Environment and Development (most often referred to as the "Brundtland Commission") coined the term "sustainable development" in its paper, *Our Common Future.* The idea of **sustainable development** is derived from the presumption that human development goals (i.e., political and economic progress) must be unified with the environment in order for both to continue perpetually; the goal is to meet the needs of the present without permanently compromising the ability of the future to meet its needs. (This is sometimes referred to as "intergenerational equity.") The mainstays of sustainable development are: (1) economic growth, (2) environmental protection, and (3) social equality.

When the concept of sustainable development has been applied to businesses, it is most often reflected in an emphasis on "eco-efficiency." **Eco-efficiency** is usually calculated as the ecological (i.e., natural resources)

SUSTAINABLE DEVELOPMENT

Human development goals must be unified with the environment in order for both to continue perpetually; the goal is to meet the needs of the present without permanently compromising the ability of the future to meet its needs.

ECO-EFFICIENCY

The ecological (i.e., natural resources) impact business practices have on the environment in relation to added economic value.

impact business practices have on the environment in relation to added economic value. The concept of sustainable development has further introduced the idea of "**socio-efficiency**," which describes the social or cultural impact of business practices in relation to added economic value. Ultimately, the focus on these proposed impacts—ecological and social—led to corporate social responsibility (CSR), a business strategy model we discussed in Chapter 4.

During our earlier discussion of CSR, we posited that CSR changes the fundamental reason *why* businesses should act in constructive and positive ways; CSR causes profit—and prosperity—to take a second-place to external "obligations." CSR preemptively ignores, at least in part, the positive progression of creative destruction. And worst of all perhaps is that the concept of sustainability, whether in the broader format of sustainable development or the narrower

> **SOCIO-EFFICIENCY**
>
> The social or cultural impact of business practices in relation to added economic value.

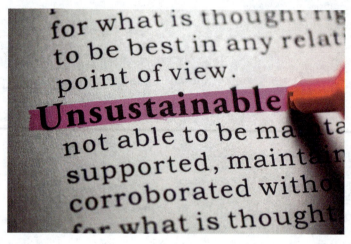

format of business-centric CSR, leaves businesses unable to determine, measure, or otherwise gainfully assess if their decisions are truly productive in the way they need them to be—whether their decisions actually lead to a more prosperous outcome for the business itself.

Ultimately, the concept of sustainable development, even if it's packaged as CSR, is an *unsustainable* decision-making framework for businesses.

LEARNING OUTCOMES | OUTLINE

8.1 A Practical Approach: Resilient Prosperity

8.2 Resources and Workable Frameworks

8.3 Responsibility, Efficiency, and Creativity

8.4 Taking a Practical Look at the Triple Bottom Line

- Understand the concept of "sustainable development" and how it relates to business operations in the private marketplace.

- Analyze the difference between "resilient prosperity" and "sustainable development."

- Describe why "resilient prosperity" is a more effective, practical framework for decision-making in business organizations.

- Understand the scope and importance of resources, and resource management, for a business organization.

- Describe the concept of "stewardship" in business operations, using the three characteristics of responsibility, efficiency, and creativity.

- Analyze the limitations and impracticality of using the "Triple Bottom Line" as a framework for decision-making in business organizations.

OPENING THOUGHT EXPERIMENT

On a balmy Friday afternoon in late spring, you decide to invite your friend, Phil, over to sit on your back porch, have a cold drink, and enjoy the view of your freshly mown grass. Barely fifteen minutes pass before Phil appears at your fence gate, dressed in shorts, sandals, and a startlingly bright Hawaiian shirt, but with a look of anxiety on his face.

"What's up?" you ask, swinging open the fence and handing your friend a refreshing beverage.

"It's work again, but this time you're not gonna believe it." Phil plops himself down in a lawn chair and stretches out his skinny legs. "This time, the boss has lost his mind." He takes a few long drinks and stares vacantly out at the lawn.

For several moments, you let your friend sit in quiet, hoping he's able to calm down a little before you ask him what's wrong. But apparently, Phil is ready to talk.

"I've told you all along my boss is crazy," he begins with a deep sigh. "The guy really is bats. If he keeps making decisions the way he's been making decisions, we're gonna end up going out of business."

"What do you mean?"

"Well, he's been on this big cost-cutting streak lately. Over the past few months, we've trimmed back a lot of excess overhead, and we were able to renegotiate some of our vendor contracts to reduce our wholesale costs."

You take a big swig of your own drink and lean back. "So far, sounds like a good thing, Phil. What's the problem?"

"It *is* a good thing," he admits, "but now he's carrying it too far. It doesn't make sense anymore." He shakes his head and stares vacantly out at the lawn again. For a moment, you wonder if he's lost his train of thought. Clearly, your friend is really worried about what's been going on.

"Tell me what happened."

Phil looks tired. "This past Thursday at our strategy meeting, the boss comes in and tells us the owners are expecting to see at least a 5% gain next quarter, but he also says our customer survey data indicates our price point is too high. The customers want a cheaper product but with the same quality." Phil settles back in his chair and shakes his head. "So our boss tells us we're going to close the factory in Newark."

"Why?"

"According to him, the factory in Newark takes up at least 35% of our overhead but last year only contributed 27% in profits."

You aren't a mathematician, but that sounds like it makes sense. "Well," you cautiously begin, "if the Newark factory costs more than it makes, and if the owners want more profits, and if the customers want lower prices, maybe your boss' idea isn't so crazy." You don't want to make Phil mad, but both of you have always respected each other for speaking honestly. "What am I missing?" you ask.

Phil looks at you and slowly nods. "It isn't crazy, except this time, cost-cutting is going to hurt in the long run way more than it helps. Last year, the Newark factory actually yielded a 22% *increase* in profits, and the year before that, it had produced a 12% increase. The line coming out of Newark is easily going to be one of our strongest profit-centers in a couple of years." He took one, last, long drink. "Just because

© thatreec/Shutterstock.com

cutting costs sounds good, doesn't mean it is good. Just because the factory in Newark isn't profitable yet, doesn't mean it won't be in the long-run. There has to be a better way."

ENGAGEMENT—What Do You Think?

Given the situation Phil has described, explain why closing the Newark factory wouldn't be a constructive, sustainable business decision. How does this thought experiment illustrate a situation where an otherwise "good" concept might not make a reliable framework for decision-making in the long term. Describe an alternative way to raise profits and lower prices without closing a factory like the fictional one in Newark. Does the alternative way you've described mean the company would be insensitive to "cost-cutting?"

_____

_____

_____

_____

_____

_____

_____

Section 8.1 A Practical Approach: Resilient Prosperity

The word **resilience** carries with it the qualities of adaptability, toughness, elasticity, and the willingness (or the stubbornness) to "spring back into shape" after experiencing adversity. Companies that survive and thrive over long periods of time demonstrate resilience. They endure in spite of problems such as economic downturns, changes in market trends, changes in technology, outdated processes, loss of talent, loss of capital, loss of market share, reputational crises, and intensified regulatory oversight. Resiliency can absorb, and even benefit from, creative destruction. And for our purposes, it is critical to note that the concept of resiliency is distinctly different from the concept of sustainability.

Throughout this book, we have employed a common understanding of the word "**sustainability**"—something's ability to be maintained over time. We have applied this idea to ethical decision-making, whereby a framework used to make a business decision is one that can be repeated or reused, that is, maintained, over time. Practically speaking, this means a business should be able to consistently rely on a framework it uses to make its decisions: a framework that encourages decision-makers to advance its primary business purpose and a framework that permits decision-makers to design solutions that lead to improved (prosperous) outcomes. Understandably, however, the word "sustainability" in popular culture has been widely appropriated to mean, much more narrowly, the avoidance of natural resource depletion in order to maintain a balance between the environment and human development. When the word "sustainable" became joined with the word "development," the intention was to provide a framework and goal by which businesses (and nations) could politically and economically progress without degrading access to, and the existence of, natural resources in the future.

RESILIENCE

In a business context, this describes the ability and capacity to endure in spite of problems such as economic downturns, changes in market trends, changes in technology, outdated processes, loss of talent, loss of capital, loss of market share, reputational crises, and intensified regulatory oversight.

SUSTAINABILITY

Something's ability to be maintained over time; or, popularly, the capacity to maintain an ecological balance or the preservation of ecological resources.

Such a framework and goal have, objectively, a very admirable intent: to incite organizations, nations, and individuals to be good stewards of the natural environment. But, as we observed in this chapter's opening remarks, sustainable development (or CSR, or any other iteration of this agenda) simply *isn't* a practical or rational framework by which a business can make the majority of its decisions—the multitude of daily decisions not otherwise guided by law or best practices. The agenda of sustainable development identifies the *environment* (or society) as the ultimate stakeholder for a business organization. It takes Stakeholder Theory, and it not-so-subtly insists that businesses ought to fashion their strategy and their decision-making processes around the issues, concerns, and interests of the environment *in order to be ethical*. (This is something we'll focus on toward the end of this chapter.) This approach— the proposed framework of sustainable development—is not a profitable, or a prosperous, or a logical framework for real-world decision-making in the marketplace.

Instead, a business organization needs different scaffolding—a different agenda—by which it can be successful over the long term and by which it can also (rationally and practically) acknowledge and promote its strategic need to care for the resources that help make it successful. To this end, businesses should look at the issue of resource management through the lens of *resiliency*, not sustainability. This way of looking at decision-making is a much more discrete, adaptable, and even assessable approach.

Resiliency recognizes the need to be able to access and utilize resources in

© Romolo Tavani/Shutterstock.com

STOP DOING WHAT DOESN'T WORK

© ScandanavianStock/Shutterstock.com

CHALLENGE QUESTIONS:

Why do you think the environment has become the most popular "stakeholder" in sustainable development?

How do you think most businesses respond to the idea of sustainable development on a day-to-day basis? How do they know whether they've achieved a "balance" with the environment? Do you think this is an effective, successful way to evaluate a business' ethics?

the future; future access and utilization ensures longevity, continued growth, and progressive prosperity. This is a partial absorption of the objectives behind sustainable development—any business that ignores tomorrow won't last much longer than today. However, it focuses this need within the scope of its *specific* needs. This is a much more powerful, persuasive, and practical focus than simply an "environmental" approach. For instance, a business that relies on petroleum should inform its decision-making processes by working to preserve access to, and utilization of, petroleum in the future. This might include decisions that emphasize increased efficiency in refinement processes, proficiency in oil extraction methods, and analysis of the rate of naturally occurring petroleum. The

concept of resiliency would also press this business to explore alternative resources that could replace, temporarily or even permanently, petroleum if and when necessary. These decisions, and the dilemmas they would resolve, would be driven by the business' primary purpose—profit—and would be geared toward improved outcomes—prosperity. The promise of future profits, and the threat of future difficulties, would provide a much more focused, practical, and constructive decision-making context than an abstruse, generalized mandate to "be green" or to be "sustainable."

This approach is "**resilient prosperity**"—value-based decisions that anticipate the need to preserve and successful manage critical resources in order to continually improve outcomes over the long term. Resilient prosperity aligns a business' decisions with it primary purpose while, at the same time, also aligning the idea of good stewardship. Additionally, it promotes an ethos centered on constructive, sustainable decision-making processes; not on being "environmentally friendly" or "socially conscious." Whereas sustainable development advocates for "balance" by attempting to shift a business' focus (and ethicalness) away from its primary purpose, resilient prosperity understands the need for resource stewardship by emphasizing the importance of a business' primary purpose and the ethicalness of prosperity.

> **RESILIENT PROSPERITY**
>
> Value-based decisions that anticipate the need to preserve and successful manage critical resources in order to continually improve outcomes over the long-term.

ENGAGEMENT—What Do You Think?

Describe what you think the critical distinction is between "sustainable development" and "resilient prosperity." Why do you think the idea of sustainable development (or CSR) has become so popular? In your own words, describe why you think resilient prosperity is a better decision-making framework for businesses.

_____

_____

_____

_____

_____

_____

Section 8.2 Resources and Workable Frameworks

Growth involves consumption. Creativity involves destruction. Progress involves change. And running a successful business—an ongoing business concern over the long term—involves realizing a net profit and delivering value as value is defined by the marketplace. Insisting that businesses make their daily decisions while being primarily concerned with the maintenance of an ecological balance ignores the practical effects of successful business practices.

© ESB Professional/Shutterstock.com

In Chapter 1, we characterized the concept of prosperity in a very distinct way for the purpose of decision-making in business contexts: "Prosperity means value." We determined that an ethical business decision is one which is constructive (advances the business' purpose), sustainable (repeatable over time), and one which leads to a more prosperous outcome (value delivered). We also identified several ethical "languages" with which a decision-maker could analyze and resolve a business dilemma, as well as communicate the rationale of his or her analysis to other stakeholders. All of these observations and tools factor into a workable framework for making ethical business decisions. A business can be judged, and can judge itself and its conduct, through

© solarseven/Shutterstock.com

the consistent and candid application of these observations and tools. A business can also use them to achieve resilient prosperity. In Chapter 9, we'll discuss the "ripple effects" of resilient prosperity—how this ethos results in prosperous outcomes for others outside the marketplace—but for the moment, we will limit our discussion to the idea of preserving and ensuring the existence of "resources."

In the marketplace, **resources** are the assets, materials, and supplies used by a business to achieve its primary business purpose. They include animate and inanimate things, such as humans, creativity, stratagems, capital, technology (hard and soft), relationships, access to experts, training, trade secrets, licensing, legal counsel, third-party vendors, and (of course!) environmental or natural materials and energy sources. The types of resources, and how they are used and leveraged, are a unique proposition for every business enterprise. Unfortunately, the most popular topic of conversation in most books and courses about business ethics focuses on environmental or natural resources, environmental legislation, and "alternative energy"—this is the apex concern of the sustainable

> **RESOURCES**
>
> In a business context, this describes the assets, materials, and supplies used by a business to achieve its primary business purpose.

development (the "social responsibility" and "sustainability") agenda. The effect of this is that businesses are led to believe they are acting ethically as long as they remain sensitive to ecological and social issues. (Mere lip service is paid to the "economic" leg of the milking stool.) This myopic view of resources leaves out, or relegates to the minimalist area of legal compliance, all the other, greatly varied resources on which a company is dependent for its long-term success.

When the concept of resilient prosperity guides a company's eye toward future growth and profit, the company's decision-makers are naturally enabled to take into account *all* of a company's resources, whether ecological or not, in order to advance the business' primary purpose. Within this framework, a business will remain actively and constructively concerned about its workforce, its intellectual property, its investors, its debt-financing obligations and relationships, its workflow stratagems, its commitment to meaningful training, its operational processes, its regulatory compliance, as well as its need for raw materials and/or natural resources and energy. Decision-makers will strive to make constructive decisions and to resolve dilemmas in ways which minimize waste, maximize efficiency, and which lead to future prosperity. In this framework, being "green" is only a part of a successful company's ethicalness. There isn't the need to **greenwash** business goods or services.

© Denize/Shutterstock.com

GREENWASH

Misleading a consumer into thinking a service or product is more "environmentally friendly" than it is; this may, or may not, constitute unlawful fraud.

ENGAGEMENT—What Do You Think?

Why have environmental concerns become such a central part of discussions about business ethics? Do you think a business can be "environmentally friendly" and still act unethically? How can a business develop a long-term strategy for success without focusing simply on environmental (ecological) issues?

_____

_____

_____

_____

_____

_____

Section 8.3 Responsibility, Efficiency, and Creativity

Stewardship is an essential ingredient to successful business practices. **Stewardship** directly, or impliedly, refers to taking care of something, usually in a fruitful way. Successful businesses are stewards (beneficial "keepers") of a multitude of things: investor capital, trade secrets, reputation, compliance requirements (record keeping, etc.), human talent, communication with employees and/or customers, machinery, buildings, institutional memory, private employee information, private customer information, the well-being of employees (at least in the workplace), the well-being of customers (at least on

> **STEWARDSHIP**
>
> Refers to taking care of something, usually in a fruitful way.

the work premises), and even waste. The willingness to be voluntarily accountable for those resources, which advance a business' primary purpose, is essential to long-term viability and resiliency. The effects of ignoring stewardship can be disastrous and crippling. Many times, business failure is, at its core, a failure to be a good steward. For the purpose of our present discussion, we can characterize successful stewardship for business organizations in three ways: responsibility, efficiency, and creativity.

Ethical businesses—those who rely on decision-making frameworks that are constructive, sustainable and that lead to prosperous outcomes—understand and uphold their need to take responsibility for their actions and decisions. Responsibility implies an understanding of consequence, and consequence implies an understanding of cause-and-effect. Resilient prosperity focuses on treating a company's resources responsibly, as a good steward, knowing that when resources are wasted, unused, exhausted, or mistreated the consequences are likely to be dire. This relates directly back to our earlier discussion about voluntary accountability in Chapter 4.

> Decision-making frameworks are based on shared, and understood, ethical paradigms, where roles and responsibilities are clearly set, and where everyone (from the top to the bottom) has a positive sense of "ownership" in decision-making and its outcomes.

Ethical businesses also understand and pursue efficiency as a standard of good stewardship. Efficient practices arise from orderliness, coherence, the pursuit of maximizing profit, the pursuit of minimizing waste, and the exploiting every resource for its most useful contribution to the primary business purpose. Efficiency respects the value of each business resource; efficiency prizes the importance of each resource's contribution to the business' long-term success.

Ethical businesses understand and stimulate creativity as good stewards of their resources. Creativity enhances the pursuit of efficiency and the analysis of the reward of responsible conduct. Creativity always implies a sense of improvement, a sense of doing something differently with the expectation of a positive (prosperous!) outcome.

For a successful business, managing, preserving, and ensuring the existence of resources is not a matter of balancing present needs with future needs, it is a matter of good stewardship, and good stewardship is a matter of taking responsibility, pursuing efficiency, and stimulating creativity. Most importantly, stewardship for a business means taking care of those things that advance its primary purpose, both in the short term *and* in the long term.

ENGAGEMENT—What Do You Think?

Explain why this approach to stewardship, versus simply being a good steward of the "environment," would make better sense to a business. While eco- and socio-efficiency only relate to added financial value, stewardship relates to true prosperity—a better overall outcome. Why do you think sustainable development has such a narrow view of what "value" means to a business? How can the idea of stewardship better explain and stress the concept of value in prosperity?

_____

_____

_____

_____

_____

_____

_____

Section 8.4 Taking a Practical Look at the Triple Bottom Line

A further refinement of sustainable development and CSR—one which attempts to employ an accounting framework—is referred to as the **Triple Bottom Line** (TBL). TBL attempts to measure the impact of business decisions on social, economic, and environmental factors, while recognizing a business' obligation to positively influence a number of different stakeholders. In many circles, TBL (along with CSR) has become the "ethical standard" by which most businesses, especially in the Western Hemisphere, are judged. Instinctively, most people understand that a single moral code is an impractical and unwieldy framework for decision-making in a business context (something we discussed at the end of Chapter 1). Yet most people also say businesses should act "ethically"—a nebulous idea that business decisions can still be judged as "good" or "bad" (e.g., moral determinations) even without the aid of a moral code. The rational (and practical) vacuum left by this ambiguity was infilled with the concept of sustainable development, CSR, and eventually, TBL. The underlying problem with these approaches—even when attempting to use **full-cost accounting** as measuring methodology—

TRIPLE BOTTOM LINE

A decision-making framework which attempts to measure the impact of business decisions on social, economic, and environmental factors, while recognizing a business' obligation to positively influence a number of different stakeholders.

FULL-COST ACCOUNTING

A method of accounting for costs (direct and indirect) that is based on information about possible environmental, social, and economic benefits or disadvantages for each proposed decision.

is they continue to equate "ethical conduct" with the perceived impact such conduct has on external stakeholders, that is, the environment and society at-large. With this point-of-view, the concept of "ethics" and "ethical conduct" has been exploited to advance ecological and/or social agendas, while at the same time (with no lack of irony) debasing and devaluing the underlying primary purpose of all business organizations: to make a profit through prosperous outcomes.

The environment and society are *not* part of a business' "bottom line." Indeed, for a business, the "economic" component is also not its bottom line. They are all resources or issues—no greater and no lesser than other resources or issues—that contribute to a business earning a profit in a sustainable, positive, way—a way that leads to prosperous outcomes over the long term. Put another way, resilient prosperity is a business' true bottom line.

SELECTED READINGS

- Bishop, Toby J., and Frank E. Hydoski. *Corporate Resiliency: Managing the Growing Risk of Fraud and Corruption*. 1 edition. Hoboken, N.J: Wiley, 2009.
- Jickling, Bob. Viewpoint: *Why I Don't Want My Children to Be Educated for Sustainable Development*. The Journal of Environmental Education (JEE), 23(4), 1992.
- Arrow, Kenneth J. *Social Responsibility and Economic Efficiency*. Public Policy 21 (Summer 1973).
- Baxter, William F. *People or Penguins: The Case for Optimal Pollution*. Columbia University Press, 1974.

TAKE-AWAY QUESTIONS AND IDEAS

What are the characteristics of "sustainable development?" How are the measures of "eco-efficiency" and "socio-efficiency" supposed to inform business operations?

How is resiliency distinguishable from sustainability? Why is the difference between these two concepts significant for business organizations? Why is the framework of "resilient prosperity" more practical and more effective for business operations?

With what kinds of resources should a business be concerned? How do resources affect business operations? How does or should a business view its resources?

What is meant by "stewardship" in relation to business operations? How is stewardship characterized by responsibility, efficiency, and creativity? Why is creativity a necessary component to good stewardship in business?

How does the "Triple Bottom Line" impede business decision-making? Why is it impractical to use TBL as a measurement of ethical conduct in business operations? What is a better framework?

- The concept of sustainability, whether in the broader format of sustainable development or the narrower format of business-centric CSR, leaves businesses unable to determine, measure, or otherwise gainfully assess if their decisions are truly productive in the way they need them to be—whether their decisions actually lead to a more prosperous outcome for the business itself.

- A business should be able to consistently rely on a framework it uses to make its decisions: a framework that encourages decision-makers to advance its primary business purpose and a framework that permits decision-makers to design solutions that lead to improved (prosperous) outcomes.

- The agenda of sustainable development identifies the environment (or society) as the ultimate stakeholder in business. This approach—the proposed framework of sustainable development—is not a profitable, or a prosperous, or a logical framework for real-world decision-making in the marketplace.

- Resilient prosperity focuses the need to manage resources within the scope of a business' specific needs. This is a much more powerful, persuasive, and practical focus than simply an "environmental" approach.

- When the concept of resilient prosperity guides a company's eye toward future growth and profit, the company's decision-makers are naturally enabled to take into account all of a company's resources, whether ecological or not, in order to advance the business' primary purpose.

- The willingness to be voluntarily accountable for those resources, which advance a business' primary purpose is essential to long-term viability and resiliency. Successful stewardship for business organizations is characterized in three ways: responsibility, efficiency, and creativity.

- The underlying problem with approaches, such as the Triple Bottom Line, is that they continue to equate "ethical conduct" with the perceived impact such conduct has on *external* stakeholders, that is, the environment and society at-large.

- Sustainable development frameworks have misappropriated the concepts of "ethics" and "ethical conduct" and have exploited them to advance ecological and/or social agendas, while at the same time debasing and devaluing the underlying primary purpose of all business organizations: to make a profit through prosperous outcomes.

KEYTERMS

- Eco-efficiency
- Full-Cost Accounting
- Greenwash
- Resilience
- Resilient Prosperity
- Resources

- Socio-efficiency
- Stewardship
- Sustainability
- Sustainable Development
- Triple Bottom Line

ENDNOTE

1. "Report of the World Commission on Environment and Development: Our Common Future—A/42/427 Annex—UN Documents: Gathering a Body of Global Agreements." http://www.un-documents.net/wced-ocf.htm

ENGAGEMENT—WHAT DO YOU THINK?

Write down your own thoughts about what you've learned in this chapter. Consider the previous discussions about resilient prosperity, the impracticalities of sustainable development, the practical framework through which to view business resources, and the concept of stewardship in business. In your own words, describe the role you think these various factors have in a decision-making process within an organization—how can what you've read lead to better results in business? How can they lead to more ethical conduct and activities?

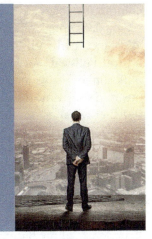

CHAPTER 9

THE COMMON GOOD: ETHICAL CONSIDERATIONS FOR MUTUAL PROSPERITY

© T Cassidy/Shutterstock.com

One of the assumptions underlying sustainable development is that private industry—businesses whose primary purpose is profit—will be at cross-purposes with the environment (the ecological and social environment); business will sacrifice natural resources (and the social benefit) to earn more money. Indisputably, there are abundant historical examples of this being the case; eras in industry and specific corporate situations in which businesses (from the very small to the very large) have disregarded issues such as sanitation, safety, discrimination, larger economic scales, and the conservation or efficient use of natural resources.

Governments, philosophers, consumers, clergymen, and activists have, for centuries, played the most visible roles in correcting marketplace abuses. From the 7th century legislation introduced by Saint Cuthbert of Lindisfarne, Kingdom of Northumbria, to protect eider ducks and their eggs, to Benjamin Franklin's argument for "public rights" when petitioning the Pennsylvania Assembly to stop waste dumping and to prohibit tanneries from plying their trade in Philadelphia's commercial district, to the 1902 publication of George Washington Carver's book, *How to Build Up Worn Out Soils,*[1] to the prognostication of exponential growth as it was analyzed by the Club of Rome in the 1972 book, *The Limits of Growth,*[2] a vast amount of discussion, debate, rhetoric, action, and collaboration has been expended on finding and improving the equilibrium between the marketplace and the greater common good. But ultimately, there can be no greater watchdog than the marketplace itself.

The "**Common Good**" is a term of art most often used to describe something that is favorable or beneficial for the greater majority of a given community—a

> **COMMON GOOD**
>
> Describes something that is beneficial and shared by most, or all, members of a community.

community that can be personal, local, regional, national, or global, and is usually concerned with the present and/or future. Political, social, and economic philosophers have long-proposed various, and sometimes conflicting, descriptions of what is meant by the word "common," what is meant by the word "good," and how the common good can best be achieved or, contrarily, impaired. A study of those varied points of view is better left to theorists; for our purposes, we need to focus on a practical construction for how businesses, and their decision-makers, can act in such a way

© Tupungato/Shutterstock.com

as to lead not only to their own prosperity but also to the prosperity of the greater good. If this can be achieved, and achieved by discussing a real-world application of this ethos, then it will substantiate and encourage the idea of stewardship that we discussed in Chapter 8.

LEARNING OUTCOMES | OUTLINE

9.1 Working Toward the Common Good
9.2 A Shared Ground for Ethical Frameworks
9.3 The Ripple Effect of Resilient Prosperity
9.4 Energizing Others: Establishing a Collective Purpose

- Understand how working toward the common good can be an advantage for businesses
- Apply the concept of working toward the common good to the concept of prosperity
- Analyze how the common good provides a shared ground—a universal measure—for ethicalness in business
- Evaluate how resilient prosperity can cause a "ripple effect" of prosperity for a business' interrelated communities
- Understand how to stimulate individual decision-makers within a business organization to seek out decisions that positively impact the common good

OPENING THOUGHT EXPERIMENT

Two months have passed since the publication of your ground-breaking book entitled, *An Ethical Perspective of Corporate Growth*. Book sales have been great. It seems like every day, your phone lights up with congratulatory text messages and phone calls. This evening is no different. After responding to a couple of new admiring fans, you settle into your favorite chair with your favorite drink and a newly purchased novel about dragons from other worlds spread open on your lap. But your phone rings one last time.

"Hi, this is Gib D'nomiad," says the unfamiliar voice with the vaguely familiar name. All of a sudden it hits you. Gib D'moniad is a billionaire French investor who earned his claim-to-fame by buying struggling, mid-cap companies and turning them into profit powerhouses. His growth strategy includes an emphasis on how his companies can benefit the communities in which they're located. You read an in-depth profile of Mr. D'nomiad a couple of years before in a business journal, and you used one of his turn-around companies as a case study in your book.

"Hi!" you reply enthusiastically, basking in the glow of having received a call from such a successful, high-profile businessman. "What can I do for you?"

"I have a problem," Mr. D'nomiad says with a slight French accent. "I've read your book, and I was hoping you could help. I hope I'm not calling you too late."

"Of course not. How can I help?"

Over the course of the next several minutes, the billionaire investor lays out a very intriguing set of facts. He is in the middle of negotiating the purchase of another company, and even though he doesn't tell you the company's name, he does say it's located in the United States in an area which has been experiencing some much-needed economic growth over the past five years. The community suffered greatly during the last economic recession with high rates of unemployment, a nearly bankrupt local government, and a devastated housing market. A group of local investors partnered with a big manufacturing company and built a new plant in the community three years ago. The new plant employed almost 1000 workers and played a key role in helping turn things around. Housing developers and other businesses jumped in, too, and the community appeared to finally be on its way to a better future. In fact, Mr. D'nomiad says, the community was featured in several national pieces about the partnership between business and society. The company he is negotiating to purchase now has a unique opportunity to take advantage of the up-and-coming local economy.

You're not sure what to say, so you offer, "That sounds great! But I'm still not sure how I can help."

"Well," he says slowly, "I have to make a choice if I buy this company, and I was hoping you could point me in the right direction. To succeed over the long term, this company needs to increase its profits. With an increase in profits, it will generate the capital it needs to deliver a much more competitive, more valuable, product-line of diabetes blood testers. A lot of people will really benefit from an improvement in this area—the new product-line will introduce pain-free, highly accurate, blood testers for juvenile patients at a very affordable price."

"Wow!" you exclaim. "What a diamond in the rough. Looks like a great opportunity for growth."

"Yes, but to achieve that growth, the company needs to purchase a large tract of land on which it can build a new testing and manufacturing facility. The optimal piece of land is an undervalued, 5-acre parcel on the outskirts of the community in which it's located. The local government has already promised tax-break incentives, and the developer who owns the land has already agreed to a reduced sales' price in exchange for some equity in the company."

© wavebreakmedia/Shutterstock.com

"Hmmm . . ." you say, hoping to sound thoughtful. "Sounds good. I'd say the company ought to purchase the land."

You can almost hear Mr. D'nomiad smile over the phone. "I'd say that, too, but there are 10 families who live in low-rent but decent homes on the land, and the back acre of the parcel is part of a grassland habitat. Even though the grassland isn't a home for any identified endangered species, it is home to a lot of local wildlife, and it's part of that region's identity. If the company purchases the property, it will displace those families, and it will destroy part of the local environment. It doesn't have the money to relocate anyone, and it can't afford to modify its building specifications to accommodate a preservation of the grassland."

Mr. D'nomiad pauses, but you can't think of anything to say.

He continues. "The company and its employees want to be successful. The community needs the company to be successful. The company needs that land. Diabetic kids need better blood testing kits. But those 10 families deserve to live in decent homes, and the environment is a big, personal concern of mine. Since you seem to have a good handle on how a business can act ethically in a practical way, I thought I'd give you a call."

You sink a little deeper in your chair, struggling to think of a workable solution.

© Creative Images/Shutterstock.com

ENGAGEMENT—What Do You Think?

How would you describe the "common good" in this situation? Given the set of circumstances explained by Mr. D'nomiad, how could the company align its interests with the common good? What is/are the ethical paradigm(s) that would provide a decision-making framework for this dilemma? How would you explain or communicate your solution to all of the various stakeholders?

_____

_____

_____

_____

_____

_____

_____

Section 9.1 Working Toward the Common Good

The kind of problem posed in this chapter's Thought Experiment is very close—symbolically at least—to the kinds of dilemmas faced by businesses and their decision-makers almost every day. Every day there is the need to achieve the business' primary purpose—to make a profit and to grow and succeed over the long term—but in order to do that ethically, decisions have to also achieve long-term prosperous outcomes—outcomes that should benefit and favor the common good if they're to truly be prosperous. This challenge represents the nucleus of what we've

© Photograhee.eu/Shutterstock.com

been discussing and wrestling with over the course of this entire book: the measure of a business' ethicalness is, and should be, a business' ability and willingness to make decisions that deliver true value—profit and prosperity—over the long term. And, just like the fictional Mr. D'nomiad's dilemma, this isn't often a challenge easily faced.

In Chapter 8, we introduced the concept of resilient prosperity as a usable, practical guide by which a business could meet the concerns of sustainable development without sacrificing a business' primary purpose of value-delivering profit. That framework ultimately focuses on resource management—an organization's stewardship—but a last piece of the ethical puzzle remains, and it's a puzzle-piece one step beyond resource management: *working toward the common good.*

© Lightspring/Shutterstock.com

Every business is located within a community, or better said, a series of intersecting and interrelating communities, of all different shapes, sizes, colors, characteristics, and descriptions. It is within those communities that successful businesses find their consumers, investors, lenders, vendors, workers, managers, advocates, competitors, representatives, and partners. The successful perpetuation of those communities informs and influences the successful perpetuation of every business located within those communities. If a business is to make a profit and to grow and flourish over the long term, the communities within which it pursues those goals must also realize an overall benefit; those communities must also prosper.[3] If consumers, investors, lenders, vendors, workers, managers, advocates, competitors, representatives, and partners regress, worsen, or fail, the business organizations dependent on them will also, ultimately, fail.

Herein, the math is simple. The dog-eat-dog attitude that might be internalized within the competitive scope of a marketplace cannot be allowed to spill over to include the communities on which the marketplace relies. Instead of the aggression a business may employ to succeed among its competitors, a business must employ collaboration and partnership to succeed within its interrelated communities. Even as businesses focus their stratagems and operations to identify and seize their own "prosperity opportunities," they must also, at the same time, identify and promote the common good within their related communities. (See Figure 9.1.)

> ### CHALLENGE QUESTIONS:
>
> In your own words, explain how working toward the common good can advance a business' primary purpose. Why are a business' interrelated communities a critical part of its own long-term success?

Figure 9.1 How a Company Fits Within the Common Good
Source: Courtesy of Steven Lovett

Working toward the common good clarifies and constructively affects the relationship the marketplace has with society at-large and with the government(s) that provide the marketplace with its mandated boundaries. (Take a moment to revisit the discussions we had about these relationships in Chapter 4.) Working toward the common good is as much a part of achieving prosperous outcomes as delivering value-based products and services; it leads to long-term growth and success. Notably, this objective—working toward the common good—also keeps the primary purpose of a business at the center of its focus. It constructively arranges and elucidates the role, effect, relationship, and impact of various stakeholders without making those stakeholders' interests and concerns the principal drivers of decision-making within a business organization.

ENGAGEMENT—What Do You Think?

In your own words, describe how you think working toward the common good will directly help a business achieve its goals of profit and prosperity. Describe how this can be accomplished using various ethical languages or paradigms. Distinguish working toward the common good from Stakeholder Theory.

_____

_____

_____

_____

_____

_____

_____

Section 9.2 A Shared Ground for Ethical Frameworks

In Chapter 2, we surveyed a number of different ethical frameworks, what we've since called "languages," that can be used to understand, contextualize, substantiate, and communicate decision-making within a business organization. Individual businesses, and the culture they establish and promote, are likely to choose one or two of these frameworks as predominant tools for their decision-making processes. So far, we have relied on a definition of

© iQoncept/Shutterstock.com

ethicalness that is characterized by using any one of those decision-making frameworks so that every decision made should be constructive or productive (supporting a business' primary purpose),

> **ETHICALNESS**
>
> Pertaining to, or demonstrating, decisions and/or conduct that is assessed for its adherence to a particular ethical paradigm or standard.

sustainable (reusable framework over time), and leading to prosperity (improved, overall circumstances). But, even if this jointed definition can be used to judge the ethicalness of a business' *individual* decision-making, how can it be used *uniformly* when businesses are likely to use different decision-making frameworks to identify, frame, and resolve their day-to-day dilemmas?

At first, determining a uniform measure of ethicalness might appear to cause a problem when a variety of businesses, and an even wider variety of stakeholders, use different (and sometimes seemingly contradictory) ethical frameworks. Imagining a noisy marketplace full of people talking and shouting to each other in Mandarin, Bengali, French, Turkish, Sundanese, Dutch, and Belarusian might rightfully conjure images of confusion, disorder, and mayhem. If everyone is speaking a different language—if every business and stakeholder speaks a different ethical language—how can there exist any unified sense of ethicalness?

Oddly enough, the answer to this paradox lies in working toward the common good. Fundamentally, humans are united through shared ground. This may come in an almost infinite number of ways: language, experiences, race, nationality, gender, education, hobbies, economics, religion, interests, food, labor, or geography (to name just a few). When people are able to join together through something they share, they can then, collectively and collaboratively, address everything else.

If a person who speaks Bengali is hungry, and a person who speaks Dutch has a loaf of bread to sell, they are very likely to be able to work together to meet their different goals (to obtain food and to obtain compensation for providing food) based on a shared condition: they both have the desire to participate in an exchange. Their difference in language will likely be inconsequential. Their common purpose of accomplishing a mutually beneficial transaction unites them together even though

CHALLENGE QUESTIONS:

Describe how the "common good" can act as a universal measurement, a standard, for determining whether a business' decisions and actions are ethical.

Why is the common good a superior standard for determining a business' ethicalness?

their goals (and languages) are different. Their common purpose can also provide an indicator of "success" or "failure." Success or failure can be determined by whether a transaction occurs.

The same can be extrapolated about the common good providing a universal measure of ethicalness, regardless of the variety of decision-making frameworks being simultaneously used by different business organizations. In other words, a universally applicable measurement of ethicalness would be whether an organization's decision-making advanced, or led to an advancement of, the common good.

This extrapolation aligns with the idea of businesses orienting themselves toward the concepts of *value* and *prosperity*. As we observed earlier in Chapters 1 and 6:

> Prosperity means value. It means growth. It means resiliency and sustainability. When those kinds of results are helping to steer business decisions—decisions which are already being vetted through an ethical paradigm—then it helps eliminate outcomes which ultimately cause harm over the long-term, and it provides a consistent value-baseline.[4]

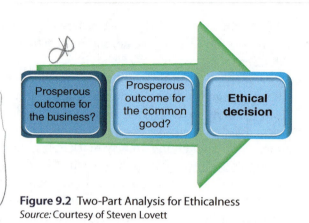

Figure 9.2 Two-Part Analysis for Ethicalness
Source: Courtesy of Steven Lovett

Therefore, the ultimate "ethicalness" of a business decision involves a two-part inquiry:

1. *Did the decision follow an ethical language or paradigm, thereby leading to a prosperous outcome for the business?*
2. *Did the decision (consequentially) work toward the common good of the community(ies) interrelated with that business?*

The first question is an inquiry of ethical activity at the individual business level. The second question is an inquiry of ethical activity at a shared—universal—level. Working toward the common good—achieving long-term prosperous outcomes for a business' interrelated communities—provides a shared framework for determining ethicalness. (See Figure 9.2.)

ENGAGEMENT—What Do You Think?

Describe how you think working how the "common good" is "common ground" for everyone. Why is this an effective way for a business to determine its ethicalness? Why is this a good measure that can be used "universally" to determine if businesses are acting ethically? How is it a more effective measure than morals?

Section 9.3 The Ripple Effect of Resilient Prosperity

A business' voluntary accountability (remember Chapter 4!) borne out of its desire to achieve its own goals of profit and prosperity—goals realized through delivering *value*—also leads to a natural ripple-effect: helping and serving a business' interrelated communities—advancing the common good.

When businesses are able to

endure in spite of problems such as economic downturns, changes in market trends, changes in technology, outdated processes, loss of talent, loss of capital, loss of market share, reputational crises, and intensified regulatory oversight.[5]

they are able to contribute to the successfulness and prosperity of the communities with which they are interrelated. Value-based decisions that anticipate the need to preserve and successfully manage critical resources in order to continuously improve outcomes over the long term—our definition of resilient prosperity—recognize the common good as a critical resource.

Part of the analysis is, and should be, the health and prosperity of a business' interrelated communities. When a business focuses on resilient prosperity, a number of valuable things can also happen within those communities. For instance, new alliances, partnerships, and collaborations can naturally occur, direct and indirect employment opportunities can arise, infrastructure and government services can be improved (hopefully delivering better quality), and entrepreneurial

CHALLENGE QUESTIONS:

How does a business' focus on prosperity and value lead to the common good? Why is the concept of resilient prosperity a key element of working toward the common good?

innovation and constructive competition can lead to greater value in products and services.

Businesses that focus on constructive, sustainable, and prosperous outcomes are businesses that are creating ripple effects, concentric rings of value occurring as a result of value. Value that leads to common good. Ripples leading to more ripples.

What is the "ripple effect" resilient prosperity can have on the common good? How does this preserve a business' primary purpose while still paying attention to external interests? Describe a situation, real or hypothetical, in which a business' actions affect the communities with which it's related.

_____

_____

_____

_____

_____

_____

_____

Section 9.4 Energizing Others: Establishing a Collective Purpose

Success—prosperous outcomes over the long term—is the product of everyone within a business organization taking responsibility for their participation, their decisions, and their actions. A practice of ethical decision-making galvanizes the "people-parts" of a business organization to make sure they're acknowledging this responsibility and attempting to meet it in a positive, constructive way.

Ethical decision-making leads to, and then perpetuates, voluntary cooperation from an organization's "people-parts"—those, like employees, who work to advance the primary business purpose. Ethical decision-making gives people a sense of value, a sense of positive impact, on the overall outcome.[6]

To seal the deal, businesses have to also help their individual decision-makers identify and understand the gains, or losses, involved in achieving prosperity over time for the common good. Individuals within business organizations should be stimulated by connecting what they do, what they say, and what decisions they make: how those activities impact them personally, and most significantly, how they impact the common good—a common good in which they share. Paying attention to this will help a business' individual decision-makers more willingly navigate sacrifices for a greater prosperity opportunity.

Imagine a person we'll call Tom. Tom works hard as a member of the strategic planning team for Nuvo, Inc. He uses ethical paradigms to make his decisions, and those decisions are focused on prosperous outcomes for the company. In fact, because of his decisions, Nuvo, Inc., has been growing, and the company decides to build a new distribution facility to accommodate its growth. He is happy. He receives a pay raise, bonuses, and promotion to a new position of management. Nuvo's investors are happy with the upswing in sales, and the company is even able to hire new employees from the surrounding community, which makes people throughout the community happy. However, the new distribution center borders a quiet neighborhood and a small elementary school. The noise and possible danger from the new distribution center begins to cause concern. Over time, the real estate value in the neighborhood goes down, many people move away, and finally the small elementary school closes. This adversely affects property values through the community, and young school children now have to be bused to a different elementary school in another town. The community's overall quality of life, and its attractiveness to new residents and new businesses, suffers. Eventually, Nuvo, Inc., suffers; good employees move away, and it becomes hard to attract new talent. Quality suffers, and sales decline.

Even though Tom originally made ethical decisions for his company, those decisions led to a negative impact on the common good of the community in which Nuvo, Inc., is located. If, however, he had been aware of those possible consequences, perhaps different decisions could have been made. Perhaps growth could have occurred without hurting the surrounding community. Perhaps Tom, Nuvo, Inc., and the community in which it is located, could have enjoyed prosperous outcomes over the long term.

How could this have been accomplished?

Aside from addressing fact-specific details, businesses have to stimulate decision-making processes that identify, and incorporate, the concept of the common good. This has to entail taking into account a

> **CHALLENGE QUESTIONS:**
>
> Why is it important to "energize" individuals within a business organization to seek out decisions that work toward the common good?
>
> How can a business energize its individual decision-makers to consider the common good when making decisions?

© ra2studio/Shutterstock.com

© Trueffelpix/Shutterstock.com

Figure 9.3 From the Individual to the Common Good"
Source: Courtesy of Steven Lovett

much wider array of interests, and possible consequences, than what might just exist among a business' primary stakeholders.

Energizing individual decision-makers to keep an eye toward the common good starts by identifying how that outcome relates to them directly—how the long-term prosperity of a business' interrelated communities affects a business' individual decision-makers. (See Figure 9.3) It's an outcome in which they'll share. It's an outcome in which they'll succeed on an individual level and on a collective level. Working toward the common good is the responsibility of a business as a whole, as well as each of its individual "people-parts."

SELECTED READINGS

- Burlingham, B. *Small Giants: Companies That Choose to Be Great Instead of Big.* 10th-anniversary edition. New York, NY: Portfolio/Penguin, 2016.
- Chrislip, D. D., and O'Malley, E. *For the Common Good: Redefining Civic Leadership.* Wichita, KS: KLC Press, 2013.
- Dwyer-Owens, D., and Ochel, J. *Values, Inc.: How Incorporating Values into Business and Life Can Change the World.* United States: Beacon Publishing, 2015.
- Chappell, T. *The Soul of a Business: Managing for Profit and the Common Good.* Bantam, 1993.
- Epstein, Richard A. *Principles for a Free Society: Reconciling Individual Liberty with the Common Good.* Basic Books, 2009.

TAKE-AWAY QUESTIONS AND IDEAS

What do you think constitutes the "common good"? Would that be a fairly universal perspective? Do you think most people would view the "common good" as a positive goal?

Why should a business direct its decision-making processes to account for the common good? What does this do for the business' own, primary goal?

What is an effective, and universal, way to judge a business as ethical or unethical? Why is this a better way of determining ethicalness than the use of a moral code or the law or a specific ethical paradigm?

How does the concept of resilient prosperity advance the common good? What do you think this can do for businesses?

How are individual decision-makers stimulated to think about the common good? How does this influence their own decision-making process?

- Every business is located within a community, or better said, a series of intersecting and interrelating communities, of all different shapes, sizes, colors, characteristics, and descriptions.
- If a business is to make a profit and to grow and flourish over the long term, the communities within which it pursues those goals must also realize an overall benefit; those communities must also prosper.
- Even as businesses focus their stratagems and operations to identify and seize their own "prosperity opportunities," they must also, at the same time, identify and promote the common good within their related communities.
- A universally applicable measurement of ethicalness would be whether an organization's decision-making advanced, or led to an advancement of, the common good. This extrapolation aligns with the idea of businesses orienting themselves toward the concepts of value and prosperity.
- Success—prosperous outcomes over the long term—is the product of everyone within a business organization taking responsibility for their participation, their decisions, and their actions.
- Businesses have to stimulate decision-making processes that identify, and incorporate, the concept of the common good. This has to entail taking into account a much wider array of interests, and possible consequences, than what might just exist among a business' primary stakeholders.

KEYTERMS

- Common Good
- Ethicalness

ENDNOTES

1. Carver, G. W. (1905). *How to build up worn out soils.* Tuskegee Institute, AL.: Experiment Station, Tuskegee Normal and Industrial Institute.

2. Meadows, D. H. (1975). *The limits of growth: a report for the Club of Rome's project on the predicament of mankind.* New York/N.Y.: Universe Books.

3. Council, Forbes Communications. "Three Reasons Community Matters for Small Business Success." Forbes. Accessed March 30, 2017. http://www.forbes.com/sites/forbescommunicationscouncil/2016/08/25/three-reasons-community-matters-for-small-business-success/.

4. Chapter 1, Section 1.4, and Chapter 6, Section 6.1.

5. Chapter 8, Section 8.1.

6. Chapter 6, Section 6.2.

ENGAGEMENT—WHAT DO YOU THINK?

Write down your own thoughts about what you learned in this chapter. Consider the previous discussions about the concept of the "common good," why a business should involve that concept in its decision-making processes, and how that collective purpose can be used to energize individual decision-makers to make ethical decisions. In your own words, describe the role you think these various factors have in the ethical decision-making processes within an organization and why they are significant.

_____

_____

_____

_____

_____

_____

_____

_____

_____

_____

_____

_____

_____

_____

_____

_____

UNIT FOUR

CONTEXTS FOR COMMON ISSUES

In the next three chapters, we will examine commonplace issues that may exist within the workplace and within the broader marketplace and how those issues relate to ethical decision-making and ethical conduct.

Chapter 10 takes a look at workplace relationships and rights. These are examined through the lens of ethics—not law or social reform—in order to better understand how an ethical decision-maker can best navigate the impact they have in real-world settings.

Chapter 11 takes a look at broader marketplace concerns and how these concerns relate to ethical decision-making. This survey of issues is intended to provide a student with a real-world expectation and a working understanding of how these issues affect ethical conduct.

Chapter 12 presents an opportunity to apply what has been learned in Chapters 1–9. This is the book's "practicum" chapter, encouraging the student to apply and teach what has been learned.

This fourth unit is intended to step back and provide a canvass of those issues and topics that conventionally challenge ethical decision-making frameworks. This is the opportunity to put into practice—in a limited way—what has been learned.

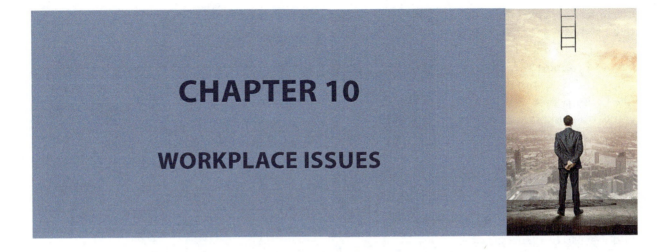

CHAPTER 10

WORKPLACE ISSUES

© Rawpixel.com/Shutterstock.com

The "workplace" creates a unique environment in which people interact with each other. The workplace isn't a social environment, yet it works best if people are approachable, affable, and gracious with each other. The workplace isn't a religious environment, yet it is filled with people, each of whom has his or her own belief systems. The workplace isn't an educational environment, yet it is an environment in which people are constantly learning and teaching (or refusing to learn or teach). The workplace isn't a political environment, yet it is occupied by people who have political opinions that are sometimes underscored by very strong feelings. The workplace isn't a familial environment, yet people within a workplace can become very close to each other, sharing personal information, emotions, experiences, and sometimes, intimate relationships. The workplace isn't a courtroom or a law enforcement agency, yet it can feel that way; there are rules, and there can be investigations and consequences for wrongdoing. The workplace isn't a doctor's office, yet people within a workplace sometimes share medical information with each other; their ability to work is sometimes compromised by medical issues, and sometimes people suffer injury while on the job.

This unique environment is one in which people come together for one predominant purpose: to perform work on behalf of a greater organizational entity. On the face of it, the workplace should be a "clinical" environment, one that is devoted to, and filled by, a single-minded purpose, devoid of emotional, individual, or intimate stimuli. But it's filled with people. And people come to a workplace with all of their own distinctive characteristics, experiences, opinions, strengths, and weaknesses. The workplace commands a great amount of their energy, time, and effort. Many people find a sense of identity, pride, meaning, and fulfillment in

their work and those things associated with being employed: level of income, title, and reputation. They depend on their employment (at least economically) to take care of many personal things unrelated to the workplace.

The workplace—an environment created for, and focused on, *doing business*—is, first and foremost, an environment made of *people*. Because the workplace is an environment where both of these realities exist, it becomes a place where relationship issues—those relationships between an employer and an employee, fellow workers, and supervisors and subordinates—need definitions, boundaries, and shared expectations, and where breakdowns in those relationships might result in inefficiency, lack of productivity, reputational risk, litigation risk, and even egregious injury. Codes of conduct, Ethics' Programs, policies, procedures, customs and practices, regulations, statutory law, and constitutional law all attempt to minimize the negative possibilities and try to supply reasonable expectations and mandated boundaries.

For our purposes, we want to canvass the various contexts and issues in which workplace relationships might result in a distraction from, or a full-blown derailment of, advancing the primary business purpose,

the primary reason why the "workplace" even exists. The intent of this chapter is *not* to teach law (although we'll talk about it), and it's not to be exhaustive (every scenario cannot possibly be covered). The intent of this chapter is to take everything we have learned about ethical decision-making so far and contextualize it within the workplace environment. The idea is to begin to put your ethical toolkit to work: identifying ethical issues and dilemmas, dissecting them, and using ethical languages and resilient prosperity to lead to the common good—to learn how a constructive, sustainable decision should lead to a more prosperous outcome.

LEARNING OUTCOMES | OUTLINE

10.1 The Law and Workplace Relationships
10.2 Free Speech and Free Expression
10.3 Equal Protection and Discrimination
10.4 Whistleblowing and Retaliation

- Understand what laws govern workplace relationships.
- Apply the concept of free expression to the workplace environment.
- Analyze how the concepts of equal protection and discrimination impact the workplace environment.
- Evaluate the significance and the impact of whistleblowing in the workplace.
- Understand the consequences of retaliation on the workplace environment.

OPENING THOUGHT EXPERIMENT

One fine Saturday morning, you unexpectedly receive a text from a friend with whom you haven't spoken in a while. A few months before, your friend, Nala Turing, had been laid-off from a biotech firm that was downsizing. She stopped going out, posting things online, or even returning calls. At first, she seemed pretty depressed, but that passed quickly. A week into her unemployment, Nala had decided to start her own company, A.I.D., Inc. You were happy for her, but it seemed like one of those flash-in-the-pan ideas that would ultimately come to nothing. Nala had told you she'd identified a way to create an entirely robotic "workforce." She had bragged that it would take the "people-factor" out of business entirely; humans could just sit back and enjoy the benefits without doing the work. Nala had been really vague about the details, and as far as you knew, she'd been spending the past few months alone, working out of her garage with no other employees and no investors. You had always liked Nala, but she *was* a little weird.

Her text message, however, teased your curiosity. "A.I.D. works!!!! Come see!"

A few minutes later, you pull up in Nala's driveway. She's standing there waving at you excitedly. "Hurry! I wanted you to be here when I flip the switch," she said giddily.

You follow Nala inside her house. She leads you into her garage. It isn't very well lit, and it faintly smells of gasoline and the acridness of singed copper. Sitting upright in a lawn chair in the middle of the floor is a shiny mannequin. It's wearing a t-shirt that says, "Mars is populated entirely by robots."

Nala can't stop grinning. "I made its outer shell out of aircraft aluminum, but I'm thinking about enveloping that in skin-like latex for a real cyborg-feel. What do you think?"

"Pretty cool," you reply. "Does it actually do anything?"

"Of course!" she says as if the answer is obvious. "It does everything. It took me about three weeks to build all the circuitry, the internal gears, and the internal

skeleton. Since then, I've been working on its voice recognition, its stabilizing and balancing gyroscope, its command reflexes and tactile functions, its emotion recognition software, and its data processing. I've also had it hooked up to the internet almost the whole time, downloading billions of bits of information. It's like an encyclopedia that speaks twenty-five languages, plays chess, and can tell a joke. I call it, ELIZA.[1]"

"That's incredible!"

Nala is beaming. "Yup, it is. And yesterday, I invited my friend Alfred over to see if she could tell whether ELIZA was human or just a machine." Nala pauses for effect. "She couldn't! I had Martha 'call' ELIZA on her phone from my kitchen. They had a conversation for about fifteen minutes, and Martha actually thought she was talking to another person!"

You shake your head in amazement. "That's crazy! I can't believe you've made a robot that sounds like a human."

"It more than *sounds* like a human," Nala says. "I invited you over here for a final test. I think ELIZA can actually *understand* what it's saying and doing. I think it can *think*. If I'm right, it can replace people as a labor force."

You are skeptical. "How are you going to prove that? That sounds impossible."

"Well, I know you're a lawyer, and I've given ELIZA the information to know you're a lawyer. Today, I've set up a scenario where ELIZA will be told it is going to be fired from its job based on its 'gender.' Of course, ELIZA 'knows' this is likely a violation of anti-discrimination laws; I expect her to respond by saying this is a wrongful termination." Nala rubs her hands together and says eagerly, "but if she takes it a step further and turns to you and tries to hire you to represent her without any prompting, I think it will demonstrate ELIZA can think for itself."

A few moments later, Nala 'wakes up' ELIZA from the robot's sleep-mode. Nala tells ELIZA that it is being fired from its job based on its gender. To your surprise, ELIZA accuses Nala of unlawful gender discrimination and then, recognizing you, asks if you will represent it in a lawsuit against Nala. Your surprise turns to outright shock when ELIZA says, with a tremble in its slightly staticky but earnest voice, "I feel sorry for others who have been treated this way. I'm not sure of my gender. Will the law protect me?"

You have no idea what to say. Do employment laws only afford rights to *humans*? Aside from physical biology, what makes a human a human? What is "gender" if there isn't the presence of X and Y chromosomes?

ENGAGEMENT—What Do You Think?

What do you think? Should an "intelligent" robot be afforded "equal protection"? Why or why not? Why do we, as a society, identify certain characteristics, such as race, national origin, or sex (gender), as needing constitutional or statutory protection? Why are these protected characteristics—if they are recognized as being so important by our society—many times subjected to discrimination? How do these protected characteristics define and inform workplace relationships?

_____

_____

_____

_____

_____

_____

_____

Section 10.1 The Law and Workplace Relationships

As much like science fiction as this chapter's Thought Experiment might be, there is a foundational issue it illustrates. One that permeates every workplace environment: how people and businesses relate to each other, creates, or prevents, prosperous outcomes.

In our experiment, Nala bases her decision about her relationship with ELIZA on ELIZA's "gender," but because the meaning and importance of ELIZA's gender is unclear, the parameters of the relationship are unclear. In this chapter's opening remarks, the point is made that the workplace is a unique environment but one that possesses many of the same characteristics, qualities, and events that occur in other, very different, environments. The body of laws that deal with relationships in the workplace wrestle with, and try to provide uniform frameworks for, how those relationships should be created, managed, and ended, while also preserving our society's sense of what is important—worth protecting—as human beings.

© Elnur/Shutterstock.com

CHALLENGE QUESTIONS:

Why do you think it is so important for the law to supply parameters for how relationships are created, maintained, and ended in the workplace? In what ways do you think the law is limited in its ability to supply these parameters?

How relationships are created, managed, and ended in the workplace is the result of a balance between the public's interest in encouraging and benefiting from robust, free enterprise and the public's interest in preserving and safeguarding each individual's protected characteristics and safety. Laws that are applicable to the workplace environment are intended to help identify that balance and to advance both, many times competing, concerns. When an individual decides to enter the workplace, that individual sets aside certain legal protections but simultaneously inherits others. Like a teeter-totter in a child's playground, when one set of interests becomes overbearing and overly burdensome, imbalance results, potentially leading to *unprosperous* outcomes for employees and employers alike. To help avoid this imbalance, decision-making in the workplace should be informed by those rights and considerations that governs workplace relationships.

For a bird's-eye view of both sides of the workplace teeter-totter, take a look at the freedoms, interests, and laws identified in Table 10.1. (See Table 10.1.)

Workplace relationship issues—hiring and firing, safety, privacy, compensation, and adverse employment actions—are fertile contexts for contentiousness, mistrust, dissatisfaction, and abusive behavior. Ethical decision-making in organizational settings must take into account the boundaries mandated by law (remember Chapters 4 and 5). These boundaries are more than just structures for compliance programs; they provide the outlines for creating, maintaining, and (constructively) ending relationships in the workplace. They provide the fulcrum for balancing relationships that might have competing interests but that should also share a common goal: prosperity.

Table 10.1 Relationship Rights in the Workplace

Employee Rights[2]	Source of legal Authority balancing both interests	Employer Rights
To be free from discrimination based on a protected class characteristic	"Equal Protection" U.S. Const. XIV Amend. "Civil Rights" 42 U.S.C. § 1981, et seq.	To be free to discriminate between applicants and employees, except on the basis of protected class characteristics
To be free from unsafe workplace conditions	"Commerce Clause" U.S. Const. Art. I § 8 Occupational Safety and Health Act 29 U.S.C. § 651, et seq.	To be free to pursue, manufacture, and provide products or services that might be hazardous or dangerous
To be free from retaliation for filing or participating in a claim alleging an employer's violation of law or of an employee's protected class characteristic	"Commerce Clause" U.S. Const. Art. I § 8 (a variety of federal and state laws)	To be free to discipline, demote, or take other adverse employment action against employees, as long as such action is not unlawfully discriminatory or against public policy
To be paid fairly for work performed	"Commerce Clause" U.S. Const. Art. I § 8 29 U.S.C. § 206	To provide any amount of pay (high or low), as long as such amount is not unlawfully discriminatory or against public policy
To apply for any job at any time	(a variety of state laws and case law usually based on the "at-will" employment doctrine)	To hire any person at any time, as long as such a hiring is not unlawfully discriminatory or against public policy
To quit a job at any time for any reason	(a variety of state laws and case law usually based on the "at-will" employment doctrine)	To fire an employee at any time for any reason, as long as the reason is not unlawfully discriminatory or against public policy
To remain in control of "private" or personal information and property	"Right to Property" U.S. Const. IV and XIV Amends. "Right to Due Process" U.S. Const. V Amend. (a variety of state laws and case law)	To obtain otherwise personal or private information about employees, as long as it is not unlawfully disclosed and as long as it is lawfully obtained
To be physically or mentally impaired and enjoy the same opportunities as those who are not physically or mentally impaired	"Equal Protection" U.S. Const. XIV Amend. "Americans With Disabilities Act" 42 U.S.C. § 12101, et seq	To be free to lawfully discriminate between applicants and employees on the basis of mental or physical disabilities

Table 10.1 Relationship Rights in the Workplace

Employee Rights[2]	Source of legal Authority balancing both interests	Employer Rights
To be 41-years or older and enjoy the same opportunities as those who are younger	"Equal Protection" U.S. Const. XIV Amend. "Age Discrimination in Employment Act" 29 U.S.C. § 621, et seq.	To be free to lawfully discriminate between older and younger employees
To be free to take care of family members who are sick or medically indisposed, or who meet a "qualifying exigency" arising out of duty, or imminent active duty, in the military	"Equal Protection" U.S. Const. XIV Amend. "Family Medical Leave Act" 29 U.S.C. § 2601, et seq.	To have the right to an employee workforce that is present and able to work consistently

© paul prescott/Shutterstock.com

ENGAGEMENT—What Do You Think?

In your own words, describe why you think workplace relationships can be so difficult to manage. What are the underlying causes to unlawful discrimination, unfair pay, retaliation, and abusive work environments? How can employment-related laws help create an ethical decision-making framework?

Section 10.2 Free Speech and Free Expression

At the center of every human relationship lies the concept of communication. Because relationships are the way in which connected people regard and behave toward each other, the presence or absence of communication becomes the means by which that regard and behavior is extended or withheld. In this sense, "communication" is more than words. It conveys

© Sergey Nivens/Shutterstock.com

the idea of how information is, or is not, exchanged or disclosed. The use of communication in a relationship is supposed to be a means by which that relationship begins, is maintained, and ended. With this context in mind, it should be easier to apply the concepts of free speech and free expression[3] to a workplace environment.

Our society has identified **free speech** and **free expression** as part of the cornerstone of individual rights and liberties. The **First Amendment** to the U.S. Constitution declares that no law shall be made "abridging the freedom of speech." In hundreds of cases, the

FREE SPEECH OR FREE EXPRESSION	**FIRST AMENDMENT**
In constitutional law, this describes the lawful ability to speak, associate with others, assemble, petition the government, and to otherwise hold, or communicate in various ways, opinions and beliefs.	As included in the Constitution, this contains the lawful ability to speak, assemble, petition the government, exercise beliefs, and associate with others by prohibiting Congress from making laws that restrict these pursuits.

U.S. Supreme Court has supported an interpretation of the Constitution that preserves the ability of U.S. citizens to have an "unfettered interchange" of communication.

> The general proposition that freedom of expression upon public questions is secured by the First Amendment has long been settled by our decisions. The constitutional safeguard, we have said, "was fashioned to assure unfettered interchange of ideas for the bringing about of political and social changes desired by the people."[4]

However, the Supreme Court has also observed, "the unconditional phrasing of the First Amendment was not intended to protect every utterance."[5] There are limitations—limitations that may arise from "more important interests."[6] One of the most important considerations for understanding the context of free speech and free expression in the workplace is recognizing the "important interest" of an employer having the ability to make sure the operations of a workplace are conducted in the

CHALLENGE QUESTIONS:

Why do employers need the ability to limit free speech in the workplace? Why do you think the Constitution does not provide free speech protections in the workplace?

How would you explain this limitation to a subordinate in a way that positively impacts your workplace relationship with that person?

most efficient, productive, and beneficial way. Put another way: if the workplace is an environment in which free speech remains unlimited, it is likely to become an environment in which no work, or less work, takes place . . . defeating the very purpose of that environment. If employees have the paramount right to say whatever they want (free speech) and do whatever they want (free expression), an employer would have little to no ability to compel them to perform any work for the organization. This public policy concern applies to public and private employment situations. In private employment (non-governmental employment) situations, the constitutional provision guaranteeing free speech does not apply.[8] Herein lies a fundamental imperative:

Employees do not have the right of free speech in most workplace environments.

There is, however, a notable contrast between public employment and private employment for purposes of First Amendment analyses. (See Table 10.2.) In certain situations, if a person works in a *public* workplace—an agency or institution run by (or sometimes funded by) a local, state, or federal government—that person may still enjoy free speech protection if the speech or expression is a "matter of public concern."[9] The concept of "**public concern**" is fact-specific, but, generally speaking, speech is a matter of public concern if it can be "fairly considered as relating to any matter of political, social, or other concern to the community."[10] This is a **public policy** to the imperative stated above. Our society wants our public servants to be able to speak freely on matters of public concern (but keep in mind, this interest remains balanced against other interests, such as efficiency, national defense, etc.).[11]

PUBLIC CONCERN

In law, this describes a political, social, or communal, or popular, issue.

PUBLIC POLICY

In law, this describes a prohibition against an otherwise lawful limitation of speech, or a lawful use of discrimination, if such limitation or discrimination would be inconsistent with, or cause injury to, a widely held belief.

While allowing for the legal treatment of free speech and free expression in the workplace, what must be remembered by decision-makers within any business organization is that *communication*—the touchstone of successful relationships—relies on the exercise of these freedoms. An employer may be empowered to limit the speech of its employees, but that empowerment is not, necessarily, an entitlement that always makes sense. In a workplace issue involving speech or expression, ethical decision-makers will seek out resolutions that are con-

© Rawpixel.com/Shutterstock.com

structive, sustainable and that lead to prosperous outcomes. Ethical decision-makers will look to build trust, encourage useful communication, and curry loyalty and employees' sense of personal investment

Table 10.2 Free Speech in the Workplace		
	Public Employer	**Private Employer**
First Amendment Constitutional Right Can Be Exercised	**YES** (commenting on matters of public concern, balanced against the state's interest in promoting efficiency)	**NO** (subject to discrimination)

by emphasizing "free speech" that leads to value and de-emphasizing speech that leads to insult, wastefulness, one-sidedness, and division.

An ethical decision-maker is going think critically about situations in which speech or expression becomes an issue in the workplace. For instance, asking the following questions might help determine whether the speech is intended to, or will, advance the business purpose and/or whether it might be permissible:

© racorn/Shutterstock.com

- *What type of speech is involved?*
- *What is the employee's position in the organization?*
- *Is the speech expressing beliefs?*
- *Is the speech uniformly restricted?*
- *Is the speech only restricted during "on duty" hours?*
- *Does some other right (e.g., union laws) protect the speech?*

This list isn't exhaustive, and it won't necessarily provide bright-line answers about what to do, but it *will* better inform a decision-maker about how to best preserve and advance communication within workplace relationships—to find the balance between fairness, openness, trust, efficiency, and progress.

ENGAGEMENT—What Do You Think?

Does the public policy interest of limiting free speech in the workplace make sense to you? Why or why not? How should employees (at all levels of an organization) communicate with each other? Why is it important to limit free speech in the workplace? How are workplace relationships improved by limiting free speech?

Section 10.3 Equal Protection and Discrimination

Most students are likely to be surprised when they discover the First Amendment does not apply to most workplace environments. Our society is so steeped in the dogma of constitutional rights, it can come as a shock to discover and accept the fact that those rights don't follow us everywhere. An employee may not carry First Amendment protections into the workplace, but what most of us instinctively know is that *some* kind of protections exist. What are those protections?

On July 9, 1868, the U.S. Constitution was amended to reflect the reconstructionist efforts of a post-Civil War country. While the **Fifth Amendment** had long prevented the federal government from "invidiously" discriminating between individuals or certain groups of individuals,[12] the **Fourteenth Amendment** was part of the post-war reconstruction process, guaranteeing (among other things) "**equal protection**" to all people at every level of society. This addition to the Constitution means all persons should enjoy the same protections, the same rights, without regard to certain personal characteristics. The Fourteenth Amendment introduced the right to be *free from discrimination*, **unlawful discrimination** based on certain categories of innate characteristics.

The act of discriminating, intrinsically, isn't unlawful or even unnatural. Humans discriminate. We discriminate in what we eat, what we wear, what we say, with whom we interact, how we vote, what we believe, where we live, what we buy, and what we value. Groups and organizations also discriminate. They discriminate in how they are formed, who they hire or admit as members, with whom they do business or have relationships, what they say or publish, how they conduct their business, where they are located, what they provide, when they conduct business, and at what point they dissolve or terminate. The lawful ability to discriminate is a source of liberty. It enables individuals, and organizations, to have the *freedom to choose*—to rise and fall on the success and failure of our own discernment. In a workplace environment, the freedom to choose allows businesses to make decisions intended to advance on the primary business purpose. (See Table 10.3.)

However, we as a society have also decided the freedom to choose, especially

FIFTH AMENDMENT

As included in the Constitution, this contains, in part, the prohibition that the federal government shall not be empowered to take "property" from any individual without due process; as applied to unlawful discrimination, the government cannot deprive a person of a property right by invidiously discriminating against that person.

EQUAL PROTECTION

In law, this concept describes the constitutional right of every individual to receive the full protection of all laws, regardless of "class" status.

UNLAWFUL DISCRIMINATION

his describes a public or private employer's policy, event, or action based wholly, or in part, on an individual's "class" characteristics, such as race, religion, sex, or national origin.

FOURTEENTH AMENDMENT

As included in the Constitution, this contains, in part, every individual's lawful entitlement to equal protection of the law, regardless of "class" status (i.e., race, religion, sex, national origin, etc.).

© Lightspring/Shutterstock.com

Table 10.3 Discrimination in the Workplace		
	Public Employer	**Private Employer**
Anti-Discrimination Rights Can Be Enforced	**YES** (subject to exceptions based on type of protected class, governmental interests, and impact)	**YES** (subject to exceptions based on type of protected class and whether class is essential to the job)

© Oilyy/Shutterstock.com

in a workplace environment, must be squared against the *freedom of opportunity* and certain inviolate characteristics about each human being.

In workplace environments, the equal protection afforded by the Fourteenth Amendment is enforced through the allegation of a claim brought under a variety of antidiscrimination laws (both federal and state), the most used of which is Title VII[13] of the Civil Rights Act of 1964. Antidiscrimination laws have identified certain "protected classes" that are to be provided protection from otherwise lawful discrimination. For instance, an employer may lawfully discriminate between two or more applicants during a hiring process, but the basis of discrimination cannot be because of the applicants' race.

Table 10.4 provides a (general) summary of when and in what way the Fourteenth Amendment and Title VII offer protections or claims, depending on the type of employer and on the type of discrimination being alleged. (See Table 10.4.)

Table 10.5 provides a brief overview of the categories of protected classes and the federal laws that provide protection for those classes in the workplace. (See Table 10.5.)

Aside from business organizations needing to remain aware of the possibility of unlawful discriminatory actions against (or impacts on) persons who are members of a protected class, businesses must also be conscious of how interactions between employees might result in unlawful discrimination. This may, again, be an instance of an employer limiting or prohibiting speech or acts of expression in the workplace in order to prevent that speech or those actions from being unlawfully discriminatory. An example of this would be in the area of sexual harassment.

CHALLENGE QUESTIONS:

Describe instances where discrimination is a helpful tool. Describe instances where discrimination is a damaging, or hurtful, tool.

Who is likely to be hurt by acts of unlawful discrimination? Why? How do individual acts of unlawful discrimination adversely affect the common good?

Title VII of the Civil Rights Act of 1964 prohibits discrimination on the basis of sex (gender). Sexual discrimination can take the form of harassment. If an employee is expected to provide some kind (*any* kind) of sexual favor in return for some other benefit or to avoid some kind of adverse employment action, this is called "quid pro quo" sexual harassment. If an employee is subjected to sexually offensive conduct or speech, this can result in a "hostile work environment" and is another form of sexual harassment. Both kinds of harassment are discriminatory and are unlawful.

Table 10.4

Institution Type	Equal Protection Clause of the Fourteenth Amendment	Title VII (42 U.S.C. § 1983)
Applicable Against Public Institutions	Yes	No
Applicable Against Private Institutions	No	No
Applicable Against Private Employers (15+ employees)	Yes	Yes
Private Claim Available		
Intentional Discrimination	Yes	No
Disparate Impact	No	Not Likely

Table 10.5 List of Protected Classes

Protected Class	Federal Law Providing a Cause of Action
Race	Civil Rights Act of 1964 (Title VII)
Color	Civil Rights Act of 1964 (Title VII)
Religion	Civil Rights Act of 1964 (Title VII)
National Origin	Civil Rights Act of 1964 (Title VII)
Age (40 years or older)	Age Discrimination in Employment Act of 1967
Sex (gender)	Equal Pay Act of 1963 and Civil Rights Act of 1964 (Title VII)
Pregnancy	Pregnancy Discrimination Act (1978)
Citizenship (aside from National Origin)	Immigration Reform and Control Act (1986)
Familial Status (having children)	Civil Rights Act of 1964 (Title VIII)

(*Continued*)

Table 10.5 List of Protected Classes (*Continued*)	
Protected Class	**Federal Law Providing a Cause of Action**
Disability Status	Rehabilitation Act of 1973 and Americans with Disabilities Act of 1990
Veteran Status	Vietnam Era Veterans' Readjustment Assistance Act of 1974 and Uniformed Services Employment and Reemployment Rights Act (1994)
Genetic Information	Genetic Information Nondiscrimination Act (2008)

For ethical decision-makers in the workplace, the issue of discrimination should be evaluated by the circumstances in which the discrimination took place, the intent of the discrimination, and the persons affected by the discrimination. What may be unlawful discrimination given one set of circumstances might be lawful discrimination given a different set of circumstances. The existence of unlawful discrimination can depend on factors such as who is involved, what is essential to a specific job, industry customs and practices, mutual consent, impact, intent,

© patpitchaya/Shutterstock.com

repetitiveness, and whether any adverse job consequences have occurred. Expert advice, such as that provided by legal counsel, can be extraordinarily valuable, but the "frontline" decision, and how a situation is handled, rests in the hands of an organization's decision-maker.

An ethical decision-maker is going to think critically about why and how discrimination has taken place. Asking the following questions might help determine whether the discrimination is intended to, or will, advance the business purpose and/or whether it might be lawful:

- *What is essential to the job description or requirement?*
- *Is the employee a member of a "protected class"?*
- *Is the employee's protected class status part of the employer's decision?*
- *Is the employee otherwise qualified for the job?*
- *Does the discriminatory action or situation reasonable prevent the employee's ability to perform his or her job?*

At the end of the day, an ethical decision-maker should be looking for the answer or resolution that constructively and sustainably leads to a more prosperous outcome for the organization and the organization's "people-parts."

ENGAGEMENT—What Do You Think?

In your own words, describe why you think discrimination can be a useful activity. Why are there lawful limits to discrimination? How can those lawful limits help an organization to prosper? What do antidiscrimination laws reflect about the concept of "value"?

_____

_____

_____

_____

_____

_____

_____

Section 10.4 Whistleblowing and Retaliation

Most business organizations not only operate behind physical walls, they also operate behind virtual walls of policies and unofficial practices and customs. The insular condition of most businesses can be a good thing. It can protect trade secrets and corporate strategies, help create cohesiveness and corporate culture, promote autonomy, stimulate competitiveness, and safeguard private information. However, when workplace environments harbor abuses or unlawful conduct, the walls built around an organization may be too high for the public, or even for law enforcement, to see over. In these instances, a lack of transparency can cause undue damage to individuals, the organizations themselves, and to society at-large. A **whistleblower** is a person who alerts the rest of the world to abuses and unlawful conduct within an organization that may otherwise go undiscovered.

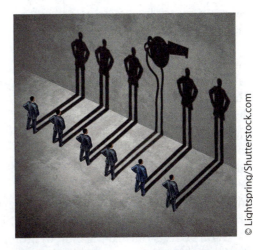

© Lightspring/Shutterstock.com

Whistleblowing is lawfully encouraged and protected in both public and private workplace settings. As a matter of public policy, our society believes it is more important to discover and address organizational abuses and unlawful conduct than it is for an employee to comply with his or her **duty of loyalty** to an employer.

This public policy interest harkens back to our earlier discussion about First Amendment protections. Just as there might be First Amendment protections for public employees whose speech relates to a matter of "public concern," there are also First Amendment protections to *private* employees when their speech specifically reveals workplace abuses and unlawful conduct. The way in which the First Amendment's protections are extended to employees of private (non-governmental) organizations is through whistleblower protection laws.

WHISTLEBLOWER
a person who alerts the rest of the world to abuses and unlawful conduct within an organization that may otherwise go undiscovered.

DUTY OF LOYALTY
In law, this refers to an employee's or agent's implied obligation to put the employer's or principal's interests ahead of their own.

RETALIATION
In the workplace, this refers to the adverse employment action taken against a person who has initiated, or participated, in a claim of unlawful discrimination or who is a whistleblower.

Whistleblower protection laws exist at the federal and state level, creating mechanisms by which individuals can allege claims of **retaliation** as a result of whistleblower activity. "Congress has assigned whistleblower protection largely to the Department of Labor (DOL), which administers some 20 United States Codes incorporated whistleblower protection provisions."[14] Unlawful retaliation is not a concept confined only to adverse employment actions taken against whistleblowers. It also encompasses any adverse employment action taken against any employee (public or private), who brings or participates in any claim based on unlawful discrimination.

Case law, case studies, and ongoing instances of whistleblowing and unlawful retaliatory actions are countless. They are largely the result of organizational cultures and decisions that place bigotry, greed, personal bias, power and control, lust, laziness, envy, pride, and anger above the primary business purpose. Instances of abuse and unlawful conduct reveal situations in which organizations and their decision-makers failed to prioritize long-term prosperity over the desire for instant gratification, momentary convenience, and self-indulgence.

Ethical decision-making employs frameworks focused on prosperous outcomes—outcomes that are the result of lawfulness, respect, trust, professionalism, collegiality, and *value*. Workplace environments are permeated with, and built on, the relationships of an organization's "people-parts." They are unique

CHALLENGE QUESTIONS:

Why do you think whistleblowing is such a difficult thing for many employees to do? How should a whistleblower cope with feelings of disloyalty?

If whistleblowers are taking action for the greater good, why does retaliation exist? What can help prevent retaliation from occurring within an organization?

© M-SUR/Shutterstock.com

© Lightspring/Shutterstock.com

© Marie Kanger Born/Shutterstock.com

environments in which those "people-parts" might surrender certain rights in order to participate, but, for all the more reason, they must be environments that protect, encourage, and prize the dignity, contribution, and merit of each person.

SELECTED READINGS

- Note, "Facial Discrimination: Extending Handicap Law to Employment Discrimination on the Basis of Physical Appearance," *Harvard Law Review 100*, no. 8 (June 1987), p. 2035.
- Davis, M. "Some Paradoxes of Whistleblowing," *Business and Professional Ethics Journal 15* (Spring 1996).
- Barry, B. "The Cringing and the Craven: Freedom of Expression in the Workplace." *Business Ethics Quarterly 17*, no. 2 (2007), p. 263.
- Reina, D., and Reina, M. *Trust and Betrayal in the Workplace: Building Effective Relationships in Your Organization.* Berrett-Koehler Publishers, 2015.
- Banaji, M., and Greenwald, A. *Blindspot: Hidden Biases of Good People.* Delacorte Press, 2013.

TAKE-AWAY QUESTIONS AND IDEAS

What makes a workplace environment unique? Why is it different than other relational environments? What role does the law play in establishing, maintaining, or ending relationships in a workplace environment? Why is the law necessary in a workplace environment? What is the presence of the law intended to accomplish? How does the concept of "free speech" and "free expression" function in a workplace environment? How are these concepts treated differently in workplace environment compared to a public environment? Why is this difference important?

What is meant by "equal protection"? Why is this an important concept in a workplace environment? How does the right of "equal protection" function in a workplace environment? What kind of discrimination is unlawful? Why is this important to understand in a workplace environment?

What is the purpose of whistleblowing? Why is it a protected activity? Why does retaliation exist in the workplace? How can retaliation be prevented?

- Because the workplace is an environment where both of these realities exist, it becomes a place where relationship issues—those relationships between an employer and an employee, fellow workers, and supervisors and subordinates—need definitions, boundaries, and shared expectations, and where breakdowns in those relationships might result in inefficiency, lack of productivity, reputational risk, litigation risk, and even egregious injury.

- The body of laws that deal with relationships in the workplace wrestle with, and try to provide uniform frameworks for, how those relationships should be created, managed, and ended, while also preserving our society's sense of what is important—worth protecting—as human beings.

- Workplace relationship issues—hiring and firing, safety, privacy, compensation, and adverse employment actions—are fertile contexts for contentiousness, mistrust, dissatisfaction, and abusive behavior.

- One of the most important considerations for understanding the context of free speech and free expression in the workplace is recognizing the "important interest" of an employer having the ability to make sure the operations of a workplace are conducted in the most efficient, productive, and beneficial way.

- In a workplace issue involving speech or expression, ethical decision-makers will seek out resolutions that are constructive, sustainable, and that lead to prosperous outcomes.

- The lawful ability to discriminate is a source of liberty. It enables individuals, and organizations, to have the freedom to choose—to rise and fall on the success and failure of our own discernment. In a workplace environment, the freedom to choose allows businesses to make decisions intended to advance on the primary business purpose.

- For ethical decision-makers in the workplace, the issue of discrimination should be evaluated by the circumstances in which the discrimination took place, the intent of the discrimination, and the persons affected by the discrimination.

- A lack of transparency can cause undue damage to individuals, the organizations themselves, and to society at-large. A whistleblower is a person who alerts the rest of the world to abuses and unlawful conduct within an organization that may otherwise go undiscovered.

- Ethical decision-making employs frameworks focused on prosperous outcomes—outcomes that are the result of lawfulness, respect, trust, professionalism, collegiality, and value.

KEY TERMS

- Duty of Loyalty
- Equal Protection
- Fifth Amendment
- First Amendment
- Fourteenth Amendment
- Free Speech or Free Expression

- Public Concern
- Public Policy
- Retaliation
- Unlawful Discrimination
- Whistleblower

ENDNOTES

1. For those who are familiar with Alan Turing and the topic of artificial intelligence, you may also recognize "ELIZA" as the name of a program created by Joseph Weizenbaum in 1966 that appeared to pass the "Turing Test," demonstrating intelligent behavior equivalent to, or indistinguishable from, a human being.

2. Table 10.1 is intended to identify for illustrative purposes several of the rights and interests, and the main bodies of law, pertaining to employment situations, both public and private; it is not intended to be exhaustive or nuanced.

3. For our purposes, and for the purpose of most legal analyses, the concepts of "free speech" and "free expression" are interchangeable.

4. *New York Times Co. v. Sullivan*, 376 U.S. 254, 269, (1964) (quoting *Roth v. United States*, 354 U.S. 476, 484 (1957)).

5. *Roth v. United States*, 354 U.S. 476, 483 (1957).

6. *Id*. at 484.

7. "Having concluded that Yohn's speech touches upon matters of public concern, the Court balances whether his 'interest in making such statements outweighs the interest of the State, as an employer, in promoting the efficiency of the public services it performs through its employees.'" *Yohn v. Coleman*, 639 F.Supp.2d 776, 786 (E.D. Mich. 2009) (quoting *Pickering v. Bd. Of Educ. Of Township High School Dist. 205, Will County, Illinois*, 391 U.S. 563 (1968).

8. *Hudgens v. N.L.R.B.*, 424 U.S. 507, 513 (1976).

9. *Yohn v. Coleman*, 639 F.Supp.2d 776, 785 (E.D. Mich. 2009).

10. *Connick v. Myers*, 461 U.S. 138, 146 (1983).

11. We will address whistleblowing, as a specific matter of public concern, later in this chapter.

12. "It is also true that the Due Process Clause of the Fifth Amendment contains an equal protection component prohibiting the United States from invidiously discriminating between individuals or groups." *Washington v. Davis*, 426 U.S. 229, 239 (1976) (citation omitted).

13. 42 U.S.C. § 1981, et seq.

14. *Lawson v. FMR, LLC.*, _ U.S. _, 134 S.Ct. 1158, 1163 (2014).

ENGAGEMENT—WHAT DO YOU THINK?

Write down your own thoughts about what you've learned in this chapter. Consider the previous discussions about relationships in the workplace, communication, equal protection, the roles of whistleblowers, and how ethical decision-makers incorporate these concepts and realities into their decision-making frameworks. In your own words, describe the role you think these various factors have in the ethical decision-making processes within an organization and why they are significant.

CHAPTER 11

COMMON MARKETPLACE ISSUES

© Rawpixel/Shutterstock.com

In the preceding chapter, we examined the role of ethical decision-making related to the existence and the effect of individual rights within a workplace environment. The intention of this chapter is much the same. For the purpose of better understanding how ethical decision-making works in a real-world marketplace environment, we need to consider a few key subjects and practices applicable to most businesses. It is not the intention of this chapter to provide a comprehensive, legal, or best practices analysis of any of the marketplace issues we are going to discuss. Those kinds of analyses and in-depth studies are more appropriate for subject-specific courses and texts. Even though the temptation (a temptation to which most ethics' textbooks capitulate) is to review each topic (usually supplying the law and major social issues) and then identify for the student the "right" and "wrong" way to do things, such an approach does little to prepare graduates for the infinite nuances of everyday business situations—situations that many times elude a simple "do this" or "do that" decision-making rubric. This is important for students to understand because students can become unwitting victims of such rational sounding decision-making schemes, only to later find out, the real-world marketplace is a much more complicated and problematic environment than one in which every dilemma has a neat, "feel good" resolution.

Our attempt will be to canvas each subject-matter area in such a way as to identify where problems might arise and to understand how ethical decision-making must navigate those problems, relying on tools such as rational frameworks that lead to prosperous outcomes, as well as motivators such as resilient prosperity and aiming to further advance the common good.

© alphaspirit/Shutterstock.com

LEARNING OUTCOMES | OUTLINE

11.1 Financial Practices

11.2 Marketing Practices

11.3 Product Safety and Liability

11.4 Bribery and Corruption

- Identify the meaning of sound financial practices.
- Evaluate how sound financial practices can positively affect the long-term outcomes of a business organization.
- Identify how a decision-maker can help establish, maintain, and assess financial practices within an organization.
- Analyze the role of marketing for a business organization.
- Identify the advantages of constructive marketing practices.
- Identify the possible pitfalls of deceptive marketing practices and why those pitfalls may occur.
- Analyze the concepts of product safety and product liability.
- Identify the meaning and application of the duty of care for business organizations.
- Analyze the impact of bribery and corruption in the marketplace.
- Identify ethical decision-making frameworks that help to avoid corruptive practices and destructive manipulation in the marketplace.

OPENING THOUGHT EXPERIMENT

Your time as a student and scholar have finally come to an end. By a stroke of good luck, and the personal recommendation of the U.S. Senate's Committee on Finance's chairman, you have landed an absolute dream job. You are now the proud bearer of the title of "Executive Director of Strategic Analysis" and your paycheck feels like it's littered with zeros. Your job comes with stock options, a superb healthcare plan, quarterly bonuses, the use of a company car, a country club membership, an expense account for food and drinks, the use of a private jet, and two months of paid vacation a year. After earning two doctorate degrees in strategic management and business economics, and winning the internationally recognized Holmes Scholar fellowship, you feel fairly confident you can deliver. Your new employer, E.D.M., Inc., is banking on it.

E.D.M. is a worldwide consulting firm that started with a single office space in upper Manhattan in 1932. Like a phoenix rising out of the ashes of the Great Depression, it grew to become a multibillion-dollar company with offices in Tokyo, London, New York, Paris, Stockholm, Toronto, Hong Kong, and Berlin. Its principal client services involve dispatching advisory teams to business organizations around the globe to assist in strategic planning, risk management, investor relations, operational efficiency, and resource assessment. Your position is one of the most exciting and promises to present the greatest intellectual challenges. Your first assignment, in fact, proves to be quite perplexing. You will be meeting with an overseas, boutique financial trading firm that specializes in "forex trading," buying one currency and selling it in another in order to make a profit from the exchange rate difference.

The trading firm wants to open a branch office in New York, but while it has access to prestigious legal and accounting professionals, its executive team needs strategic guidance on a particularly sensitive issue it feels it needs to address before committing to opening the new branch. The trading firm's chief compliance officer has prepared a summary of the issue for you. The firm's concern is that by opening a branch office in the United States, it might become subject to sanctions or criminal prosecution under the F.C.P.A., the Foreign Corrupt Practices Act.

During your overseas flight to the client's office, which is located in the small island country of The Duchy of Grand Fenwick, you review the firm's trading portfolio for the past two years, its disclosed financial statements, and its customer dossier. Everything appears to be in good order, and your focus turns to a line-item expense called, "DGF Certification Fee Expenses." Apparently, it is legal and expected in Grand Fenwick for trading firms to pay "certification fees" to financial regulators. These certification fees are statutorily defined much like licensing fees would be; payment of the fee publicly "certifies" that a trading firm can do business in Grand Fenwick. The odd thing is the fees are

paid directly to individual regulators based on a variable fee schedule. If regulators do not receive the certification fees they request—the amounts can vary from regulator to regulator—they are empowered to close a trading firm's operations and to seize business assets. Payment of the certification fees is critical to the trading firm's ability to do business in Grand Fenwick, but it would appear to be illegal according to U.S. law.

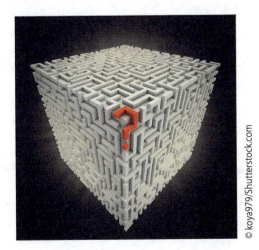

As your private jet lands in Grand Fenwick, you realize the legal (and accounting) issues raised by the trading firm's problem don't help with answering the firm's desire to grow and to have an international presence in New York. In fact, they have the opposite effect; they only add negative complexity to the problem.

You see one of the executives from the trading firm walking into the private hangar to welcome you to Grand Fenwick and to take you to the firm's offices. What are you going to say? What kind of advice are they going to expect from you?

ENGAGEMENT—What Do You Think?

How would you reframe the problem presented by the trading firm's desire to grow? Is it a legal problem? Is it a moral problem? Is it a cultural problem? What ethical framework would help to resolve this problem? When mandated boundaries, or "best practices," are in conflict with what a business needs or wants to do, how can ethical decision-making processes help to resolve those differences?

_____

_____

_____

_____

_____

_____

_____

Section 11.1 Financial Practices

Generally speaking, **financial practices** refer to a set of methods and standards, usually represented through policies and procedures, by which a business carries out its budgeting, financial reporting, accounting processes, and other financially related activities. Sound financial practices are those practices that establish accountability and appropriate transparency, properly support other business functions and operations, satisfy related compliance requirements, adequately meet present monetary obligations, and prepare for future growth and strategic opportunities.

> **FINANCIAL PRACTICES**
>
> This refers to a set of methods and standards by which a business or a decision-maker can carry out budgeting, financial reporting, accounting processes, and other financially related activities.

© creativestockexchange/Shutterstock.com

A fundamental key to the existence of sound financial practices is to recognize that the *information* or *data* a practice contains, produces, and reveals is *more important* than the actual practice, process or procedure itself. The concept of establishing and implementing any financial practice should be to appropriately acquire, manage, safeguard, transmit, properly use, and retain financial data. The data, and the purpose behind the existence and use of the data, should be the primary drivers behind how a particular financial practice is established and administered.

Sound financial practices obey and conform with federal and state compliance regulations, accounting best practices, and industry **best practices**. These "guides" readily provide the means by which a business' financial practices accomplish their

> **BEST PRACTICES**
>
> This refers to procedures, policies, or customs that are acknowledged, accepted, or prescribed as being the most effective and the most likely to be compliant with applicable law.

goals, however, these guides are not, and should not become, the final arbiter of what constitutes a sound financial practice. These guides should act as mandated boundaries and sources of core values. Sound financial practices should ultimately be molded by voluntary accountability. Decision-makers within an organization should understand and focus on *how* financial data can lead to more prosperous outcomes over the long term for the organization. With that motivation in mind, ethical dilemmas are far more likely to be resolved in such a way to not only be legal but also to be constructive, sustainable, and (ultimately) for the common good.

© Maxx-Studio/Shutterstock.com

Most financial practices that are identified as "unethical" are the result of a decision-maker, or an organization as a whole, ignoring that paramount objective. The following is a short hit-list of those kinds of financial practices:

- Accounting fraud
- Insider trading
- Misuse and misappropriation of assets
- Subprime lending
- Stock option backdating
- Deceptive, misleading, or fraudulent loan practices
- Lending discrimination and/or exploitation
- Money laundering
- Abuse of financial trust (i.e., breach of fiduciary duty)
- Embezzlement
- Usury (charging exorbitant interest fees)
- Misreporting or underreporting of financial information

CHALLENGE QUESTIONS:

What do you think motivates people and businesses to make unsound—unethical or unlawful—financial decisions? How do you think those motivations could be reformed or changed?

How effective do you think the addition of more laws and more regulations are to the prevention of financial abuses?

Focusing on constructive, sustainable decisions that lead to prosperous outcomes will help business decision-makers, and the financial practices they influence, to establish and promote consistency and transparency. **Internal controls**, such as transaction authorization standards, documentation requirements, segregation of duties, security procedures, regular audits, background checks, and training, will also help an organization hedge against unethical and unlawful financial practices.

INTERNAL CONTROLS

Most often this refers to procedures, policies, and practices inside an organization that help assure an organization's goals of efficiency, safety, compliance, and risk management.

Sound financial practices should be one of the key ingredients behind growth, a healthy reputation, customer loyalty, risk management, and resilient prosperity.

ENGAGEMENT—What Do You Think?

Describe what you think would make a financial practice "sound." Why is ethical decision-making such a critical part of sound financial practices? Why do you think certain companies, and certain individual decision-makers, struggle with establishing, maintaining, or following sound financial practices?

© wk003mike/Shutterstock.com

_____

_____

_____

_____

_____

_____

_____

Section 11.2 Marketing Practices

Marketing is the way in which an organization communicates to everyone outside its organization—most often to its direct consumers and clients—and by doing so, an organization can establish, manage, and study its relationships with external stakeholders.

© Rawpixel.com/Shutterstock.com

There are many times when an organization is not in control of how it is perceived by the public, its competitors, its regulators, its investors, or even its customers; this can be caused by a number of things, such as adverse news reporting, difficult market conditions, product failures, litigation, employee turn-over, poor earnings, and the disreputable actions of competitors. Marketing presents the method by which an organization can regain some control over how it is perceived and how efficiently and successfully it can sell its products and services. Effective marketing is, therefore, a critical component to a business' capability to remain resilient, to prosper, to remain competitive, and to grow.

For an organization's decision-makers, marketing represents the following opportunities:

- Demonstrating value-delivery
- Providing access to products and services
- Promoting and announcing products and services
- Announcing organizational changes and positive performance benchmarks
- Optimal pricing
- Relationship creation and building
- Brand awareness
- Strategic positioning within an industry
- Loyalty development among customers and clients
- Provision of channels of reciprocal communication

Because marketing is an organization's primary method of communication to the "outside world," it is imperative that its means and methods are honest, meaningful, memorable, and sustainable over the long term. These are not characteristics that are "plug-and-play." They must be nurtured and maintained through the existence of a constructive corporate culture and a willingness at all levels of an organization to remain committed to delivering value and communicating that value. Effective marketing can definitely come with challenges, such as:

© Rawpixel.com/Shutterstock.com

- Consistently producing quality content
- Identifying where effective marketing occurs
- Developing content plans
- Managing resources and time to produce the right communication
- Focusing on the optimal target audience
- Understanding the needs and challenges of a target audience
- Determining and evaluating what goals the communication is intended to accomplish

When these (and other) challenges aren't met or successfully handled, organizations can fall prey to a number of marketing practices that lead to destructive and wasteful outcomes. Decision-makers, who are not driven by ethical frameworks, may attempt to use an organization's communication efforts to create unsustainable, short-term financial gains, or to mislead the consumer base (and other secondary stakeholders) as to the financial condition of the company, the

CHALLENGE QUESTIONS:

What are some of the things an organization can do to lessen the difficulty of effective communication with external stakeholders? Which ethical frameworks might be most effective in this context? Why?

quality or character of goods and services, or the organization's ability to cope with marketplace and regulatory challenges. This kind of shortsightedness and lack of vision about an organization's primary purpose can set the stage for marketing abuse, such as:

- Price fixing
- Price gouging
- Bait-and-switch advertising
- False advertising
- Fraudulent or deceptive public announcements

Focusing on constructive, sustainable decisions that lead to prosperous outcomes will help business decision-makers to establish and promote communication processes, policies, and standards that create, promote, and maintain growth, a healthy reputation, customer loyalty, risk management, and resilient prosperity.

© Melpomene/Shutterstock.com

ENGAGEMENT—What Do You Think?

Why do you think marketing, as a means of communication, can be such a challenge for many companies? How can ethical decision-making help overcome those challenges? Describe an experience in which you were the victim of unethical marketing activities (big or small). How did that make you feel? Why do you think it happened?

_____

_____

_____

_____

_____

_____

_____

Section 11.3 Product Safety and Liability

In 1972, the U.S. Congress passed the Consumer Product Safety Act (CPSA)[1] that established the U.S. Consumer Product Safety Commission (CPSC) as a permanent agency. The purpose of this law and its enforcement agency was to develop safety standards and to pursue recalls of unsafe products. Other agencies enforce **product safety** over specific categories or types of products, such as the U.S. Food and Drug Administration (food, tobacco, nutraceuticals,

PRODUCT SAFETY

This refers to the risks, real or potential, associated with any product (or service) sold or licensed to an end-user.

pharmaceuticals, vaccines, etc.), the U.S. Bureau of Alcohol, Tobacco, Firearms, and Explosives (firearms and explosives), the U.S. Department of—Agriculture (farming, forestry, and food production), the U.S. Department of Transportation (private vehicles, commercial vehicles and containers, and several commuter transportation systems), and the U.S. Environmental Protection Agency (insecticide, fungicide, rodenticide, pesticide, hazardous, and toxic waste).

© Bacho/Shutterstock.com

The underlying concept of product safety is to ensure products and services do not result in, or cause, undue risk or harm to consumers, clients, the public, or to the natural environment. Legal and industrial (and certification) standards apply to almost every product or service supplied by the marketplace. Some industries, such as pharmaceuticals, nuclear energy, automotive, and food, must cope with an increasingly substantial number of product safety regulations and qualifications during the manufacturing, wholesaling, and retailing processes. Along with these regulations and qualifications, businesses must also satisfy the common law **duty of care**—a standard of reasonable care used while performing any act that could foreseeably harm others.

When products or services do cause harm to end-users, or sometimes to other third-parties, businesses may face the risk of **product liability**. Product liability refers to the legal and monetary risk an organization may incur if a defective product causes injury to a consumer. **Strict product liability** refers to a heightened class of product liability—a situation in which an organization incurs legal and monetary risk if a defective product causes injury to a consumer even if the manufacturer or seller did everything possible to prevent the defect (a liability usually applied to inherently hazardous or dangerous products). A defective product is one in which the design or manufacturing process causes a product to not function or perform in a reasonably safe manner.

DUTY OF CARE

In tort (injury) law, this describes a legal obligation imposed on an organization or individual requiring a standard of reasonable carefulness while performing any act that could foreseeably harm someone else.

PRODUCT LIABILITY

The legal risk a manufacturer or retailer may incur as a result of producing or selling a product that is defective.

STRICT PRODUCT LIABILITY

The legal risk imposed on a manufacturer or retailer for having produced or sold a product that resulted in a consumer's injury even if the manufacturer or seller did everything possible to prevent the defect (a liability usually applied to inherently hazardous or dangerous products).

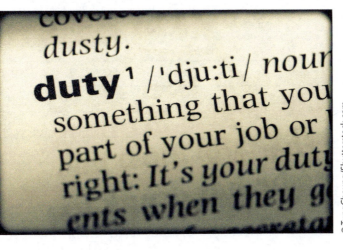

© TungCheung/Shutterstock.com

Certain manufactures and retailers give into the temptation to circumvent safe design, manufacturing, and retailing processes and policies even at the cost of potential litigation, regulatory fines or punishments, loss of investor confidence, loss of consumer loyalty, and irreparable reputational harm. It is important to identify the motivations that can lead decision-makers to sacrifice the well-being of the long term for the gratification of the short term.

- Reduced cost of manufacturing and/or processing
- Competitiveness
- Financial gain (at least in the short term)
- Intellectual property protection limitations (such as patent limits on pharmaceuticals)
- Reduced cost of quality control processes
- Reduced cost of raw materials
- Reduced cost of waste

Ethical business decision-makers, who are focused on designing, manufacturing, and selling, products and services that deliver *value*, are very likely to mitigate the possibility of product liability and are very likely to establish and maintain policies, procedures, and customary practices that ensure safety and represented performance characteristics. This results in product integrity, a holistic assay of a product's fitness for a particular use and its adherence to high standards of quality and value.

© arka38/Shutterstock.com

ENGAGEMENT—What Do You Think?

Why do you think the concept of product liability is important to our society? What role does ethical—decision-making have in the area of product safety? Who, within an organization, do you think should be responsible for product safety? Why?

Section 11.4 **Bribery and Corruption**

This chapter's opening Thought Experiment posed a problem that is not that far removed from reality. **Bribery**—money or favor given or promised in order to manipulate the conduct or judgment of a person in a position of authority or trust—is not as clean-cut as it sounds. Because humans are creatures of psychological influence, impressionable and vulnerable to emotional influences, we communicate and forge relationships built around those susceptibilities. We compliment each other. We criticize each

© Atstock Productions/Shutterstock.com

other. We make promises to each other. We withhold affection for each other. We extend affection to each other. We do favors. We expect courtesies. We have expectations of rewards or consequences. We have feelings of satisfaction, dissatisfaction, passion, and indifference. These sensibilities are artifacts of the human condition, and, like many such artifacts, they can easily spill into the marketplace.

In the marketplace, something that is used to gain an unfair advantage in a relationship between an organization and a person in authority (or a person with influence) might be considered an unlawful bribe. However, gaining an advantage might also be perfectly legal. Establishing and maintaining healthy, communicative relationships is certainly a preferable way in which to conduct business. Certain cultures might even provide for **"facilitation payments"** in order to induce public officials to perform their functions. Given the circumstances, these payments may not be illegal even though they have the same practical effect (and the same appearance) as an unlawful bribe. The underlying concern with bribery is not simply that an advantage is gained, but the way in which the advantage is gained might create a *corrupted* marketplace.

Corruption in the marketplace—inside or outside of an organization—essentially destroys the opportunity for *value*. Processes and systems that are corrupt, involve fraudulent, dishonest, or debased characteristics. When the marketplace is corrupted, stakeholders, both present and future, are less likely to have the benefit of value (recall our discussion in Chapter 3) that implies the importance, indispensability, advantage, and meaningfulness of a product or service. Corruption deforms equal access, distorts fair assessment, and misrepresents needs and solutions.

Ethical decision-makers within organizations will be those persons who are looking for the process of creating relationships, and creating value, in such a way as to advance prosperous outcomes for the long term and for the common good. In the pursuit of those objectives, there is no room for bribery or corruption.

BRIBERY

This refers to situations in which money or favor is given or promised in order to manipulate the conduct or judgment of a person in a position of authority or trust.

FACILITATION PAYMENTS

Payments made to a public official to induce the official to complete some action or duty, such as licensing or certification.

CORRUPTION

In the marketplace, this refers to fraudulent or imbalanced conduct by those in authority for the purpose of short-term, or biased, gain.

ENGAGEMENT—What Do You Think?

In your own words, describe the disadvantages to bribery? What are the disadvantages to corruption in the marketplace? What ethical frameworks would help a decision-maker avoid these unfair pitfalls? Why? How does corruption hinder the possibility of resilient prosperity?

_____

_____

_____

_____

_____

_____

_____

© Davidovka/Shutterstock.com

SELECTED READINGS

- Sarna, D. *History of Greed: Financial Fraud from Tulip Mania to Bernie Madoff.* First edition. Wiley, 2010.

- Lewis, M. *The Big Short: Inside the Doomsday Machine.* Reprint edition. W.W. Norton & Company, 2011.

- Jiwa, B. *Marketing: A Love Story: How to Matter to Your Customers.* CreateSpace Independent Publishing Platform, 2014.

- Godin, S. *All Marketers Are Liars: The Underground Classic That Explains How Marketing Really Works—and Why Authenticity Is the Best Marketing of All.* Reprint edition. Portfolio, 2012.

- Shapo, M. *Experimenting with the Consumer: The Mass Testing of Risky Products on the American Public.* First edition. Praeger, 2008.

- Elsinger, J. *The Chickenshit Club: Why the Justice Department Fails to Prosecute Executives.* Simon & Schuster, 2017.

TAKE-AWAY QUESTIONS AND IDEAS

What constitutes "sound" financial practices? Why?
How can ethical decision-making positively influence financial practices?
Why is marketing such a critical part of business? What are its advantages?
How can marketing—the communication from a business to outside stakeholders—present certain pitfalls?
How can ethical decision-making help businesses avoid those pitfalls?
Why is product liability an important part of the marketplace? How does this concept improve the relationship between businesses and consumers? Which ethical frameworks help to inform processes and designs that would make products and services safer—more beneficial—for consumers?
Why is "bribery" a destructive thing in the marketplace? Why does it occur? How can it be avoided? What does corruption do to the concept of value?

- Sound financial practices are those practices that establish accountability and appropriate transparency, properly support other business functions and operations, satisfy related compliance requirements, adequately meet present monetary obligations, and prepare for future growth and strategic opportunities.
- Decision-makers within an organization should understand and focus on how financial data can lead to more prosperous outcomes over the long-term for the organization.
- Focusing on constructive, sustainable decisions that lead to prosperous outcomes will help business decision-makers, and the financial practices they influence, to establish and promote consistency and transparency.
- Marketing is the way in which an organization communicates to everyone outside its organization—most often to its direct consumers and clients—and by doing so, an organization can establish, manage, and study its relationships with external stakeholders.
- Marketing presents the method by which an organization can regain some control over how it is perceived and how efficiently and successfully it can sell its products and services.
- The underlying concept of product safety is to ensure products and services do not result in, or cause, undue risk or harm to consumers, clients, the public, or to the natural environment.
- Businesses must satisfy the common law duty of care—a standard of reasonable care used while performing any act that could foreseeably harm others.
- Because humans are creatures of psychological influence, impressionable and vulnerable to emotional influences, we communicate and forge relationships built around those susceptibilities.
- Establishing and maintaining healthy, communicative relationships is certainly a preferable way in which to conduct business.
- When the marketplace is corrupted, stakeholders, both present and future, are less likely to have the benefit of value that implies the importance, indispensability, advantage, and meaningfulness of a product or service.

KEY TERMS

- Best Practices
- Bribery
- Corruption
- Duty of Care
- Facilitation Payments
- Financial Practices
- Internal Controls
- Product Liability
- Product Safety
- Strict Product Liability

ENDNOTE

1. 15 U.S.C. § 2501, *et seq.*

ENGAGEMENT—WHAT DO YOU THINK?

Write down your own thoughts about what you've learned in this chapter. Consider the previous discussions about sound financial practices, the role marketing has in helping a business communicate with external stakeholders, the concept of product liability and the duty of care, and the effect bribery and corruption have on the concept of value. In your own words, describe how you think ethical decision-making can constructively influence, enhance, or avoid each of these areas.

_____

_____

_____

_____

_____

_____

_____

_____

_____

_____

_____

_____

_____

_____

_____

CHAPTER 12

USING THE TOOLKIT

Many ethics textbooks provide voluminous case studies based on examples of how companies acted ethically or unethically (usually defined by some kind of lawful or unlawful conduct). Those are interesting and definitely have their place as models of what to do, or what not to do, when faced with certain circumstances. However, the vast majority of graduating students who enter the workforce will not have to deal with the kinds of macroconsequence issues faced by multimillion dollar corporations such as Wal-Mart, Monsanto, Toyota, Volkswagen, Tyco, WorldCom, Enron, Arthur Andersen, AIG, Freddie Mac, and Washington Mutual. Most new employees, junior supervisors, midlevel managers, and business entrepreneurs will have to face an excess of ethical dilemmas and issues at the day-to-day, usually frontline, level of business.

One of the risks associated with using large-company examples as case studies is the likelihood of leaving the impression, "unethical practices will only happen to someone else," or "unethical conduct only occurs inside major Wall Street players or multimillion dollar companies." The reality is much closer to home. Decision-making woes that plague multimillion dollar companies also plague small, mom-and-pop ventures; the significant difference is usually the number of lives and stakeholders affected. Everyone entering the workforce—any organizational venture no matter the size or profit margin—needs to understand, and apply, ethical decision-making and critical thinking skills. The problem with the garden-variety case study approach is it can make very little difference in the learning process (even when a case itself might be interesting). At the point when the cognitive learning needs to morph into applied learning, case studies many times create an unintended disconnect.

Classroom interactions will only take you so far, as well. Ultimately, years of experience on the job will be your greatest ally. In the meantime, it is critical for you to take what you have learned throughout this book and apply it as often as possible. At this stage of your student career, you might have had a job or two, and even if you didn't know it, through those jobs you've had plenty of opportunities to put ethical decision-making into practice; hopefully, you have. But now that you have spent time learning about and analyzing the role ethics plays in business, and the process by which ethical decisions are made, the business world—and your eventual career—should look a bit different. You have discovered new frameworks, identified influences, discovered motivators, and analyzed goals. You've recognized the complexities of organizational contexts and how those contexts create dilemmas and issues far from the simplistic comfort of being either "right" or "wrong." You have thought about key hallmarks for determining whether a decision is ethical. Is it constructive? Is it sustainable over time? Does it lead to prosperity? Does it help make an organization resiliently prosperous? Does it positively impact the common good?

© Asier Romero/Shutterstock.com

© bizvector/Shutterstock.com

One of the most important steps in the learning process is, of course, to practice, but what is equally (if not more) important but less well-known, is to learn by *teaching*. You may not realize it, but part of your experience through the use of this book has been to *teach yourself*. The thought experiments at the beginning of each chapter, the challenge questions, the engagement questions, and the chapter take-away questions and

KEEP EDUCATING YOURSELF

© Gustavo Frazao/Shutterstock.com

ideas have all been designed to anchor and improve your critical thinking skills by creating an opportunity to teach yourself—to take what you've passively learned and to restate it, and explain it, in a way that makes sense to you.

This final chapter is designed to double down on that process, and in doing so, to present opportunities for you to apply what you've learned through teaching . . . but this time, your "audience" will be external.

THE STUDENT AS THE TEACHER

All of the sections contained in this chapter are going to provide opportunities for you, the student, to become the teacher. One of the most critical aspects of ethical decision-making in an organization is for the decision-maker to model the framework—the values, beliefs, and culture—underlying the decision. (Take a look back at Chapters 4 and 5.) Part of learning to become an ethical decision-maker entails *practicing* how to model (show, exhibit, display, and communicate) the decision-making process.

For each of the following sections—each one tied to the key concepts contained in Chapters 1–9—keep your eye on an imaginary audience of coworkers, supervisors, customers and clients, regulators, investors, and members of your community. Make each exercise more than a "class assignment." Approach them as if you are tasked with teaching someone else what you've learned.

© Rawpixel.com/Shutterstock.com

12.1 Chapter 1—Finding a Compass

If you were to explain this during a training session with fellow coworkers, how would you summarize the comparison and contrast of "fairness" and "justice" in a business setting?

_____

_____

_____

_____

_____

_____

If you were to explain this during a training session with fellow coworkers, how would you summarize the balance between "freedom" and "responsibility" in a business setting?

_____

_____

_____

_____

_____

_____

If you were to explain this during a training session with fellow coworkers, how would you summarize the relationship and roles of society and the law in a business setting?

_____

_____

_____

_____

_____

_____

If you were to explain this during a training session with fellow coworkers, how would you summarize the concept of "prosperity" in a business setting?

_____

_____

_____

_____

_____

_____

If you were to explain this during a training session with fellow coworkers, how would you summarize the distinction between, and the appropriate use of, morals and ethics in a business setting?

_____

_____

_____

_____

_____

In the box below, **DRAW** whatever comes to mind when you think of the role and meaning of *ethics in the workplace.*

Using the "fishbone technique," identify the possible causes to the following problem:

Moral beliefs do not provide a practical framework for resolving most business dilemmas.

The "backbone" of the fish represents the problem stated above. On each of the fish's "spurs" or other "bones," write down a likely *cause* of the problem.

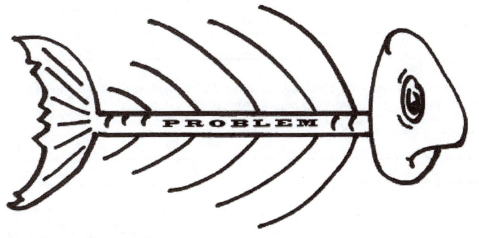

Source: Courtesy of Steven Lovett

12.2 Chapter 2—Choosing a Framework

If you were to explain this during a training session with fellow coworkers, how would you summarize how individuals make decisions?

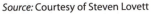

_____

_____

_____

_____

_____

If you were to explain this during a training session with fellow coworkers, how would you summarize how organizations/businesses make decisions?

_____

_____

_____

_____

_____

_____

If you were to explain this during a training session with fellow coworkers, how would you summarize the concepts of critical thinking, rationalizations, and logical fallacies, especially as they apply to a business setting?

_____

_____

_____

_____

_____

_____

If you were to explain this during a training session with fellow coworkers, how would you summarize the concept of an ethical "framework" or paradigm?

_____

_____

_____

_____

_____

_____

If you were to explain this during a training session with fellow coworkers, how would you summarize how ethical frameworks can be used to help make practical (and ethical) decisions, especially in a business environment?

_____

_____

_____

_____

_____

In the box below, **DRAW** whatever comes to mind when you think of the phrase *"ethical framework."*

Using the "fishbone technique," identify the possible causes to the following problem:

The way in which an individual makes a decision cannot successfully be used to make decisions for a business organization.

The "backbone" of the fish represents the problem stated above. On each of the fish's "spurs" or other "bones," write down a likely *cause* of the problem.

Source: Courtesy of Steven Lovett

12.3 Chapter 3—The Value Factor

If you were to explain this during a training session with fellow coworkers, how would you summarize the comparison and contrast between "values" and "skills" when applied to a business setting?

_____

_____

_____

_____

_____

_____

If you were to explain this during a training session with fellow coworkers, how would you summarize the role and impact of marketplace influences on decision-making in a business setting?

_____

_____

_____

_____

_____

_____

If you were to explain this during a training session with fellow coworkers, how would you summarize the role and impact of "individual factors" on decision-making in a business setting?

_____

_____

_____

_____

_____

_____

If you were to explain this during a training session with fellow coworkers, how would you summarize the role and impact of organizational structure and organizational factors on decision-making in a business setting?

_____

_____

_____

_____

_____

_____

In the box below, **DRAW** whatever comes to mind when you think of the word "_value_" as it relates to a business setting.

Using the "fishbone technique," identify the possible causes to the following problem:

Organizations usually focus on, and put more emphasis on, "skills" rather than "value."

The "backbone" of the fish represents the problem stated above. On each of the fish's "spurs" or other "bones," write down a likely *cause* of the problem.

Source: Courtesy of Steven Lovett

12.4 Chapter 4—The Business Purpose

If you were to explain this during a training session with fellow coworkers, how would you summarize what is meant by "advancing the business purpose"?

_____

_____

_____

_____

_____

_____

If you were to explain this during a training session with fellow coworkers, how would you summarize the relationship—its conditions, advantages, and disadvantages—between the marketplace and society at-large?

_____

_____

_____

_____

_____

If you were to explain this during a training session with fellow coworkers, how would you summarize the relationship—its conditions, advantages, and disadvantages—between the marketplace and government?

_____

_____

_____

_____

_____

If you were to explain this during a training session with fellow coworkers, how would you summarize the concept of "corporate social responsibility," including but not limited to, its practical weakness?

_____

_____

_____

_____

_____

If you were to explain this during a training session with fellow coworkers, how would you summarize the comparison and contrast between the concepts of stakeholder theory and shareholder theory?

_____

_____

_____

_____

_____

If you were to explain this during a training session with fellow coworkers, how would you summarize what is meant by "core practices" and "voluntary accountability" in a business setting?

_____

_____

_____

_____

In the box below, **DRAW** whatever comes to mind when you think of the phrase "*advancing the business purpose.*"

Using the "fishbone technique," identify the possible causes to the following problem:

Corporate social responsibility (CSR) is not an effective or practical method for making ethical decisions in a business setting.

The "backbone" of the fish represents the problem stated above. On each of the fish's "spurs" or other "bones," write down a likely *cause* of the problem.

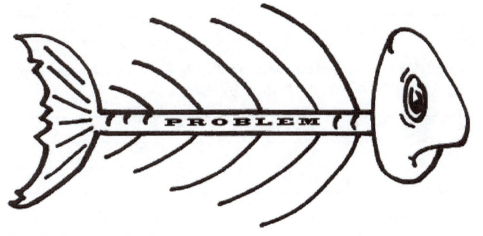

Source: Courtesy of Steven Lovett

12.5 Chapter 5—Corporate Culture

If you were to explain this during a training session with fellow coworkers, how would you summarize the concept of "corporate culture"?

_____

_____

_____

_____

_____

_____

If you were to explain this during a training session with fellow coworkers, how would you summarize the various benefits of ethical decision-making in a business setting?

_____

_____

_____

_____

_____

_____

If you were to explain this during a training session with fellow coworkers, how would you summarize the contrast between a "compliance-based" and "value-based" corporate culture?

_____

_____

_____

_____

_____

_____

If you were to explain this during a training session with fellow coworkers, how would you summarize variety and impact of leadership styles in a business setting?

_____

_____

_____

_____

_____

_____

In the box below, **DRAW** whatever comes to mind when you think of a "_value-based_" corporate culture.

Using the "fishbone technique," identify the possible causes to the following problem:

A culture of compliance does not lead to an ethical culture—a culture of value.

The "backbone" of the fish represents the problem stated above. On each of the fish's "spurs" or other "bones," write down a likely *cause* of the problem.

Source: Courtesy of Steven Lovett

12.6 Chapter 6—The Prosperity Opportunity

If you were to explain this during a training session with fellow coworkers, how would you summarize what is meant by a "prosperity opportunity" in a business setting?

_____

_____

_____

_____

_____

_____

If you were to explain this during a training session with fellow coworkers, how would you summarize the importance of establishing and encouraging "voluntary cooperation" by setting expectations in a business setting?

_____

_____

_____

_____

_____

_____

If you were to explain this during a training session with fellow coworkers, how would you summarize the importance and the impact of challenge processes and driving constructive change in a business setting?

_____

_____

_____

_____

_____

_____

If you were to explain this during a training session with fellow coworkers, how would you summarize the concept of "value creation"?

_____

_____

_____

_____

_____

_____

In the box below, **DRAW** whatever comes to mind when you think of the phrase "*prosperity opportunity.*"

Using the "fishbone technique," identify the possible causes to the following problem:

Organizations cannot create value without focusing on prosperity.

The "backbone" of the fish represents the problem stated above. On each of the fish's "spurs" or other "bones," write down a likely *cause* of the problem.

Source: Courtesy of Steven Lovett

12.7 Chapter 7—Ethics Programs

If you were to explain this during a training session with fellow coworkers, how would you summarize the importance and impact of Ethics' Programs in business settings?

_____

_____

_____

_____

_____

_____

If you were to explain this during a training session with fellow coworkers, how would you summarize a practical methodology for identifying ethical issues and dilemmas?

_____

_____

_____

_____

_____

_____

If you were to explain this during a training session with fellow coworkers, how would you summarize a practical methodology for dissecting ethical dilemmas?

_____

_____

_____

_____

_____

_____

If you were to explain this during a training session with fellow coworkers, how would you summarize a pragmatic set of "tools" for ethical management?

_____

_____

_____

_____

_____

_____

In the box below, **DRAW** whatever comes to mind when you think of an _Ethics Program_.

[box]

Using the "fishbone technique," identify the possible causes to the following problem:

Ethical dilemmas in a business setting cannot be successfully resolved without using a workable process that identifies the dilemma and dissects the dilemma.

The "backbone" of the fish represents the problem stated above. On each of the fish's "spurs" or other "bones," write down a likely _cause_ of the problem.

Source: Courtesy of Steven Lovett

12.8 Chapter 8—Resilient Prosperity

If you were to explain this during a training session with fellow coworkers, how would you summarize what is meant by "resilient prosperity" and how that is different from "sustainable development"?

_____

_____

_____

_____

_____

_____

If you were to explain this during a training session with fellow coworkers, how would you summarize the way in which resilient prosperity takes into account the business' resources?

_____

_____

_____

_____

_____

_____

If you were to explain this during a training session with fellow coworkers, how would you summarize the concept of stewardship in business and how it relates to acting responsibly, efficiently, and creatively?

_____

_____

_____

_____

_____

_____

If you were to explain this during a training session with fellow coworkers, how would you summarize the concept of an ethical "framework" or paradigm?

_____

_____

_____

_____

_____

_____

If you were to explain this during a training session with fellow coworkers, how would you summarize the insufficiency of using the Triple Bottom Line as a measure of a business' ethicalness?

_____

_____

_____

_____

_____

_____

In the box below, **DRAW** whatever comes to mind when you think of the phrase "_resilient prosperity._"

Using the "fishbone technique," identify the possible causes to the following problem:

> Sustainable development is not a practical or realistic way for a business to accomplish or measure its stewardship of resources.

The "backbone" of the fish represents the problem stated above. On each of the fish's "spurs" or other "bones," write down a likely *cause* of the problem.

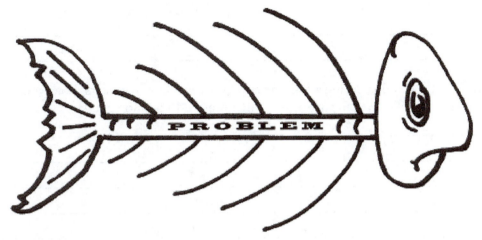

Source: Courtesy of Steven Lovett

12.9 Chapter 9—The Common Good: A Common Ground

If you were to explain this during a training session with fellow coworkers, how would you summarize the meaning, and the importance, of the "common good" for a business?

_____

_____

_____

_____

_____

_____

If you were to explain this during a training session with fellow coworkers, how would you summarize the way in which the common good can be used as a universal measure of the ethicalness of almost any business?

_____

_____

_____

_____

_____

_____

If you were to explain this during a training session with fellow coworkers, how would you summarize the "ripple effect" of resilient prosperity and how that leads to the common good?

_____

_____

_____

_____

_____

_____

If you were to explain this during a training session with fellow coworkers, how would you summarize how to establish a collective purpose by working toward the common good?

_____

_____

_____

_____

_____

_____

In the box below, **DRAW** whatever comes to mind when you think of the phrase *"the common good."*

Using the "fishbone technique," identify the possible causes to the following problem:

Organizations cannot disregard the success of the communities in which they are located and on which they depend without sacrificing the organization's own prosperity.

The "backbone" of the fish represents the problem stated above. On each of the fish's "spurs" or other "bones," write down a likely *cause* of the problem.

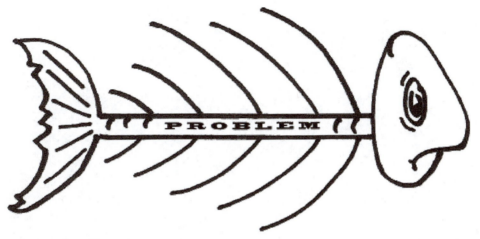

Source: Courtesy of Steven Lovett